Boris Lanin, Nikolau Nikolaevich Karazin

The Two-Legged Wolf

A Romance

Boris Lanin, Nikolau Nikolaevich Karazin

The Two-Legged Wolf
A Romance

ISBN/EAN: 9783744676168

Printed in Europe, USA, Canada, Australia, Japan

Cover: Foto ©Thomas Meinert / pixelio.de

More available books at **www.hansebooks.com**

THE

TWO-LEGGED WOLF

A Romance.

BY

N. N. KARAZIN.

(ILLUSTRATED BY THE AUTHOR.)

TRANSLATED FROM THE RUSSIAN BY

BORIS LANIN.

————

CHICAGO AND NEW YORK:
RAND, McNALLY & COMPANY.
1894.

CONTENTS.

PART SECOND.

THE TWO-LEGGED WOLF.

CHAPTER I.

THE TWO-LEGGED WOLF.

In the hot, yellow sand stood a wooden stake, painted red. The lower portion of this stake, imbedded in the soil, was shod with iron; at its upper end there was a short crosspiece, and upon it sat, its feathers bristling, a handsome hunting-falcon, dreaming — the sharp, rascally eyes covered by the opaque, transverse eyelids.

The bird seemed the embodiment of perfect immobility. From the little red cap fitted to its small shapely head down to the little silver chain which fastened its leg to the crosspiece it resembled a thing carved. He never moved; not one of the little bells which adorned the collar around the bird's neck gave forth a sound, and, as if drawn by hand, the short bluish shadow cast by the bird lay sharply defined upon the reddish-yellow background of sand.

Two greyhounds, lean, gaunt, and nearly hairless, with inflamed tongues protruding, lay flat upon their sides, and but for the barely perceptible movement of their clearly defined ribs they would have been taken for carrion rather than for living animals ready at the first motion, at a single faint summoning whistle of their master, to jump up and scan the boundless steppe — to fly like arrows over the wave-like, friable sands, which to the eye appeared to have neither ending nor beginning.

A handsome, showy horse — a blooded Turkoman stallion — covered, in spite of the scorching heat, with a heavy blanket, also stood motionless near by; the clean, sinewy fetlocks of its forelegs hobbled with a thin woolen rope. The costly bridle, ornamented with silver, turquois, and carnelians, was lightly attached to the horn-shaped bow of the saddle, maintaining the graceful bend of the swan-like neck. The remainder of the horse-trappings were lying close by, arranged in the most scrupulous order. It was evident that a very experienced hand had placed them thus, and that the same hand was ready with a single motion to swing the whole load upon the horse's crupper and fasten it on in spite of its apparently complicated nature. There was a pair of "korshuns," or saddle-bags, made of the costly Khivan carpet known as "kisil-tirnak"; a leather case with cups, the so-called "kalmyk-bash" or "terkesh," ornamented with long rawhide tassels; a gourd-kalyan, or water-pipe, with silver mountings, a long reed stem, and a skillfully embossed copper bowl; a goatskin water-vessel, warped and wrinkled from long exposure to the heat; a pair of long-barreled Persian pistols, the muzzles resting in sockets; and a bag of woolen tissue for oats, half-filled.

In addition to the falcon, the horse, and the greyhounds, there was still another living creature, though it was difficult to regard it as such. Why should a living being lie so long in such an evidently uncomfortable position?

This other being was a man. He lay stretched out at full length, with his arms under his head, his eyes piercing the boundless gray depth of the burning, scorching sky overhead. The broad brim of his slashed felt hat protected a pair of oblique, blinking eyes, and cast a shadow dividing the bronzed high cheek-boned face into two distinct parts.

The man was dressed in a loose cloak of camel's-hair cloth, under which garment another, bright red in color, was visible, with edges embroidered in gold braid. The glaring pattern of his voluminous red trousers, also embroidered in silk of various colors, shone in the sunlight. The feet were clad in soft leather socks, with green heel-pieces, and shoes with high, narrow heels shod with silver-notched steel.

Beside him lay a costly "klynch," or saber, in a scabbard of black shagreen-work, and with a white bone hilt, set with stones of various colors, chiefly turquois, and ornamented with tassels; a double-barreled gun of Russian make, and a Russian revolver in leather case, which was attached by a white cord to the wide metal-plated belt. In addition to these arms there was also a whole collection of knives suspended from the belt, and various smaller articles needed in warfare or on the road—flints and steel, wire primers, etc., and, finally, a wallet of red "safian" leather, embroidered in silver.

A little removed from this motionless group, at the bottom of a shallow ravine overgrown with dry acanthus thorns, lay another horse, without saddle or bridle. The eyes of this horse were staring wide in the chill of death; its long-benumbed legs, shod in the Turkoman fashion, were stretched out at full length after the last convulsive scraping through the heated sand.

This was no temporary immobility. Here was a real corpse. All doubt on this subject was easily dispelled by observing the dry, wide-open nostrils of the animal and noticing the myriads of small desert ants making their unceremonious entry into their uttermost cavities and emerging again, unhindered, into the light of day. It was not even necessary to enter into such details; to inhale the tainted air was quite sufficient.

"Ah ! may the dog catch me, but that smells good, especially upon an empty stomach! After having nothing to eat for the last four days this seems perfectly delicious. From which side can I best get at it?"

Thus, probably, thought a stunted desert wolf who had long since been attracted by the tainted air, but who had not yet summoned up sufficient resolution to emerge from the rubble at the farther end of the ravine and draw nearer to the tempting morsel, which was evidently destined for the salvation of such as he, with stomach debilitated from long fasting and tormented by the pangs of hunger.

"And what has *he* planted himself down there for, *with his dogs?*" thought the wolf, as he lay flat upon the ground, his sharp snout barely distinguishable from the gray soil. " He has rested, he has eaten, and he has fed his horse — now he should go on his way and not keep others from eating. With what an air of importance he spreads himself out, the rascal! as if the whole desert existed only for his benefit. Well, if he felt such gnawing in his entrails. Ah! if I could snatch just a wee morsel! He may not notice it."

And the wolf began to move gently forward. He had barely stirred when he glanced about. The horse moved its well-shaped ears: the red, bloodshot eyes of the dogs opened slowly. A muffled, ominous growl was heard. Mortal fear seized upon the small four-footed rover, pervaded his whole being, and suddenly suppressed the vivid calls of biting hunger.

The wolf drew back, and once hidden from view, he crawled back farther; then, springing to his feet, away he flew behind the sandy ridges and hillocks. For a long, long time he could not summon sufficient courage to draw nigh again to the spot from which the tempting smell spread through the hot desert air, causing a nervous twitching of his sharp-pointed, cunning snout.

An hour passed by, and still another, and with them the fears of the wolf. The hunger gnawed more viciously than ever at his vitals. He drew nearer once more and looked. The horse still stood motionless; the dogs still lay stretched out in exactly the same spot. Like a stuffed bird, placed there as a decoy, the falcon sat upon his crosspiece, and without moving a single muscle or changing his position in the least, like a lifeless corpse, the resting warrior lay extended upon the sand.

Again the starving animal began to ponder. "Why, in the devil's name, does he lie there ever since morning? Does he imagine the fallen horse will ever get upon its legs again? Is he waiting because he dreads to go on with a single horse?"

The blazing sun began to decline in its course toward the west; beneath it purple shadows began to gather, and a faint approach to coolness became perceptible in the air. A tint resembling the reflection of a distant conflagration gradually overspread the horizon, and the summits of ridges and hillsides appeared as if smeared with fresh blood along their margin, while the more prominent heights and isolated rocks scattered over the desert cast long, growing shadows over the gray, level sands.

The warrior half-raised himself, sat up, and glanced around. He rubbed his eyes with his knuckles, straightened the broad-brimmed hat upon his head, and suddenly sprang to his feet, mechanically seizing his weapons.

The horse whinnied and strained at his halter; the dogs jumped up as if bitten by a snake, and barked furiously; the bells on the falcon's collar resounded faintly.

"Ready for the road! I must push on alone, since that one will never get up again — the Russian jade!" muttered the warrior to himself, and went, staggering, over to his pile of trappings, among which the most conspicuous object was the long stem of his costly pipe.

Here he put his smoking-apparatus in order, cleaned out the bowl, filled it with fresh tobacco from his embroidered chamois pouch, struck fire, and soon was sending forth dense clouds of whitish smoke over the desert.

Around him it grew darker and darker; the red glare which had lighted up the summits of hills and ridges went out; a bluish mist rose from the bottoms of ravines and gullies.

The warrior was dreaming, while his dim, sleepy eyes stared into the desert through the dense swaths of tobacco-smoke.

When a solitary horse sees or hears another horse approaching, it acts as if beside itself; it strains at its halter — shifting from side to side, stretches its long neck, extends its nostrils, pricks up its ears, whinnies softly and in a friendly tone, and then again assumes an expectant, statuesque attitude, listening to the approaching clatter of hoofs, noting from afar the flourish of tail and mane of the strange animal.

The dogs, also (if they notice it), can not keep still at the approach of a strange rider. Their bark is heard at once, either threatening to strangers or glad and in welcome to friends, and they rush forth to meet the new arrival. There is no need of urging them to such action.

In this instance both horse and dogs remained perfectly quiet, while at the same time the bivouac was being approached quietly and noiselessly by a horseman. The dreaming warrior saw him plainly between the clouds of smoke which covered the steppe before his eyes.

He saw and noticed the even progress of a fresh horse straight toward him, without picking its road; upon its back sat the rider, half-naked, clad only in leather trousers. The crooked legs rested upon the wooden, felt-lined stirrups. The hands held neither bridle nor whip; they hung, as if paralyzed, motionless at the sides of the body, which, in turn, appeared as if strung upon wire. There was no hat on the head of the rider, and the warrior could plainly see his purplish, blood-shot face and protruding eyes with yellowish whites, the swollen end of the tongue convulsively pressed between the decaying, uneven teeth. At the nape of the rider's neck could be seen a knotted woolen rope, and from the knot, along the back, hung the end, frayed and tattered from constant friction against the wooden saddle-tree, not covered with cloth, as is the fashion of Kirghiz saddles. The thin chestnut horse, hanging its head and nodding its white-starred forehead at every step, advanced without any apparent lifting of its legs, which did not seem to touch the earth. The dry grass and thorns did not bend or rustle under its feet. It came across the ravines without descending to the bottom, as if passing through the air from one ridge or hillock to the other.

There was something uncanny about the progress of this strange rider. It seemed as if he ought to have reached the warrior smoking his water-pipe long ago, but all the time the distance between them had neither increased nor diminished. The rider apparently remained stationary, but the horse's legs kept up their purposeless motion, and up and down bobbed the white-starred forehead.

One pair of eyes only, staring straight into the smoke, saw this rider. Neither the Turkoman horse, nor the dogs, nor even the falcon from under his red cap saw him at all. They did not hear him or feel his approach. Before them the boundless space extended in death-like stillness, and they remained quietly in their places. What did it matter to them if under the stupefying influence of his strong tobacco their master saw a vision?

"Leave me, Yunus! leave me!" muttered the warrior, in scarcely audible tones. "Why do you always haunt me? What do you want of me? Of course, I am guilty before you — I sold you! sold, yes, sold you! Go, go, go! leave me!"

And the warrior overthrew his pipe by a sudden backward movement. He trembled, resting his elbows upon the ground, never removing his eyes from a certain spot, and paying no attention to his surroundings. He did not notice the smoking and smoldering of his camel's-hair cloak, upon which a live coal had fallen from the bowl of his pipe.

CHAPTER II.

GOOD PEOPLE IN A GOOD PLACE.

" MIRZA! "

" Aye ? "

" You're not asleep? "

" Why should I sleep.   I've slept all day."

" Do you see anything good? "

" Below, only darkness; above, the stars — there. is nothing else to be seen."

" You will never see him! "

" He'll come.   If not this night, then to-morrow. That is sure! as sure as that they call me Osman and you Sharip, and your pock-marked countryman Saïd Bey."

" That will do!   All the same, one may come from the Tekke Oasis in four days, and here we have seen the sun set six times already.   As for me, I fed the last handful of oats from my bag to my horse yesterday evening."

" Perhaps something happened to him on the road. On the road anything may happen — good or bad! "

" The bad comes oftenest, especially when the black spirit roosts on one's shoulders."

" Spirit! nonsense! "

" Why not?   They roam from one end of the desert to the other.   Perhaps I have seen them — and not I alone —"

" What did you see, Mirza? "

" What?   It is night now — in the daytime I will tell you all about it."

"That is foolish babble. Ha! ha! ha! All goes according to Allah's will!"

"Dawn will soon break; it is beginning to feel colder."

"Yes, the wind is beginning to stir above. Do you hear the rustling of the thorns? You can always hear that toward morning."

Thus talked, from sheer loneliness, the bandits of the desert, Osman and Sharip, who flattered each other with the aristocratic title of "Mirza."

One of them lay flat on his face at the very top of the rocky bank of a dry ravine, covered from head to foot with his cloth mantle, and looking out from beneath, striving to see something in the foggy shadows of the impenetrable darkness of night in the desert. The other "Djigit," or desert-rover, was lying a little lower down on the slope, also bundled up in his warm cloak.

Neither of them slept—no more than the other four men, whose somber, uncertain shadows could be discerned below, at the very bottom of the ravine, where the remains of a camp-fire still shone in ruddy glow, faintly reflected in the metallic portions of their arms and accouterments.

This was a small party of roving "Yow," or desert people, who had been bivouacking for several days in the valley of Utch-Kuduk (three springs), named thus because there were, and still can be found, in this neighborhood three holes, half-filled with sand, in which a small quantity of turbid, brackish water gathers periodically—enough, perhaps, to satisfy about ten thirsty stomachs.

This water was very bad—*djaman-soo;* people had to be driven beyond all restraint of squeamishness, or to be nearly dead with thirst, before they would drink of it. Horses swallowed it unwillingly, in small sips, evidently only from necessity; camels alone seemed to enjoy it, and licked up, with evident satisfaction, the fetid, slimy ooze which covered the bottoms of the wells.

All around lay the sun-burned desert, gray and stern of aspect. The winds roamed over it in a fitful, unsteady way, driving before them in all directions columns of dust, which filled the eyes of travelers, and picked up in their flight bits of the gray sage-brush, shaping them into spherical "desert-witches," together with pieces of dry dung, bird-feathers left from some vulture's meal, and pieces of paper dropped by passing travelers.

In the summer there were solitude, heat, and ashy dust, gaunt, hungry wolves, and absence of all food and water. In the winter, solitude and frost again find the same gaunt, hungry wolves, driven by famine to throw themselves upon each other for the sake of a piece of dry, sinewy flesh.

This uninviting, deadly region does not enjoy a good repute, and no wonder. The large caravans describe a long circuit around this cursed place; they pick their route, be it ever so much longer, where water is more plentiful. The small caravans have other fears, and prefer to shape their course through more inhabited regions. And why should they not dread it when they were liable at Utch-Kuduk to run against such good people as are now found there encamped? From such good people the farther away the better.

"We'll soon have a long road before us," began Osman, after a brief silence. "Eh, Mirza, do you hear me?"

"Oh, yes! I was dreaming a little. Did you say there was anything stirring?"

"May Satan carry thee away upon his crooked horns!
I say we shall have to undertake a long journey."

"We'll not go far; we will not go all the way with
him; we will wait for Sadik at Adam Krilgan. And
then, you know, the Khan has given orders not to
trouble the Russians as long as they can not get their
long tail (baggage train) out of the sand."

"The sand is death to them and death to us!" muttered Osman.

"Well, we shall not perish — we belong to the country. Do you hear?"

"What?"

"A horse running."

"'Sh! Don't stir!"

Both the rovers bent their ears to the ground and
listened attentively. For about three seconds a deathly
silence reigned, broken only by the faint crackling of
the fire below and the sighing of the wind that always
precedes the dawn.

"Four feet — there should be eight," said Osman, as
he lifted his head.

"Four," confirmed Sharip.

Having exchanged these brief remarks, the men
again set themselves to listen.

A faint streak of light began to extend along the
horizon. Fainter and fainter grew the twinkling stars,
disappearing entirely before the rapidly spreading belt
of light.

The red morning dawn sweeps from the vault of
heaven all the small sparks of light — only one star
struggles a little longer, flashing like a diamond and
darting its twinkling beams. But this one also disap-
pears. Half the sky lights up in rosy reflection; a

GOOD PEOPLE IN A GOOD PLACE.

golden light pours over the steppe, driving before it
the blue, smoky shadows of night.

" There he is!" shouted Osman.

" He is coming," concurred Sharip.

These exclamations at once brought to their feet all
their companions, and caused them to climb up out of
the ravine.

" One horse — there is no man; it's his horse, the
bay racer — the white horse is not there; the saddle
hangs on one side — there's something wrong.   Allah's
will be done!"

While giving vent to these broken observations
Osman tightened his belt, girded up his cloak, and
gradually approached his horse, which was tied not far
away.

Three of the men had already started their horses at
full speed toward the solitary racer, with the costly saddle hanging at his side.

The frightened stallion glanced at them cautiously,
pricked up his ears, drew back, snorted, and then stood
still, having at last recognized old acquaintances in
both horses and men.

They brought the racer to the camp, surrounded him,
and began a close inspection.

" There's no blood — no bullet has touched the horse,
no sword or lance; the horse has been in no fight,"
Osman gave as his opinion.

" Yes; the horse has not been fighting," remarked an
old white-haired robber, after having carefully looked
into the large black eyes of the blooded animal.

" But is it his horse?" queried another, dressed in
an old rusty coat of mail.

Nobody replied a word to this question. All only
looked askance at the queer fellow, shrugging their

2

shoulders contemptuously. Who of their brother
rovers of the steppe did not know the warrior Atam
Kul, who had run away from the Russians? Who had
not seen him on this very mettlesome racer, which had
not its equal on the whole right bank of the Amu?

The "yow" were puzzled and somewhat disconcerted
— grave doubts began to weigh upon their minds.
They were here, waiting for Atam Kul. Word had been
brought to them from him that he would be at Utch-
Kuduk at this time. "The Mirza is coming," they had
been thinking, "to get us together. At the 'Three-
legged Camel' [the name of another watering-place] he
will get seven more. Farther on, at Ka-la-at, another
party is waiting. Well, Mirza Atam Kul will gather
them all under his standard. He'll lead us — where will
he lead us to? Ah! Allah knows where. We know nothing as to that — that is his, Atam Kul's business. But
now — what shall we do now? In place of the captain
only his horse has come. What shall we do now?"

The frightened, doubting rovers consulted for a long
time, until Osman helped them out of their difficulty;
and upon his command they mounted their horses,
seized the riderless racer, and set out at a gentle trot
upon the tracks made by the iron-shod hoofs of the
horse of Atam Kul.

"Perhaps we'll find out what we want to know," said
Osman. "Perhaps we may find him," he continued,
hopefully.

"Dead?" queried curtly the white-beard.

"And if he be dead," broke in suddenly he of the
rusty coat of mail —"he had good clothes, a saber and
daggers; he has a bag with money — why should all
that be lost?"

In this view of the situation the wolfish nature of

these rovers revealed itself, and full play was given to their brutal instincts.

A pack of hungry wolves is racing along in single file — an old, experienced wolf is in the lead. Paff! a shot. The animals jump aside and look about; they pay no attention to their trail or the enemy in sight, but throw themselves upon their leader, who is perishing from a piece of lead under his left leg. "Why should the meat be left to spoil? Farther on we may find nothing, but here is food all ready for us."

In this frame of mind the pack which emerged from Utch-Kuduk set out in the same direction in which Osman and Sharip had been watching all night, to throw themselves upon their leader, Mirza Atam Kul.

CHAPTER III.

BEFORE THE STORM.

Four years ago, just after the devastation of Bokhara, alarming premonitory rumors began to spread all over the steppes.

In all the independent, roving camps, which had sided more or less openly with Khiva, the people were convinced that they would speedily take up arms again and resume the conflict, of which God only knows the beginning or when the end will be. They felt sure that the battles of Samarkand and Zarabulak, which caused the downfall of the Emir of Bokhara, would not remain without consequences for their own Khan, whom most of them blamed for his feeble support of the neighboring ruler during his war with the "white blouses." *

The tribes hostile to Russia felt convinced that this submissive and undecided action of the Khan was taken intentionally.

"Just wait! The Russians will get after you too, and then the Bokhara people will pay you back in the same coin!" Such expressions could be heard among the nomad tribes. They were echoed under the felt roofs of their "kibitkas," and carried by the wind over the steppes, reaching finally the more luxurious felt houses and stone dwellings of those nearest to the Khan.

The tribes of Chodor, Solor, and even the distant Tekke, talked openly of war. The peaceful "Uzbeks," the farmers and gardeners of the Khivan Oasis, also took up arms. The latter, however, scarcely knew against whom they would use their weapons — their antediluvian matchlocks, their crooked, sickle-shaped sabers, and reed lances — whether against the white blouses, who had not yet made their appearance, or against their boisterous roving neighbors, the Turkomans, who had more than once exhibited their readiness to take up arms either for the faith and the prophet, for the preservation of their ancient customs, or simply for the sake of war, skillfully concealing their true motives under the mask of duty and feudal submission to the Khan of Khiva.

The Khan's condition at this time was peculiar, and not entirely devoid of a comical aspect.

Shah Nazar of Persia, in a verbal discussion of the

---

* "White blouses" or "white shirts" is the name given by the Central Asiatics to the Russian soldiers on account of their white canvas campaigning uniforms.

state of affairs at the court of Khiva, painted the situation as follows:

"The Khan Saïd Mahomet-Rachim has two ears and but one brain; two hands and but one body. With each ear he hears a different story; with one hand he drives the Turkomans into the field, with the other he keeps the Uzbeks at home. What would the Khan do? He must cut himself in two or incline to one side or the other. Which side was the strongest? The Uzbeks prayed, 'Do not go, do not stir! remember our fields, gardens, and orchards, our houses and families.' The Turkomans—the great-grandchildren of Satan, whom nothing can restrain, cried, 'Go on! What are you afraid of? Do you not know us? Haven't we been bringing you our saddlebags full of Russian heads for the last two months? Haven't we strewn the sands of the desert with white blouses? If you do not go it will be the worse for you. You have received our earnest-money, and you know what kind of an army we can put into the field.'"

At the Khan's summer residence, in the meantime, complaints came pouring in from the peaceable Uzbeks. Here the Chodor tribe had driven off stock; there the Karas had sacked a whole village, carrying all the girls and young women away with them. In another place all the boats on the Amu Daria had been seized, and such exorbitant charges made for ferriage that suffering and disorder resulted. What could the Khan do against them?

"Wait!" he wrote to the nomads on the left bank of the river. "If the Russians are coming, we will meet them in war. I shall not make peace. If they do not come, I shall not begin war, and then I shall have my hands free for the others."

The Uzbeks secretly rejoiced when they heard of this letter. They felt convinced that the white blouses would not initiate hostilities. " They will soon be here! " consoled themselves the Turkomans. " But if they linger, we will hurry them up; we'll cut them to the quick, and thus call them." And then there was inaugurated a very effective system of " cutting to the quick."

Khivan emissaries, sent out by the party desirous of war, began to scatter over the steppes and to show themselves in the midst of the roving tribes who had been subjected to Russia for more than ten years. These adroit agitators, who, according to the written instructions found upon some of them, were expected to have "long noses and glib tongues, the daring of the tiger, the persistence of the wolf, the cunning of the fox, and the speed of the hare," overran the sandy region between the Caspian and Aral seas. They even penetrated into Emba, and stirred up the Kirghiz, instigating them to open revolt, promising the most active support and protection from Khiva.

The nomads listened to these emissaries with much curiosity and the greatest attention. The old men smiled and shook their heads incredulously. They well remembered their unfortunate experience of former years. The young men would perhaps have answered the call, but were restrained by the doubts of their elders, who outweighed them in council; and a majority of the agitators met with no success, though they gathered around them a few audacious individuals in whom the inborn thirst for plunder and violence was only slumbering, leaving a constant desire for the changing fortunes of war and brigandage in preference to the monotonous routine of peaceful times.

In the sands of the " Little Horde " and " Great Horde " small bands of " sheepskin caps " began to form and to " explore " the caravan routes of Kazalinsk. Rumors of disorders on the roads became more and more frequent at the military stations. Attacks were reported upon the postal stations of the Orsk-Kazalinsk district. A few stations in the Kara-Kum also suffered, the horses being driven off and the Cossacks guarding them carried into captivity. The wounded and killed were carried to Kazalinsk from the various roads, and a general panic ensued.

The merchants called for armed forces for their protection, and not receiving them, suspended trade. Small mounted detachments sent out into the steppes chased in vain " the wind over the ground," as the Cossacks aptly expressed it; they exhausted themselves and their horses, and returned to their stations without having attained any definite results.

All the plundered merchandise, the stolen cattle, and captured prisoners were taken to Khiva and neighboring settlements, where they found eager purchasers in the local markets.

Entirely independent of the Khivan agitation, a revolt broke out in the steppes of the " Middle Horde," in 1870, and found the most active support on the banks of the Amu. Disaffected individuals, tribes guilty of breaches of the peace, and camps of nomads fled to the river to escape just punishment. The name of Sadik, a relative of the well-known Ablai Kenissar, and famous as a warrior, began to be heard again in the steppes, attracting to his familiar standard the houseless rovers from the utmost confines of the desert.

In answer to inquiries from the Russian authorities, the Khan replied that he was not the cause of all these disorders, and that he was a sufferer himself from the warlike spirit prevailing; that he was not able to cope with the Turkomans. "Perhaps the Russians themselves would like to measure swords with them!" added he, not altogether without a double meaning.

At that very time couriers were daily leaving the Khan's summer palace with letters and costly presents for the Emir of Bokhara. Saïd Mahomet Rachim-Khan inquired of Emir Mosaphar what the latter intended to do if the Russians should go to Khiva through the outskirts of his own dominions. The war party at Bokhara also began to lift its head and to murmur. But the Emir Mosaphar distinctly remembered the disasters of 1868. He could not forget Samarkand and Zarabulak, and he could not ignore the gallant revenge of Karsh and Shegrisiabs. The Emir knew well what he would do — a few troublesome heads severed from their bodies soon quieted the warlike agitators.

Over the endless steppes the "ominous mist" was getting thicker and thicker, and before long this ominous mist began to be tainted with a decided flavor of blood.

These troubled times dragged along for months and years. The storm was gathering overhead, the atmosphere was sultry, and there was no break in the clouds. Some reaped advantage from the unsettled state of affairs and some suffered. The latter, dreading to leave their felt-roofed houses, drew nearer about them their scattered droves and herds; the former roved about over the steppes, chiefly in the direction where the first encounter with the white blouses was to be expected.

The deserts of Kizil-Kum began to fill up with people; that was patent to everybody. Even the wolves and vultures began to increase in these fateful regions.

Four-footed and winged robbers scent their quarry from afar.

And there from the east, beyond the Nuratin-Tow, the gusts of desert-wind came laden, not only with sand and dust, but with the alarming cry:

"The white blouses are coming!"

CHAPTER IV.

"BEGINNING TO BOIL."

THE band from Utch-Kuduk did not advance very far. After halting once to give their horses a breathing-spell, they were about to set out again, when, far away along the uncertain, wavelike horizon of shimmering, mirage-laden desert-air, there appeared a few diminutive black dots.

The sharp eyes of Osman were the first to notice them; he bent back in his saddle and, trotting ahead, gave warning: "What is that over there?"

"Ours," replied the rider next to him, turning as pale as the dust of the road, and preparing to unfasten the matchlock from behind his shoulder. The rovers, now thoroughly alarmed, gathered in a group and stood still.

"What is the matter with you?" said Osman, grinning through his teeth, while looking to his weapons. "How will you have it? Are they our people?"

"They are running fast! Somebody is after them — that's sure. Ah! look, look! how they whip their horses."

"Retreat!" shouted Sharip, shaking in his saddle with laughter.

The little band of "sheepskin caps" obeyed this cry only too willingly. They wheeled around at a full gallop, but when they noticed that Sharip himself did not stir, they reined in their horses and turned around again, one by one.

"Easy, my friends, easy! Oh, what warriors! Ha, ha, ha!" shouted Sharip. "Oh, you cowards, you children of Satan!"

"You are one of his sons yourself! Perhaps you have never been near the white blouses, or you would not talk so foolishly," snarled one of the bandits.

"Ha, ha! I see how you will fall upon the Russians as soon as Mirza Sadik gives the word of command. You will charge as you did just now — the wrong way! I see how it will be."

"It would be better for you to look over there. Don't you see? Those are our men from the Three-legged Camel, but behind them you'll see other people."

"Those from the Khala-at are also with them. There is Vaïtak, my chum; I can tell him by the gallop of his horse. Oh! how he jumps — like a goat. There, there! Well, something must be wrong."

The distance between the flying horsemen and those awaiting them was rapidly growing less. The color of the horses could already be easily distinguished, and it was possible to see how furiously the men lashed their exhausted steeds.

"Why do they press them so unreasonably?" muttered Osman.

Two of the advancing horsemen were much ahead of the others, and kept nearly side by side. The saddlebags of one had become detached by the rapid gait, or perhaps they had not been fastened well because of hurry, and the rider kept them in place with one hand. The faces of both of them showed alarm — the eyes shifting from side to side as if trying to discover something on the distant horizon. Their lips, dry and cracked from the rapid motion through the air, were half-open; the hair of their scanty beards stood on end, and was thickly powdered with the dust of the desert.

The horses, covered with lather, breathed laboriously, especially one of them, from whose inflamed nostrils drops of blood were issuing, together with a shrill, spasmodic whistle.

"He's done for!" exclaimed Sharip, who had recognized the ominous sound from a distance.

"What is the news?" bawled Osman at the top of his voice.

The foremost horseman bounded ahead, after trying in vain to rein in his horse. He attempted to say something, but succeeded only in pointing with his hand toward Utch-Kuduk as he hurried along.

"Russians!" yelled the other as he went flying over his horse's head, plowing up the deep, dusty soil with his red, perspiring face. The unfortunate overdriven animal had not strength enough left to arrest its mad gallop, and involuntarily discarded its master.

An alarmed discussion at once arose in the little group of horsemen, which the other fugitives joined one by one, until there were about twenty of them together.

Among the arrivals were two Turkomans from beyond the Amu Daria, wearing striped cloaks. Both came in some distance behind the others — not because their horses were more exhausted, but because they

purposely held them back. Their bridles were drawn
tight, the thin chain-bits cutting the mouths of their
tired horses, which were still striving to forge ahead.

"Make haste for Utch-Kuduk!" shouted one of the
men.

"We'll talk as we go!" added the other, turning to
Sharip.

"Are you Atam Kul's men?"

"Maybe we are," replied he, evasively.

"Where is he?"

"Ah! we wanted to ask you that question."

"H'm!" grunted the Turkoman, and slackened his
bridle. "Hurry up! get along!" shouted the other; and
the whole band was soon in full flight.

"The Russians have come to Khala-at; Mat Murat
was too late to close the road for them. Nias and
Sadik are said to be awaiting them at Min-Bulak,"
said one of the Turkomans, gruffly —"the ravens! The
Cossacks came to the Three-legged Camel and beat off
our men. They'll make for Utch-Kuduk next, and then
we'll be without any water. We need a day to feed the
horses and let them drink, and fill our bags with water;
if they don't catch up with us before, the 'giaours!'
They march early, without tiring themselves, but they
cover a great deal of ground in a day. They have no
wagon-trains, but many camels; one can't pass their
columns in two hours with the fastest horse. So many
stomachs require a great deal of water. If they drive
us from the wells, ten Sadiks could not prevent them
from reaching the Amu without any battle."

"Water in the steppe is life; no water is death,"
laconically added the other Turkoman, and these words
had a strange effect upon the hearts of these rovers of
the steppes. A great dread came over them. Many of

'them shuddered as they glanced furtively about them.
All, without exception, urged on their horses.

The panic which had seized upon the fugitives from
the Three-legged Camel communicated itself to those
from Utch-Kuduk. They were all running, running as
if flying before a prairie-fire or an advancing flood;
they were flying like a giraffe before the whistle of
the hunter's bullet — flying like wild horses before the
threatening slipnoose of the lasso. They strove to
seize upon the small store of rotten salt-water — which
was life, and timidly glanced at the scorched, sun-
dried steppe — which was death.

In other parts of the desert, also, small mounted parties were running, and single scattered horsemen were
spurring their steeds.

They had been waiting for the white blouses, and
now they had come almost unexpectedly. It was a surprise, though a surprise for which the whole steppe had
been preparing for the last four years.

" Water means life — no water, death ! " These words
of the Turkoman were truly prophetic.

CHAPTER V.

THE CAMP OF THE WHITE BLOUSES.

THESE yellow, drifting sand-dunes, over which the
hot wind blew in gusts, sweeping together and scattering
again the loose dust of the surface, had never seen such
numbers of people — people altogether strange to the
country, and unfamiliar; clad in short white blouses and

red leather trousers, armed with Berdan rifles; people
who came to these places for the first time, but bore
themselves as masters, as if entirely at home on the
sand-hills.

Their bivouac covered a vast space. Everywhere
along the foot of the ridges could be seen the glistening
bayonets of stacked arms, and the red rags of weather-
worn guidons, flapping gently. Here and there small
fires were burning, and tents loomed up in many places.
Immovable, buried in sand almost to the axles, stood
the field-pieces; behind them rows of green caissons,
and back of them again rows of stunted, clumsy horses
at the picket-ropes. Then more rows of stacked muskets, more guidons, and more sheds and tents. And in
the midst of all these — some sleeping or dozing, in
groups or singly, others squatting or sitting, doing
something, as busy and restless in bivouac as they are
calm and collected in action — could be seen the white
blouses.

Isolated infantry sentries loomed up on the outlying
ridges of the higher sand-dunes; farther away, and
barely visible through the dust and the smoke of
camp-fires, were the mounted pickets; single horsemen
trotted from one vidette to the other, occasionally
ascending the more prominent sand-hills and looking
long and carefully into the distance as if they expected
something that must surely appear along the greenish,
wavelike horizon.

More than anywhere else the people gathered about
the gaping black apertures — the wells; here the talking and turmoil were loudest. There was constant
coming and going. They came running, swinging
their empty kettles, buckets, teapots, and every imagi-
nable vessel that could be carried on the march. From

the wells they went slowly, and not hurrying in the
least — balancing carefully the precious fluid obtained
with so much difficulty.

The wells were not all in one place; they were scattered along the winding gullies. By connecting these
points with lines, one could obtain an irregular figure
corresponding exactly with the outline of the whole
bivouac, if observed from above, from the point of view
of those two vultures that have followed the expedition
from its first camp, and now seem to feast their eyes
on their prospective prey.

All this activity of the bivouac, all its social life and
all its living interests, center at the wells — they are its
nerve-centers.

The Turkestan expedition had arrived in the region
of Khala-at only yesterday. All knew that it was
impossible to move forward from here very soon, and
therefore all strove to establish themselves as quietly
and conveniently as possible, if quiet and comfort were
not out of the question in this terrible god-forsaken
country.

Ahead of them, that is, in the direction in which
pointed the muzzles of the cannon, now closed with
wooden tampions, there spread out an entirely unknown waste — terrible according to its misty traditions
and the tales of disaster which filled the hearts of all
with a secret and almost superstitious dread.

" Look there! Do you see it? " one of the native
train-servants whispered to his Russian *tamyr* (friend,
chum).

" What is there to see? " replied the other after taking
a heroic pull at his strong pipe. " There is only sand
— nothing else."

" Look! Here you see hills now, and yonder

ravines," said the Kirghiz, pointing far afield with his claw-like, black and almost charred finger. "If a storm should come up in the night, you will see what there is to-morrow. Where the hills are now there will be hollows, and where the hollows are now there will be hills."

"Well, there is some kind of a road?" inquired the chum.

"Road? There's no road; no roads at all. The roads are those upon which the will of Allah may lead you; there is no other road."

"Nu! what a country!"

"What do you want to go there for?" You must not! No man, or camel, or horse can stand it."

"That will do."

"I've heard," here chimed in a young voice from another group of white blouses—"the fellows in my company told me—that once the Emir of Bokhara led his troops into this place, and that his whole army was buried in the sand, and that nobody knows now where they perished."

"Tell us some more lies!" gruffly interrupted an overgrown non-commissioned officer, with bristly and pimpled face.

"They call it Adam Krilgan," comes from a third group; "that means in our tongue 'Man's Perdition.'"

"Well, we shall have a look at this Man's Perdition!" bragged a boisterous bugler. "It is just such a road as that to the Holy Land. Now, Brother Kossolapkin, did they drive you away from the wells with your tea-kettle? What are you carrying an empty vessel for?"

"Chase me away?" grumbled the dissatisfied Kosso-lapkin; "no, indeed. Some riflemen captured my water and drank it up for me on the way. 'You can go again,' they said; 'we must go to the picket-line'—the rascals!"

THE CAPTIVE.

" What a shame!   I'd like to drench them! "

And again a timid, constrained voice could be heard;
" No bird flies over it, brethren, and no animals run
into it."

" First of all comes Providence, and second, our superiors. If they order us to go, we'll go; and suppose a
bird doesn't fly there; well, let him keep away — we do
not need him at all."   Thus struck into the conversation a stately orderly sergeant, with two crosses of St.
George on his breast.   "Spread your felt-mats and
talk no more nonsense.   Second relief, fall in!   Lively,
there! " he shouted, seating himself upon a bale that
had not been unpacked.

The soldiers were not alarmed — at least that
would have been the impression of anybody looking upon these faces; faces with and without mus-
taches — some sun-burned and almost bronzed; others dead-white, as if consumptive; others, again, red
and bloated and framed in bristly side-whiskers; all,
without exception, evidently occupied with their every-
day necessities — the cleaning out of the old water-
holes half-filled with sand; the digging of new wells;
the procuring of water, the demand for which was
never satisfied and seemed to be increasing, the wells
scarcely yielding a sufficient supply.

On the top of a natural tumulus a small fortification
was being erected — a few protective bastions were
gradually rising from the sand above the surrounding
desert.   Somewhere a drum was beating, and from
another direction came the shrill, melancholy notes
of a bugle.   A chorus of singers * attempted to start

---

* Each Russian regiment has a trained chorus of singers to
cheer the men on the march and in camp.— TRANSLATOR.

3

up a song with hoarse, half-strangled voices, but they
gave it up — evidently they were not up to singing yet.

In spite of all this outward appearance of calm, an
uneasy feeling oppressed everybody's heart. These
blinking eyes, inflamed by heat and dust, oftener and
oftener lifted themselves from the work in hand and
gazed into the distance, over the endless, shifting sands,
in the direction of Adam Krilgan — which means
" Man's Perdition."

In the officers' tents, also, this underlying anxiety was
noticeable. All in the Russian camp dreaded those-
fatal sands, and all strove to get into them. Behind
them lay the blossoming settled regions — full of life;
ahead of them stretched the sands — where death reigns
supreme. If each of them had been offered the free
choice, to go back or to go ahead, not a single man
would have been found wishing to return. They were
building fortifications — that meant the detachment of
a small garrison to guard them. All knew that this
was necessary, but they dreaded being selected to stay
behind in safety more than they feared the sands, more
than the burning heat, the deathly thirst — more than
anything else in the world.

The sick declared they were gaining strength — they
put on a bold face and feigned to be well; the weak
strove to outdo the strong. They built the low mud
walls and bastions all the same, cursing the while the
unwelcome toil.

They were all Russian soldiers — the old battalions
of the Turkestan expedition. In their ranks could be
found the heroes of Tashkent, Uratube, Dshuzak, Ird-
shar, Samarkand, Urgut, Shegri-Sabsa, Karsh, and
Zarabulak. It was unusual to meet a white blouse
belonging to this corps unadorned with a dirty, frayed,
striped piece of ribbon.

CHAPTER VI.

THE CAPTIVE.

A PLATOON of Ural Cossacks which had been dis-patched three days before upon a reconnaissance in the vicinity of Khala-at had just returned to the camp.

The Cossacks were leading about their sweating, dusty horses and stretching their own legs, cramped from long riding. A small group of them, five or six, still remained in their saddles, surrounding a strange horseman. The costume of this rider was very dif-ferent from that of the men around him. He kept in the saddle not by his own free will — his feet were bound with a rope under the horse's belly; his hands were pinioned behind his back. Like a captured wolf, he cast furtive, suspicious glances from side to side un-der his wide-brimmed felt hat. The camel's-hair cloak he wore was torn and blood-stained in places. The shreds and stains, the blue marks on his face, and swollen eyes spoke eloquently of the desperate resistance he had made before falling into the hands of his enemies. In addition to these discolorations and scratches, his whole face was thickly covered with dust, converted into a layer of grease by admixture of sweat, so that it was difficult to discern the lines of this high cheek-boned face under its disgusting mask. Two grey-hounds kept close to the prisoner's horse — one of them with a broken leg — lifting their pointed noses and whining plaintively at sight of their master.

One of the Cossacks carried upon his shoulder a hunt-ing-falcon with a red cap; on the saddle of another the trappings and arms of the captive were tied in a clumsy bundle.

The officer in charge of the platoon proceeded to the commander of the expedition with his report, while from the whole camp the infantrymen, artillerymen, and Cossacks began to assemble to look at the captured warrior. The native allies also came, the Kirghiz drivers and packers from the camel-train, to look and ascertain what kind of a wild beast had been caught by these bearded Ural Cossacks. They came from the right, from the left, from the rear, and from the front, examining everything, and not at all backward in touching the man and his belongings with their hands. They began to question the Cossacks.

"Where did you hook him?" inquired a lanky artilleryman who was staring and feeling the angular knee of the prisoner, who seemed to shrink from the contact.

"What a beast!" exclaimed an undersized infantryman while scratching his sunburned neck.

"I should call it about forty versts from here," said one of the Cossack guards. "He fought desperately when we took him. We had all we could handle."

"Did you catch him unawares, or how?" asked the artilleryman.

"We came upon him when he was asleep; we could never have caught him otherwise. His horse was a mettlesome, powerful racer; he was hobbled, but broke loose — the son of a devil! — and off he flew over the sand; we could not begin to catch him."

"He bolted — what a pity!"

"We captured him with his whole outfit, you know," explained another "Uraletz" (Ural Cossack). "His kalyan (water-pipe) was ready for a smoke; all his trappings were laid in order. He was lying down flat, his nose in the air, and sound asleep in the open steppe. We would have bound him while he slept, but his dogs there — may some evil spirit fly away with them! — spoiled the game for us. Well, he woke up, and as he sprang to his feet he made for his horse. Sissoyek, the sergeant over there, who was in command, flew at him; the horse broke away and ran off, and both men came down together to the sand."

"His only friend failed him, and now he sits here!" sententiously observed one of the Cossacks.

"Ah, what a flyer he was! We had such a chase after him!"

"A she wolf or bear are gentle compared to him. We beat him and beat him! We wanted to shoot him; Bassun already had his carbine at his shoulder, taking aim, when the lieutenant — God help him! — told us to take him alive without fail. Well, then the rumpus commenced again." ·

"But he — didn't he shoot at all?"

"He fired twice — and hit, too. He gave me a scratch on the hip. That cross-eyed fellow over there threw a rope over him from behind — that fixed him."

"Where does he belong?"

"From beyond the Amu Daria, he said, but you can't believe him. All kinds are running loose in the steppe now. There was no end to the tracks we saw."

"Last night," remarked an infantryman, "four came up in front of our picket-line. They stood and stood on a sand-hill, and away they went again!"

"We went as far as the Three-legged Camel. There they had another camp. One well they filled up, the rascals; into the second they threw a dead dog; the third was left all right. The cursed band of robbers! Pfoo!" The Cossack pretended to lift his hand against the prisoner, who only blinked his eyes and shivered convulsively. "Be quiet, you fool; I won't touch you," the Cossack said to reassure him.

A few in the crowd of spectators laughed, and one by one they began to disperse, their curiosity satisfied.

The lieutenant returned from the general's headquarters. The unlucky warrior was lifted from the saddle and his legs untied; the hands were left pinioned. The man sank heavily upon the sand, where he curled himself up, drawing his torn cloak over his head. Two Cossacks, dismounted, were placed as sentries over him; the others led away their horses to the picket-ropes.

At this moment one of the native trainmen separated himself from the dispersing crowd of spectators. He was nearly naked, with a sheepskin cap on his head, and with short leather trousers, almost worn through in places. He advanced within three paces of the prostrate man, squatted down upon his heels, and, resting his chin upon his hands, began to gaze, never removing his eyes from the place where the face ought to be, under the sheltering folds of the cloak. All the strength of his eyes was centered upon this point.

"What are you doing?" grumbled one of the Cossack sentries.

"Am I in your way?" asked the Kirghiz in a whisper.

"Let him sit there," said the other sentry, "as long as he does nothing else."

"All right; let him sit," consented the first.

Everybody in the camp knew old Dostchak, the Kirghiz. They knew him in the cavalry as well as in the infantry lines. He was known also in the artillery division. All knew him, and felt convinced that he would never do anything bad, while he was known to have done much good, even in his humble position as camel-driver.

The Cossacks saw nothing suspicious in this last whim of his. Dostchak sat there without troubling anybody, and nobody troubled him or drove him away. He never relaxed his watch upon the captive warrior, who slept, or perhaps only feigned sleep.

CHAPTER VII.

THE SISTER OF CHARITY.

THE hoarse, disagreeable bellowing of camels, their sickly, malicious snorting, the disgusting noises of rumination; the neighing of horses; the whining and barking of dogs; gruff and hoarse voices of men; occasional shots in the distance; the stamping of hoofs; heavy footsteps upon the hardening sand; the clatter and thud of the sappers' shovels and mattocks — those were the sounds which filled the air throughout the Russian camp and spread over its *triste* surroundings, together with the wind, sand, and dust. There was nothing in them that was joyous, nothing that would be in the least agreeable to the ear or that could relieve or refresh an anxious, troubled heart.

Everything here bore witness to the fact that all these living beings had not been brought together for purposes of peace or joy. Nevertheless, a strange note sounded through the heated air. The sound was feeble and barely audible; but it was unexpected, and of a nature to surprise and perplex any ear to which it pen-

etrated. This note was altogether out of accord with
all other sounds, and strangely inappropriate in the
midst of all the eye could see. In the general chorus
it produced an apparent discord. All surroundings
spoke of war, but this sound reminded one of its very
opposites — of family, of love, and of peace. It was the
cry of a child.

And this sound at once evoked another, equally
fresh, caressing, full of powerful, charming harmony —
the voice of a woman.

At about twenty paces from one of the wells, and
sheltered from the wind by a protecting ridge, stood a
small conical tent, shaped in native fashion. In its
outward appearance the tent had nothing to distinguish
it from others; the same tightly drawn ropes, the same
coarse seams running from the top of the cone to the
very bottom, the same accumulation of sand on the
weather-side. All this could be seen about any of the
many tents dotting the ground.

Nevertheless, this tent appeared to exert some
special moral influence. All who passed by the other
tents did so with perfect equanimity; no change of
expression was noticeable in any of the passers-by
beyond the customary mechanical motion of the hand
toward the visor of the cloth caps, and that only took
place when through the narrow three-cornered opening
of some tent an officer's epaulette became visible, or
gilded buttons glistened, or a foot in spurred boot protruded — or in case of some other infallible indication
of the presence of a superior.

An altogether different phenomenon could be
observed here. To this tent all eyes were attracted;
all ears were bent toward it; hurried steps were
restrained. Stern, scowling looks softened and bright-

ened; on parched lips there gleamed something very
nearly approaching a smile.

But whenever the entrance-flap happened to be
lifted, the common raising of the hand to the visor
seemed out of place and without meaning. As before
something to be worshiped, something holy — as before
the altar — the close-cropped common soldiers' heads
were bent low and the ill-shapen but strongly made
caps removed.

The interior fittings of this tent differed very much
from those of others. In the first place, the total absence
of arms struck the eye — for the present inmates they
were entirely unnecessary. Further, the carpets and
mats which covered the ground were cleanly swept,
and not strewn, as usual, with ends of cigars and cigarettes, with loose cards and pieces of chalk, or leavings
and scraps from the table. The inner walls of the
tent, of striped *adrassa* cloth, were not soiled. A large
iron folding-bed, its blankets covered with a clean
white quilt and white pillow-cases, fairly shone with
freshness. Large leather-covered packing-boxes bound
with iron served as divans and settees. In one corner
stood a wooden tub with water, covered and protected
from the sand and dust which penetrated even this
neatly kept domicile. Every trifle bore the impress of
comfort and neatness; the small mirror, the towel
hanging from a peg, the traveling teakettle and glasses,
the hamper with dishes — in all there was visible the
careful, experienced hand of the housewife, the hand
of woman.

In a light-gray cotton dress, almost short enough for
an apron, with a white muslin kerchief over her head,
the mistress of this home sat on the bed, talking to a
child, a boy of two or three years, who was perched on

her knee. The boy fretted and whimpered, evidently without any particular cause, simply because he wanted to whimper and worry a little. The woman was striving to divert him from his childish trouble and to disperse his little cloud of gloom. Her beautiful large gray eyes looked upon the child with such kindliness, with an expression so profoundly loving, that it was easy to recognize the tie between them. Only a mother can look like this; only a mother can have such eyes.

With her somewhat toil-worn, but scrupulously neat, hands the woman stroked the boy's bright flaxen hair, and caressed his round, rosy cheeks. Her slender fingers tickled him under the chin. A smile glided over her sunburned face — a smile full of love and gentleness, pleasing and restful, but in which there was nothing approaching, even remotely, joy or merriment. Nor was there grief in this smile, or anything harsh or bitter — but there was in it something strange and unearthly.

Angels possibly smile like this; and this woman was really an angel to all who came in contact with her.

She was our old acquaintance* Natalia Martinovna Chishikof, the daughter of an old gunner who lived in retirement at Chiniaz, on the Syr Daria, a heroine who had braved the privations and dangers of this difficult campaign, and boldly taken upon herself a heavy but sacred task.

The history of her life was brief, but sad. She had been carefully brought up by her simple and honest parents, living peacefully in rural retirement, with old Dementy, also an old soldier, as their only servant. What social life there was in this remote region

---

* Referring to the story "Among the Reeds," by the same author.

depended chiefly upon the officers of a few troops of cavalry stationed along the border-line. A few years ago, however, an officer of the Guards, belonging to a prominent St. Petersburg family, had been sent to the " border-swamps " on special duty. This military dandy, finding time hanging heavily upon his hands, amused himself by making love to Natalia Martinovna, who was then just budding out in youthful beauty. Accident made her his nurse while under treatment for a gunshot wound, and fascinated by the handsome officer's distinguished manners, and deeply impressed with his fine attire and luxurious habits, the innocent girl freely gave him her whole heart, and in an unguarded moment was betrayed under promise of marriage. The aristocratic scoundrel, whose name was Rovitch, soon tired of his plaything and deserted her. Several months after his departure a child was born in the little home on the border. Both the aged parents, bowed down with grief and shame, died within a year. In her loneliness and desperation Natalia resolved to take service in the field, as Sister of Charity, with the army of Central Asia, then actively engaged. Unable to bear separation from her boy, she took him with her. Old Dementy would not abandon his young mistress, and was allowed to attach himself to the command and look after her safety and comfort.

Natalia knew well that in the most painful moments of bodily suffering, in the anxious minutes of death-agony, at times of dejection and hopelessness, her mere presence, her kind caresses and quieting words of holy love and hope had more than once brought consolation to the unknown heroes, so rough in outward appearance, but sensitive in their simple hearts — the same who, in their soiled white blouses, their worn leather trousers, in boots shrunk out of shape by the heat, took off their cloth caps and linen havelocks in reverence when passing her tent.

A mother's love for humankind, especially for suffering humanity, induced her to go; a mother's love for her infant would not permit her to separate from him.

These were the causes which explain the presence of mother and child in this rough, warlike camp, pitched in the midst of desert-sands, under the burning, nebulous, colorless sky.

CHAPTER VIII.

IN THE OFFICERS' CIRCLE.

It was growing dark. In the air a slight movement was becoming noticeable, bringing with it a barely perceptible feeling of freshness.

In front of one of the officers' tents a large variegated carpet was spread over the sand, and upon it sat or reclined nine or ten officers. They were drinking their muddy, brackish tea, and between sips blew clouds of tobacco-smoke into the air.

The prospective comparative freshness of the night had called them from their sultry tents, and loneliness had driven them together. Conversation was carried on in a drowsy, lifeless manner — no new subjects of talk had turned up for ever so long. Not far away, two "denshtchiks" (orderlies) were heating up small traveling "samovars," by putting little fragments of dry dung into the furnaces, which spread around them the disagreeable burning-smell peculiar to this kind of fuel.

Upon an iron grating some meat-compound was stewing, with boiling foam flowing over the rim and sides of the smoke-begrimed saucepan. The flames of candles were shining through the canvas of one of the tents, throwing upon it the dark shadow of the back and elbow of somebody engaged in writing, to judge by his movements. A mongrel, tailless dog, with tongue protruding from one side of his mouth, and with bleared eyes, was faithfully sitting up, though nobody had asked him to exhibit his proficiency. A stray mule, with flopping ears, was wandering around, continually stumbling over and getting entangled in the tightly drawn tent-ropes. The soldiers' fires gleamed at a respectful distance from those of their superiors, and beyond them, back of the encircling groups of sitting and reclining human figures, red metallic lights sparkled from the bayonet-points of stacked rifles.

"It's impossible to have one's sleep out on such a day — and at night there is no sleep for us at all; it is very tiresome!" exclaimed Major Pugovitzin, at the same time nearly dislocating his jaws with a yawn that opened his mustached mouth from ear to ear and brought some moisture into his sleepy eyes.

"It's death!" confirmed his friend, Major Birnaps. " No diversion but the work on the fortifications, which, if I am not mistaken, are rapidly approaching completion.", Major Birnaps was born in Russia, or rather in Siberia, but he always spoke Russian with a German accent and not very correctly — a peculiarity which could only be explained by the law of heredity.

" Do you know, gentlemen, what I would like to have now?" said Lieutenant Kustikof, half rising, and then, becoming confused, subsided again.

" Prokhor — tea!" shouted the deep voice of an officer with red side-whiskers.

"We shall remain here until the detachment comes from the big fort," said Adjutant Lokhmatof, lying on his face and jingling his spurs.

"In order to continue the proposed movements with joint forces," explained Major Birnaps.

"Do you know, gentlemen," once more began Lieutenant Kustikof.

"Yes, my boy; stop there!" interrupted Pugovitzin. "I want to ask you something. Why did Natalia Martinovna pull your ear to-day?"

All laughed at this.

"I struck Shadrin, the drummer, in the mouth. Natalia Martinovna must have seen it; she called me up, and —"

"And gave you a love-tap — splendid! Prokhor — tea!"

"Gentlemen, there was some firing on the right flank to-day. Did you hear it?"

"The devil may know. Perhaps the pickets did it from sheer lonesomeness; or, as three days ago, they shot at an eagle, I suppose."

"They alarmed the whole camp for nothing!"

"It was not an eagle. The Turkomans are coming very close," remarked the adjutant. "I saw three in the distance myself. They went along over there where our camels are taken to pasture. The general ordered a platoon out to meet them."

A Cossack lieutenant on crutches came up to the group of officers and stood behind them, listening to the conversation.

"My native militiamen told me," he began, when all turned toward him. "Yes, the natives told me that Sadik has come and stationed himself at the next wells. He has about fifteen hundred men, and Atam Kul is with him also."

" Which Atam Kul?" began the major; "the same who —"

"Yes, the same," interrupted the Cossack. "Our Atam Kul. If we could but capture the scoundrel!" Here the Cossack's face was distorted by a painful grimace. He had stumbled and hurt his injured knee.

"How is your leg?" asked he with the red side-whiskers.

"Oh, it's all right. I can not walk much, but on horseback I do not feel it. Perhaps —"

"Such a beast of a man!" exclaimed Pugovitzin, returning to the previous subject. " He was a son of the devil — a common native, like our trainmen. They gave the animal a cross and made him an officer. He became completely Russified — and then, suddenly, he cleared out!"

"I heard he got into debt when he was sent out to collect tribute from the nomad tribes."

"He simply stole," remarked the Cossack. " Now he is considered one of their head men."

" I remember," began Birnaps, "on the march to Samarkand, we were playing cards at Major Gorlas-toi's —"

"Oh, nonsense!" broke in Pugovitzin. "Do you remember any march on which we did *not* play cards?"

" I say that I remember I had the bank. Many of the staff and line officers were betting —"

"Well?"

"Together with them Atam Kul was betting, and he was behind one hundred and ten rubles, which to the present day —" The end of the sentence was drowned in general laughter.

"You have an excellent opportunity now," a voice exclaimed from the tent; " capture and prosecute him."

" I should certainly prosecute him," replied the major, quite seriously.

" What will be done with him, gentlemen, if he is captured? Will he be hung or shot?" inquired Lieutenant Kustikof.

" Shot, since he has been an officer."

" But, in addition," cut in the side-whiskers, " he should be strung up for at least fifteen minutes for non-payment of a card-debt." He laughed long and loud at his own humor.

The others ceased talking for a time.

" Oh, by the way," began the adjutant, " Natalia Martinovna should be informed to-morrow."

" Of what?"

" As to Atam Kul. He was one of her most devoted admirers. I remember he used to become speechless whenever he saw her. His eyes used to burn like fire, and he trembled all over. At one time Spelokhvatof and I had to drag him away by force."

The lame Cossack here tried to insert a remark, but thought better of it.

" He asked her to marry him, at any rate, and offered her ten thousand sheep as dowry."

" He once nearly stabbed me with his knife, from jealousy," said a fusileer officer. " It was a dark night, and late; you could not see a thing. We had spent the evening at the commanding officer's. Well, Natalia Martinovna asked me to escort her to her quarters, and that beast followed us — he was simply furious. It was lucky that Trubatchenko and Babadshak caught up with us —"

" I would have killed the dastard on the spot," broke in the Cossack. " I would —" He did not finish his sentence, as he nearly fell, leaning too heavily upon his

THE SISTER OF CHARITY.

crutch, the iron point of which sank suddenly into the sand.

" He is only a wild animal — why should you kill him?" came from a well-modulated voice somewhere in the crowd.

" At any rate, he must be first captured. When he's caught, an example ought to be made —" Major Birnaps here made an expressive gesture.

" Three hours ago," continued the same quiet voice, " I thought that Atam Kul had already fallen into our hands. I talked to him, or at least tried to. He didn't answer. To recognize his physiognomy was almost impossible. His face was all scars and blood and dirt. I will look at him to-morrow when they have washed him a little."

" I noticed him myself," said the adjutant. " When they took him off the horse he limped. You'll remember he used to drag his right leg a little. Well, now —"

" Now that can scarcely be considered as proof," interrupted Pugovitzin. " After a man has had his legs tied with a rope under a horse's belly for several hours, there is nothing astonishing in seeing him limp a little; that is no proof."

" Are you speaking of the warrior the Ural Cossacks brought in? How can he be Atam Kul? I remember him very well indeed. This one is of lower stature, and speaks no Russian at all; and as to his features — well, these cross-eyed fellows are all made after the same pattern."

" That is true," confirmed Major Birnaps. " I can distinguish but three of my natives, and them only by their cloaks."

" But, all the same, the circumstance is suspicious,"

4

sententiously remarked an officer wearing the epaulets
of the general staff. "The matter should be fully
cleared up. He must be questioned and the facts
ascertained; in a word—"

"Stuff!" said the red side-whiskers, as if speaking to
himself.

The staff officer raised his head and frowned, and
disdainfully shrugging his shoulders, he said, audibly,
but as if to himself, "The pig!"

"Gentlemen, gentlemen!" said Pugovitzin, raising
his voice, restraining at the same time side-whiskers'
hand, which was reaching for a bottle. The bottle was
empty. They all knew this, but they also knew what
he wanted it for; the major acted wisely, indeed, in
preventing side-whiskers from putting the bottle to an
improper use.

"Skilomordin, drop that! This promises to be a fine
night, gentlemen — somewhat cooler than last night.
Vassa, can't you give us 'The summits of the mountains?' Tune up!" .

"It's all right!" muttered the insulted officer, as he
rose to his knees and gazed out into the darkness.
"The devil knows what kind of a man he is. I'll watch
him!"

" The summits of the mountains sleep in the mist of night,"

began Kustikof in his tenor voice.

" In the silent valleys,"

chimed in a few voices in discordant chorus.

"I'll give you a pig!" The side-whiskers could not
yet control himself, but he came in with his deep bass:

" The leaves are still and quiet."

   *   *   *   *   *   *   *

"Well, they began to hammer him," whispered one orderly to the other, relating some episode of his former rural life.

"What for?" asked the other.

"Oh, because —"

"Was it on account of the woman, his daughter-in-law?"

"That was the trouble. When he became her father-in-law, of course, there was an end of it. There was his son, of course — and the crowbar stood handy in the corner."

"That's so. Oh, look at that brown thing in the sand!"

"Kill it! kill it! Take your boot — now, once more! Draw away the carpet; it will get under the trunk. Now then, it's done for!" Such were the energetic expressions accompanying the killing of a scorpion — one of the plagues of camp-life in the desert. All joined in the hunt by the light of lanterns, and the disgusting insect was dispatched after a persistent chase.

CHAPTER IX.

SHADOWS.

THE Cossack on crutches, in the meantime, wandered through the bivouac, tacking skillfully between the rows of sleeping soldiers, stepping over the tent-ropes, and carefully circling around the officers' horses, tied to stakes, which pricked up their ears and looked suspiciously at the dark, limping figure passing by. He passed through the whole left wing of the bivouac, and,

turning around a sandy ridge, found himself near the
water-holes, where, in spite of the late hour of the night,
there was still a bustling crowd of thirsty individuals.
Above the din of human voices, the squeaking of blocks
and ropes and the splash of water being poured into
buckets could be distinctly heard. He stopped one of
the soldiers with a bucket half-filled, drank from it, and
remarked, "It is getting a little clearer and fresher."

"That's so, your honor, it is getting sweeter now;
but at the first beginning — damn it, wasn't it salty!"
answered the soldier.

"Well, go on! Thank you!"

"To your good health!" Coming to a half-front and
lifting his free hand to his cap, the soldier walked rapidly away. The officer stood still as if lost in thought,
and then proceeded in the same direction, now disappearing in the darkness, and then again thrown into
relief by the light of fires, alternately vanishing and
reappearing. He went the whole length of the camp,
and at last halted just opposite a small tent, at a distance of about ten paces from it.

Here he seated himself carefully upon the sand,
adjusting his injured leg in the most comfortable position, and gazed thoughtfully at the objects before him.

The tent was lighted within. On the surface of its
reddish-gray cloth dark shadows appeared, as if
thrown from the lens of a magic lantern. There
were two of these shadows, and though their outlines
were not altogether distinct, the most careless observer
would not have hesitated to declare that one of the
figures was a woman, the other a child. The child was
held in the woman's arms. At times she lifted
it up, seizing it under its arms — thus children are
thrown up in play; and during these movements the

little legs struck out vigorously into the air, throwing droll shadows upon the walls of the tent.

Both shadows frequently assumed strange, and even monstrous, misshapen outlines. A nose would suddenly stretch to an unusual length, or be broken by a crease in the cloth, or by a seam, and turn off in another direction; or a hand with fingers extended like a gigantic claw would cover the whole side of the tent. The folds of the handkerchief around the head, or a whisp of hair hanging over the brow, would suddenly be transformed into odd-shaped horns, and then again assume their natural form. Passers-by paid no attention to these weird phantasma, but if any one had cared to observe them closely he could not have refrained from an amused smile, or perhaps would have broken out into Homeric laughter.

I remember observing once a similar scene after a battle, during which blood had been flowing over a distance of ten versts. It was the result of one of those colossal fatal panics which will not be forgotten for centuries to come, and in the course of which, thanks to the growing perfection of the arms of civilization, very few of our men perished, but vast multitudes of "the others."

In the night, not long before dawn, I sat exhausted by the bloody scenes of the preceding day, upon a camp-stool, not far from the tent of one of the wounded officers, looking at the thin canvas lighted from within. What misshapen, comical caricatures were thrown upon the dirty, blood-stained cloth!

"I am dying; yes," whispered the wounded. "I have a daughter. Ah! she is alone among strangers. O Heavenly Father! Ah, how it burns! Save me, doctor —can't you? I do not want to die. I can not; I dare not."

"Well, all right, all right. You'll get over this. What are you fretting about; it's only a trifle," murmured the doctor, striving to console him. Then the solemn, admonitory voice of the priest could be heard: "After this brief span of life — dark, full of suffering, and grief, and trouble — there is another, an eternal one."

"What do I want with the other life! I want to live now — now! My daughter — Nadia!" shrieked the weakening voice, in which the death-agony could already be distinguished. But upon the cloth of the tent the most absurd and comical profiles were thrown, up and down and from side to side — a weird shadow-dance, with the superscription, "*Memento mori!*"

The eyes of the lame Cossack fixed themselves upon the tent, following all the movements of the shadows. He did not notice the unnatural shapes; he saw through the folds of the double cloth what nobody else could see. His eyes beheld graceful, pleasing forms; his ears were filled with gentle, cherished sounds.

Men who for prolonged periods have seen nothing to remind them of woman, and who are living under conditions which predispose them to excitement of the passions, with the whole system abnormally stimulated by scenes of blood and violence — such men would naturally be expected to be roused into a train of passionate, cynical imagery by the sight of a being of the other sex; but here they bore patiently the presence of a woman — a young and beautiful woman — in the midst of their camp.

The presence of this woman in the bivouac pitched in the sandy desert on the road to Adam Krilgan roused no such feelings. If anybody's mind had given birth to an impure thought, he would have striven to suppress it before it could assume definite form, fearing to be figuratively stoned by his fellow-man for sacrilege.

The restraint was, of course, only of a moral nature; but God knows that the most reckless among them would not have ventured to draw upon himself the mute reproach which would have blazed upon him from every passing face.

Ascetic monks, within the dark walls of their sanctuaries, often gaze upon the pleasing lines of female beauty as displayed in the images of the Holy Mother. Do those beauties inflame their blood? Do they waken the passion slumbering in their souls?

Natalia, with her calm, sorrowful smile; with her kindly eyes, always to be found where grief and suffering reigned — Natalia, the mother with her little son in her arms, was not a mere woman in the eyes of those surrounding her.

And thus the feeling of profoundest love which shone from the lame Cossack's eyes was worship rather than human love.

The heathen worshiper looks with such eyes upon his good idol when he asks for protection against another god, not less powerful, but evil.

The voices subsided, the light was suddenly extinguished, and the moving shadows disappeared, but the Cossack was still in the same place. Leaning upon his elbow, he stretched himself at full length upon the soft sand, which was still warm, in spite of the comparative freshness of the night.

"What do you want?" he gruffly addressed somebody.

"It is I, your honor; I brought your felt-mat and your saddle-cushion," replied a tall, dark figure stand-

ing before him.   The Cossack recognized the old servant of Natalia's father, the inseparable attendant and
watch-dog of the daughter.

"Thank you, Dementy — thanks!" he said, smiling
faintly.

"It is far to the Cossack camp," said Dementy,
spreading the mat, "and you'll be just as well off here.
I am going where the horses are tied."

"Well, how is Natalia Martinovna; how is Petka?" the
Cossack began again.

"Thanks be to God, they're all right," replied the old
man, going away, and smiling under his shaggy gray
mustache.   "Oh, what a man — watching there all
night!"

———

CHAPTER X.

WHAT OLD DOSTCHAK TOLD HIS COMPANIONS.

A LITTLE aside from the camel-train, in a gully
affording some protection from the wind to the flames
of their fire, already burning low, a few half-naked figures, dark as ancient bronzes and thin as skeletons, were
grouped together. The bodies appeared entirely black,
but, whenever the fire was hidden from the eye of the
observer, a reddish glare glided over them, defining
in distinct outlines the dark shadows between the ribs
and underlying the prominent muscles. The ends of
some cloth wound around a head would flash out, and
upon the handles of knives gleaming reflections were
thrown, and as quickly vanished. A bony hand would
appear reaching toward the fire, throwing into it a

handful of dry dung, and disappear again in the shadow of the dark southern night.

They were conversing in subdued, guttural tones. A low saucepan was hissing and spluttering on a small tripod, the reddish steam barely rising above it. The kalyan (gourd water-pipe) bubbled and squealed, passing slowly from hand to hand. Somebody gave vent to a long-drawn sigh, as if trying to recover from the effects of the hot, tiresome day; another expectorated the saliva collected during his long pull at the pipe, and coughed; a third hummed in half-tone an endless song, with the unavoidable refrain of "Ada-laïga," but stopped suddenly after the first line of his improvisation. Several mouths began to yawn together; and Allah and his prophet were duly remembered. Again they subsided into low, desultory conversation. At last only the crackling of the fire could be heard, and the rustle of some invisible thing moving over the sand out of the shadows into the deceptive light of the camp-fire. These "lautchi" (native allies and laborers) had assembled here to pass away the summer night, having had a sufficiency of sleep during the day.

" Has Dostchak come? " spoke up one of them.

" He has not come," answered another.

" He has not come," confirmed a third. And once more silence reigned.

The world "moved on." The Pleiades appeared above the horizon, in Orion's girdle sparkled its three stars, and the Great Bear had almost turned backward. Soon a grayish streak appeared along the eastern horizon — the herald of dawn. Light steps were approaching over the soft sand toward the fire, and a dark figure loomed up not far away.

"Dostchak — is it you?"

"It is I," answered the figure. "Yes, it is I, Dostchak; just as thou art Alaï, thou Uzen, and thou Sharip — each of us has his name. Over yonder lies somebody whom the Cossacks captured, and are now guarding — only not very carefully — who also has his name."

"Are you hungry?"

"I — am I hungry? Very hungry! And that one over there is also hungry, but he does not dare to speak of it; he does not dare to show his face — he is afraid. He is afraid because his name is not Dostchak like mine, nor Alaï like yours, nor Uzen or Sharip like yours, but quite another. Why should he be afraid to be called by his name?"

After this long peroration, Dostchak sat down before the saucepan, took off the cover, and put in his hand to feel if it was hot; then, drawing it out again, he licked his fingers clean.

"Who lies over there?" asked Alaï.

"What is he called?" added Sharip.

"Dostchak will tell us," confidently asserted Uzen.

"He'll tell," briefly uttered Sharip, and began to eat.

The others also moved up to the kettle and inserted their hands. They had been waiting only for Dostchak's arrival before beginning to attack with their chopsticks the mess of flour, brackish water, and a handful of army-crackers purloined by Uzen from a broken bale of the camel-train.

After the meal Dostchak began his tale:

"At that time we lived near Tokmak, on the river Chu, but our huts stood higher up in the mountains. I had no hut of my own, and no household goods. After the death of my second wife I did not wish to keep house again. I took refuge with a rich man — he was a bey —"

" He was called Biketaï," Uzen interrupted him.

" Biketaï. Well, I lived with him. I was overseer over all his cattle and horses, and lived in great friendship with old Biketaï himself. It was good for him and good for me. Yes, those were happy times! "

Dostchak here took breath and a draw from the pipe; then he expectorated, and went on:

" Biketaï had two sons. The oldest was then just twenty years old — the younger only fourteen. The old man loved the younger, but not the oldest. Nobody could have loved him; he was a very bad man. He spat upon the beard of our Mullah, old Hassun. The father wanted to beat him; he pulled out his dagger, and said, ' Just touch me with your little finger!' The robber!"

" Aye, aye!" The listeners shook their heads.

" Yes. How much trouble, how much evil came to our village through him! Our neighbors also suffered not a little. Ours is a mountainous country, and wooded. Most of the people have no permanent abodes, and roam about, and for such people — just like wolves they are — you must look out. We soon learned that the oldest son of Biketaï made common cause with these rovers and depended upon their support. Then robberies and plunder began on the Russian frontier, as it then was. They said it was our fault. They sent soldiers against us, and we suffered ruin and desolation. All this was caused by that cursed one. Then they turned to old Biketaï. 'Take him away,' they said; 'you are his father.' 'Take him yourself,' answered Biketaï; 'I renounce him.' Well, they tried to take him, when another outrage was committed. In a neighboring village a bride was stolen at night; a good young woman and beautiful. They followed the tracks, but could not catch up. The girl perished miserably, and after a time we learned that Atam Kul had a hand in the business. The young husband came to the father, and said, 'Your son has done me a great injury; I must kill him.' 'Kill him!' said Biketaï. 'I must not,' said the husband; 'some of your blood is still upon our family.'* 'It's all right,' said Biketaï. 'I renounce him; he is son of mine no longer.' The husband then went into the mountains to seek Atam Kul — and he was never heard of again. Two days later Atam Kul came back. 'Go and take Achmet's body away,' he said; 'somebody has killed him — or maybe he killed himself!' Well, they went after the body.

"For a long time he thus troubled all of us. He was looked upon in our villages as equal to the black pestilence. He was always called the 'cursed one.' For seven years we suffered from him, and during the eighth he went away of his own accord.

"At that time the white blouses first passed by Tokmak. They were going to fight against Aule-Ata. A general led them. He took every native who went to him in his service. Atam Kul went with them, and we had no more news of him — just as if he had died. Nobody heard of him, and none of us saw him. All the country was quiet then. We thanked Allah for that, and all the people went to pray at the holy shrine that stands upon a precipice on one side of the caravan road. So glad were they all to be delivered from the 'cursed one.'

"Then there remained to Biketaï only his younger son, Yunus. He was a good boy, honest and kind, and called me uncle. I loved Yunus no less than his old father loved him.

"Another year passed by, and another, and then a

---

* The vendetta exists among these roving tribes.

third; the time passed just as almighty Allah ordained. Old Biketaï died, and all he left behind him went to Yunus by his will. To the oldest, Atam Kul, he did not leave a single scabby sheep. We all concluded that that was as it should be. Another year went by, and another. Yunus betrothed himself to a girl from a good family. Then there came news of Atam Kul.

"We learned that our cursed one had become a great man among the Russians. They gave him a title, and gold epaulets, and a cross with a bird upon it, and finally gave him some command. Those who saw him said that he had become very great — greater than the Bey of Almatinsk, who also had gold epaulets. Yunus became uneasy, and no longer talked of his betrothed. He would not drink kumiss, nor eat, and he slept but poorly. He always sat in his house, thinking.

"I knew what he was thinking about, but was afraid to say anything. I did not dare to think, even. My heart felt all the evil that was before us.

"I kept silent and waited. At last Yunus spoke himself. He said: 'What am I here? Only a common Kirghiz. What does it serve me to have cattle and plenty of everything when all belongs to me alone?' 'As to that,' I answered him, 'you will marry and have a family of children, and you will live as your father lived, rich and comfortable.' 'I shall join the Russians with my men,' he said; 'they are at war over there. I am no worse than my brother, who got up among the great people.' He cut me to the quick with those words. I talked to him for a long time; and not I alone — many old men came to talk to him. Within a month he began to get ready."

"Yunus?"

"Yunus. I also got ready. I would not leave him,

and vowed never to take my eyes off him. It was right for him to go — why not? — had it not been for his older brother. At the same time we heard that this older brother was very angry with Yunus because the inheritance had gone to him alone and had not been divided between them. Most of all I feared Atam Kul; but, trusting that Allah would not allow evil to prevail, we went."

The narrator took breath and again refreshed himself with the pipe. The faint streak of light in the east spread and spread, and in contrast with this pale, yellowish light it seemed to grow darker below, especially in the ravines. Here and there, like scattered posts, the sentries could be seen looming up darkly, moving slowly back and forth on the short paths they had trodden during the night.

Dostchak continued: "At that time much land was taken by the White Tsar, though we did not know much about it then. We passed by Antye-Ata, where the Russians had long been settled; then we came to Chimkent, where they were building a new fort, and then to Tashkent. Here they had built a whole new town, larger than the old one that belonged to Bokhara. Then we asked, 'Where is the war?' 'At Samarkand,' they answered; 'still farther away.' We went on to Samarkand. I don't remember how long we were on the road, but, thanks be to Allah, we got there safely.

"The commander at Samarkand at that time was very strict. He had a black helmet on his head, and on his nose he wore round glasses with a golden frame. I remembered then that I had seen him before, at Almalakh — only he was younger then. First of all we went to the commander and inquired after Atam Kul. They told us: 'He is here, but he has gone away about a hundred versts or so; he'll soon be back.' We concluded to do nothing until we had seen Atam Kul. We wanted to win him over by telling him: 'You are the older brother — tell us what to do!'

"At last Atam Kul arrived.

"We did not recognize him at once. He seemed to be a head higher in stature. Some of our people were with him — quite a number. He also had Russian Cossacks under his command — a whole company. He spoke Russian, and drank wine with the big officers; he even shook hands with the general.

"Well, I went to see him first, and told Yunus to wait. I thought I might find out first what thoughts he harbored in his soul. 'What have you brought me?' shouted he at me. I told him. 'Well,' he said, 'my brother Yunus is a rich man now, but he lets a common dshigit speak for him; that seems strange.' When he said that he smiled in such a way that it made me feel cold all over, but I kept silent and waited. 'Well, all right,' he said; 'he can go along with my other men, and later I will speak to the general about it. Where is he staying?' he asked. 'In a bazaar behind the town,' I said. 'There is an empty house, and a yard with three poplars in it — there we have put up.' 'Well, in the evening I will go there myself. Good-by, you old dog!' That he meant for me — the word cut me to the soul, and had it not been for Yunus I should have jumped at his throat, though he had cut off his beard, the renegade, in Russian fashion. Well, I went away, but I heard him cry after me: 'Eh! did the old fool, our father, leave much property behind him?' I made no answer to this.

"In the evening the brothers met. There was no

trouble — they embraced even — only Atam Kul's lips were pressed together very hard, and he looked upon Yunus with an evil eye.

"Two days later we heard that the Russians were getting ready to march — not against the Emir, but for him. They were to take back the city of Karsh, which the Emir's eldest son had taken away from his father. We went with them. We marched through the country, and our people roamed about through the enemy's villages. We all know what war is. They began to drive off cattle, and the people of Bokhara complained to the general about it, and he told them they should not be troubled. The general was that kind of a man that when he ordered anything, nobody dared to disobey him. A day passed by — our people were encamped at Dshama — and new complaints came in. That made the general very angry, and he inquired who was doing it. The officers told him Atam Kul's people. Atam Kul was called, and came. He stood there pale and trembling, for all his being such a big man. The general ordered him to tell his people that the first man who stole cattle would be hung, as an example to the others. We heard of it only afterward, but all our misfortune sprang from this.

"As soon as we got to Karsh, firing began. Our men were all scattered. Atam Kul was with the general. I was looking for Yunus, but he was not with us; then I was seized with such fear that I did not feel the horse moving under me. In the evening I looked around again — there came Yunus driving four cows before him and leading a camel by the halter, passing straight by the general's staff. The strict general shouted, 'Hang him!' I nearly fainted. With the general to say a thing was to do it. I got our people together at once and rushed up to the general — there were fifteen of us — and we all fell upon our knees. 'Forgive,' we said. 'It is the first time, and he is very young. He knew nothing of it; his brother never told him of your strict orders.' 'What brother?' asked the general. 'Atam Kul,' said we. 'I did not know he had a brother. Is that your brother?' he asked Atam Kul; but he — the cursed one — may his bones never find rest on the earth or under the ground! may a fiery pestilence devour him! — he denied him. 'No,' he said, 'I do not know him; he is not my brother.' 'All right; hang him!' said the general without looking up. They brought on poor Yunus. Again we began to beg, and we swore that that was Atam Kul's brother who was serving with him. 'Is that your brother?' the general asked again. Atam Kul smiled, and said, 'I can find many such brethren. Any new-comer may call me brother!' The general frowned, and gave his last command: 'If he is your brother, I will pardon him.' Then we all fell at Atam Kul's feet; we kissed his boots, and adjured him by all that is holy — then we waited. But the Cossacks were already preparing the rope. They dragged Yunus under a tree — all was ready, and we were waiting still for Atam Kul to speak. He stood there staring at the ground, silent. His face was as dark as the earth beneath him. He glanced sometimes at the general and sometimes at the place where Yunus was bound.

"Then we began to pray to almighty Allah. The general turned away and went into his tent, but before he entered he turned and looked at Atam Kul, and asked, 'Well?' We all held our breath. 'No, he is no brother of mine,' said Atam Kul, talking very low — his lips scarcely moved; but all of us who stood there heard his last words.

"They hanged Yunus. I then left the Russians and
went away, only watching from afar. I never lost
sight of the rascal; I have followed his every step, and
wait to see when just Allah will send him his punishment."

Dostchak ceased talking, and threw another piece of
dung upon the fire.

"Well, what else?" asked Uzen.

"I wait," said Dostchak, and nodded his head.
The men who had listened to him also nodded their
heads. They all understood now why he who was
bound over yonder was so much afraid that somebody
might know him — might know his name.

Drums now began to beat, and bugles sounded from
the picket-ropes. The sky in the east flamed up
brighter and brighter. The rays of the rising sun
already gilded the summits of the sand-hills, then
descended lower and lighted up the bayonets of the
soldiers' muskets. The camp of the white blouses
began to stir and to take up its ordinary pursuits.

Having passed away the summer night, the native
"lautche" scattered over the camp, wherever they
wished to go; but soon they began to collect in one
place. Old Dostchak was also there, and many others
crowded around the bound man. He was made to get
upon his feet, and taken to the general's headquarters
to be questioned.

CHAPTER XI.

A DESERTER.

In a shallow ravine between two rows of sand-dunes, about four versts ahead of the line of double sentries, a small outpost of ten riflemen with an officer was stationed.

It was getting near morning, and a grayish light already began to spread along the eastern horizon. A slight movement began in the camp, which was invisible to those of the outpost, because of it being hidden from them by hills and smoky fog, but the stir was easily perceptible to trained ears.

The soldiers felt very tired after a night of prolonged and earnest struggle with an almost unconquerable desire to sleep. If a sentry, standing or walking, can scarcely keep from nodding, how much more difficult must it be for men stretched out in comfortable positions and wrapped up in warm greatcoats! But it was necessary to struggle all night, and that all the twenty-two eyes should look sharply at the line which but imperfectly defined the horizon, to watch whether suspicious black dots did not appear against the comparatively bright streak of sky. It was necessary for all to listen intently for the stamp of horse-hoofs or the slightest rustle of a body dragging itself over the sand.

But in this outpost all were volunteers, fond of nocturnal and all other adventures, and consequently it was altogether unnecessary for the officer in charge to watch his subordinates, whether any one of them should fall asleep, lulled and overcome by the death-like stillness and immobility.

With the dawn the outposts were permitted to return to camp, as they could be of no use during daylight. They had the privilege of sleeping throughout the day after their wearisome night, which easily explains the satisfaction with which the soldiers observed the extending sphere of morning brightness, as well as the stir and movement in the camp, which increased with every minute.

" Look!" whispered one of the riflemen, very faintly, as if to himself, without turning to his companions or changing from his reclining posture, and looking steadily ahead to some point in the distance.

All would have looked without this warning, and in fact all observed simultaneously what the speaker saw. They all seemed to strive to sink themselves still deeper into the sand, so flatly were they clinging to the ground, holding their breath — only the fingers of the left hand strongly grasped their gun-barrels, and the forefinger of the right barely felt of the smooth surface of the trigger. Thus tigers crouch, watching their victim's approach to the watering-place, with the same complete extension of the body, the same deathlike immobility — only these were bipeds and gray, not striped quadrupeds.

On the very summit of a ridge which lay in dark outline before the eyes of the riflemen a black spot appeared — a horseman. He stood for a second, and disappeared again. An unexperienced eye could not have ascertained with any certainty where he was hidden, whether he had retreated behind the ridge again or turned aside; but the trained watchers clearly saw that the latter was the case.

After this a whole group of black dots appeared upon the ridge, but they did not hide ; they stood and took possession of the height, and then rode along it in various directions.

"Listen!" again whispered the first rifleman, but again his warning seemed superfluous, for all were listening intently without it.

They heard a horse's hoofs in rapid motion, but it was the gait of a tired horse, frequently breaking from its gallop. The noise was coming nearer every second.

Six men of the outpost, throwing off their greatcoats, quickly rose, and ran to intercept the rider; the others never moved their eyes from the sandy ridge.

The horseman was now quite near, looking around attentively. His horse snorted, and also glanced about suspiciously, stretching its slender, handsome head into the wind and pricking up its ears. The rider was armed, but he unfastened his weapons and gathered them in a bundle, as objects he did not intend to use.

"A deserter," whispered one of the riflemen to another.

"Very likely," whispered the other. "Those over there were chasing him, but didn't catch him. They're afraid to follow him farther. They've stopped."

The rider urged on his horse, which fell back on its haunches, striking out vigorously with its forelegs. In a second he was dismounted, or rather pulled from his saddle. He could not cry out, because muscular palms covered his mouth; he could not move, because a thin, elastic rope was quickly twisted about him, cutting here and there into his dusky, bronze-like body.

A silvery strain sounded through the morning air; from the camp the bugle called, "Draw in your outposts!"

"Well, thanks to the Lord!" sighed one of the riflemen, with evident satisfaction, "this night we did not
wear ourselves out for nothing. The Lord sent us some
game, though we can't eat it!"

The captive was taken into camp and duly inspected.
The face was not that of a Kirghiz or an Uzbek, nor did
it resemble a Turkoman's. The eyes were large and
black; the eyebrows thick and arched; the beard long,
thick, and curly, and though it was now gray with dust,
it was black as tar by nature. The man was clad
very poorly in a ragged "khalat," or cloak; the feet
were bare and chafed to bleeding by the iron stirrups.
His weapons also were of the meanest description: a
saber in a worn-out scabbard and a short flint-lock
musket. The horse, however, could not easily have
been bought for 500 "teel" (Khivan gold-piece, worth
nearly $2), and bridle and saddle were ornamented in
rich patterns with silver and turquoises. The rider
and his horse did not match, and that was a suspicious
circumstance.

"I am an Irane" (Persian), said the prisoner. "I
served in Mat Murad's own stables. I heard that the
Russians were near, and that they came to liberate my
countrymen. I ran away from my master, and stole a
horse with all its trappings. They pursued me a long
time, almost to your camp; but they couldn't catch me,
because the horse I had under me has not its equal in
Mat Murad's stables. If they had caught me they
would have skinned me alive, and if I were to fall into
their hands again I'd be lost. The Russians are my
only salvation, and I will serve them faithfully. I'd give
every drop of my blood for the Russians. I can be of
use, too. I know all the roads well, and I know all that
is going on there — what troops they have, and how

many cannons. I know all that; and so as to remember well I have put everything on paper." And the capt- ured Persian — fugitive or deserter, as the soldiers called him — drew from his bosom a ragged, yellow piece of paper, closely covered with fine writing in neat Persian script.

Then the riflemen of the outpost were questioned. They said, "About ten men were chasing him — per- haps more; we saw them."

"One of them shot me," continued the Persian. "See, here is the mark of the bullet — look!" He drew the cloak from one of his shoulders, and all could see the red, scald-like mark made by a bullet grazing the body.

"All right," said the general. "Don't be afraid. Serve us well, and it will go well with you — we will not give you up to the Khivans; but if you betray us, we'll hang you — I want you to know that."

An interpreter translated this short speech to the Persian, who made a low obeisance, placing both hands upon his heart, and visibly brightening up with joy. He asked only one favor — that his horse be not taken away from him. This also was granted. He was given to understand, however, that he would be closely watched until he should convince them of his faithful- ness.

The Persian was then ordered to join the camp of the native militiamen, and, very well satisfied with his reception, he passed through the whole camp, accom- panied by two dismounted Cossacks. He held up his head straight, while his eyes roved from side to side, taking in everything within the camp. He noticed a sentry standing up, and near him, crouching in the sand, sat the man who was "afraid to tell his name." The head of this man was bent upon his knees; his face was not visible.

"A dirty people are the Khivans! May they all perish, from the oldest to the youngest!" said the Persian,
loudly, and laughed disdainfully. Hearing these words,
the crouching man raised his head, looked up, and trembled, with his eyes wide open.

"Allah will help thee the day after to-morrow; watch
and be ready!" said the Persian; but now he spoke in
Persian, while at first he had used the Uzbek dialect.
The Cossacks escorting him understood all he said at
first, but the last sentence was unintelligible to them.

"He is abusing him, I suppose," remarked one of the
Cossacks to the other. "Surely, these Persians do not
love the Khivans."

"Who'd love the whip and stick?" replied the other,
not altogether without pertinency.

The crouching man again lowered his head, and
nobody noticed the animation that flashed up in his
face for a second, lighting in his heart a spark of hope
for rescue.

On the same morning Dostchak visited the camel-
camp, and then went to look again at the man who was
afraid of his own name.

"Well, how is it?" inquired Uzen.

"What simple people these Russians are! Allah preserve them! Every runaway blown here by the wind
they pick up and believe his every word. One must
look sharply or something bad may happen!"

There was much work for the native allies this morning; the camels—two thousand of them — had to be taken
into the steppe to pasture. Fortunately, all was quiet
there, and the scouts brought the most reassuring
reports.

"Everything is quiet — nothing stirring."

CHAPTER XII.

LABORERS FROM A PLUNDERED CARAVAN.

THREE days had passed since the unknown warrior had been brought in by the Cossacks. He had been questioned, and all that could be expected from a captured common native had been ascertained, and for a time he was left to himself like any ordinary prisoner. Rumors, however, began to spread more and more through the camp as to the personality of this prisoner. There were many who had known Atam Kul personally when he was in the Russian service. Among them were some who had been quite intimate with him, and could scarcely be mistaken, meeting him now when only five years had elapsed, but — ah! there seemed to be innumerable "buts" interfering with definite assertion — all the more since a decisive recognition of Atam Kul's identity was equal to a sentence of death for him; and who would willingly take such a sentence upon his conscience as long as there existed the most infinitesimal spark of doubt?

The reasons for explaining everything by a simple resemblance were many. Who would, for instance, expect to find in the open-hearted, rough, and somewhat vulgar Atam Kul, as they all had known him, such self-possession and presence of mind under such trying circumstances; such subtle skill in disguising his face, his customs, and familiar movements — in a word, all that could possibly betray him?

He was called loudly from behind, entirely unexpectedly — he did not turn or betray himself by the

slightest motion of his shoulders. He was interrogated
on various subjects, gradually leading up to decisive
questions, but nothing suspicious appeared in his
answers.

His face, it was true, resembled that of Atam Kul,
but the thin Kirghiz beard was different. The other
was red-cheeked, stout, and smooth-skinned, with an
impudent look and self-satisfied bearing; this one was
thin, pale, with prominent cheek-bones, and appeared
much lower in stature. Then the scars in his face
almost obliterated his features and gave them a different expression. The other spoke gruffly and loudly;
this one lowly and painfully, as if the words were forced
up from the very bottom of a worn-out, consumptive
chest. But in spite of all this there were many who
said:

" However, the devil take him! how much they are
alike, the beasts! " And this " beast " remained a common "dshigit " of Sadik's band; had heard something
of Atam Kul, but had never seen him in person. Only
two individuals in the whole camp had no doubt as
to his identity. One of them was our old friend
Dostchak, who kept silent to await the proper time;
the other, Natalia, was prevented by humanity from
speaking.

In the meantime other strangers came into the Russian camp. On the road by which the Russian expedition had arrived there appeared four men on foot. One
of them had been wounded on the head by some sharp
weapon or instrument; the other three were uninjured.
They were all nearly without clothes, only leather
trousers covering their nakedness. All were completely worn out with long marching, sinking to the
ground exhausted as soon as they reached the Russian

picket-line. They were taken and brought to the camp.

They appeared to be from Bokhara, laborers in the employ of one of the merchants who had gone with a caravan from Nur-ata, and had been plundered by a roving band. They stated that about a hundred mounted " dshigits " fell upon them, took their camels and goods, killed two men outright and wounded one — there he was — who had come with them, and robbed them of all their clothes, leaving only the trousers. They begged the Russians, before everything else, for something to eat and drink. That was the second day they had been without water and food. After that they would ask for an asylum — that is, for permission to go with the Russians until an opportunity should offer to return to their own country.

It happened that rumors had already reached the camp that some caravan from Bokhara had been plundered by the Turkomans, and it was naturally believed that these men had belonged to it. The new-comers were given food and drink, and permitted to remain. They seemed to be much pleased, thanked the Russians, and implored Allah to shower all blessings upon them.

The Persian deserter made up to these people at once, questioning them, and telling them his experience, and they became friends from the first. Two of the new arrivals turned out to be also Persians, his countrymen, and that seemed to satisfactorily explain the intimate relations springing up between them. The Russian soldiers always treat the natives very kindly, especially when they are suffering, and on the very first day many of them addressed them as "tamyrs" (chums).

On the same day, also, the victims of robbery seemed

to forget their sufferings, wandering freely through the camp, looking at everything, and not failing to notice the prisoner, and even trying to converse with him.

Again it was only old Dostchak who, grumbling and growling, was very much dissatisfied with the condition of affairs — so much displeased that he resolved to overcome his timidity and to communicate his fears to the highest authorities. After attiring himself in his new red cloak, he prayed long, on his knees upon his little felt-mat spread upon the ground, and his hands uplifted. Then he proceeded through the camp, shaping his course toward a large tent where a red ensign with seven white stars, tattered and bleached by sun and rain, fluttered gently in the breeze.

CHAPTER XIII.

THE REPORT.

Dostchak trudged along until he caught sight of the tent, the object of his journey. It was necessary to pass by long rows of stacked arms along which pensive sentries were pacing; in another place bales of supplies were piled up — these also had to be avoided. He described a great circuit around the artillery-park, and came upon the hospital-tents, and was again forced to make his way around. In doing this Dostchak stumbled over ropes and dragged at tents, for which he was soundly scolded. Soldiers whom he knew spoke to him kindly, and many to whom he was unknown looked up at him.

"Eh, friend, where are you going?"

"Ah! my old chum; you piece of an old picked bone! Won't you have some tea? Come here, you red devil — I'll give it to you, with sugar. Sit down!"

"Look, boys, he's got a medal — there it dangles on his cloak. Dostchak, good luck to you, you honest soul!"

"Careful, you old devil; you'll upset the guns!"

Similar greetings showered upon Dostchak from all directions; but he went on and on, not saying a word to anybody, or acknowledging any of the calls and invitations. At last he got to his destination.

There was the red flag! How frayed were its edges — it must have been over a great deal of country. And there stood the sentry — a rifleman. A copper saucepan was simmering in the sun; steam was rising from it, and a small fire glimmered under the iron tripod. An orderly was opening a bottle, wiping the neck with the skirt of his tunic. A Cossack officer who had just come out of the tent jumped upon his horse, which backed and gave him some trouble, but he gained his seat, not, however, without nearly trampling upon old Dostchak. Then somebody else emerged from the tent, rattling his saber; he dropped some papers out of a portfolio, and the wind carried them away. Some Cossacks ran up and began to pick them up. Dostchak got his hands upon one of the papers, trying to say something, but his timidity kept his lips sealed.

"Well, there is some wind this morning," some one remarked; "it fairly howls!" "The commander of the cavalry perfectly agrees with me," comes from a pleasing baritone voice within the tent. "Cut it into small pieces and put it in," somebody was explaining behind the tent.

"What do you want?"   .

Dostchak was overcome with confusion. A mustached physiognomy looked him straight in the face, without taking its eyes off him. It was terrible! The mouth opens wide, with grinning teeth, and — down goes Dostchak on his knees with his red cloak, his medal, and his tall sheepskin cap, which he twists in his trembling hands.

"I should know that face," thinks Dostchak; "I've seen him with the train. Once he struck me with the whip — but not very hard. I want the genderal — *arzimbar*" (I have a request). He spoke up loud and resolutely, seating himself upon the sand opposite the very entrance, and resumed his customary respectful attitude.

Dostchak spoke Russian very badly, being barely able to make himself understood at all; but in view of the great importance of his present business, he had made up his mind to carry on his conversation with the general in Russian, in order to avoid the use of an interpreter, in whom the natives generally repose but very little confidence. He had only just succeeded in pronouncing his explanatory words when the general himself emerged from the tent. The red khalat at once attracted his eyes.

"What do you want?" inquired the general.

Dostchak went straight to. the point. "When will you hang Atam Kul?" he asked, rising to his legs and making a deep obeisance.

The general laughed until his white vest and gold chain fairly shook over his stomach. "Catch him and bring him to me; then I will hang him," he replied, still laughing. "I remember this fellow — the sworn enemy of Atam Kul. I remember him — some one told me —"

"Exactly, your Excellency," some very small body behind the general's back replied, very respectfully. "It was, with your Excellency's permission, on the march to Nur-Ek. Fires had been lighted to warm up our freezing men —"

"Genderal," broke in Dostchak — "Genderal, why you no hang Atam Kulka? Why you catch and no hang? He will run away, Atam Kulka — no can hang him then. Atam Kulka soon run away. One day, two days, run away. There's bad people in the camp. One man no good; four men no good. Atam Kul take them and run away. Right away hang Atam Kulka, genderal; then Atam Kulka no run away."

The old native's request, in spite of the comical phrases in which it was couched, had in it so much earnestness, so much honest enthusiasm and persistence, it breathed so much conviction and truth, that the general involuntary contracted his brows and considered for a minute.

"Why do you say that *that* is Atam Kul? Perhaps it is not he," said the general.

"Let Atam Kul be brought. Dostchak will show you."

"See about that!" said the general to the small man behind him. "Sit down!" turning again to Dostchak.

The old man immediately seated himself, squatting down upon the sand, more like a manikin than a living man. The general returned to his tent; the little man hurried away somewhere.

"Allah, all-powerful, all-wise, and just! allow not the wicked to triumph over the good. Do not place black dirt upon my clean head. Great Allah, you are the only god over this whole world, and there is no other!" Thus softly muttered Dostchak, scarcely moving his dry, senile lips.

CHAPTER XIV.

ATAM KUL.

NATALIA, accompanied by several officers, emerged from her tent and sauntered through the familiar camp. The lame Cossack, limping along on his crutches, kept abreast of her, joking with little Petka. The child held tightly to his mother's clothes, striving to adjust his short little legs to the steps of the grown people. This was, however, not very difficult for him, because Natalia accommodated her movements to those of her son, and the whole group of promenaders advanced very slowly.

They had long since discussed all subjects of interest, and being for the moment without any material for conversation, they went along silently. Some one hummed a march, the others mechanically keeping step to the tune.

"Petka," the Cossack broke the silence, "come and sit on my shoulder. I'll carry you. Climb up, young man! Kustikof, set him up here."

"Don't want to!" replied the child, clinging still tighter to the clothes. "I walk! walk!"

"Never mind; let him get used to walking," said Natalia. "Well, how is your back, Karpof?" turning to a young soldier of the line who not long since had sprained his back drawing a heavy tub of water from the well.

"It's all right, little Mother Natalia Martinovna, as if taken away by your hand," pleasantly replied the soldier, springing to his legs and standing at "attention."

"They are cured by a single word from you!" joked the old doctor, coming out of the nearest tent, in his gray nankeen blouse, and joining the promenaders. "You simply take all the practice away from us doctors!"

"Well, to a soldier a kind word and a gill of whisky are more beneficial than a whole pood [forty pounds] of your dirty apothecary's stuff," remarked one of the officers. "My mouth is still bitter from the last dose you gave me."

"My leg here is getting worse and worse," gruffly broke in the Cossack "It may have to be cut off yet. I would have long since put a bullet through my forehead were it not—"

"Natalia Martinovna, cure him with a k——," began the same officer; but he stopped, and swallowed the remainder of the sentence, under the influence of a severe look from Natalia.

"The dysentery is subsiding," reported the doctor, hurriedly—"it is much less virulent; there were eight scorpion-bites; the drummer's forefinger was amputated to-day; two bottles of port-wine were stolen from the dispensary."

"Oh, look there, gentlemen!" exclaimed Kustikof. "What a crowd there is gathering at the general's! What a lot of people! Let us go there!"

"Let us go," calmly replied Natalia. The whole group, passing by the long picket-ropes of the artillery, directed their steps to the general's headquarters.

In front of the general's tents a considerable multitude was indeed assembling, forming a half-circle facing the principal tent, and observing with undivided attention something that was going on there. The foremost ranks of the crowd were occupied chiefly by officers; behind them stood some infantrymen with loaded arms, and in rear of them a dozen or two of Cossacks and a great crowd of native militiamen, lending the scene a touch of color with their bright, wide-striped cloaks. Passing horsemen halted, and, raising themselves in their stirrups, looked from their saddles over the heads of those in front. The curious were flocking together from all directions, in such numbers that when Natalia Martinovna arrived it was with much difficulty, in spite of the willingness of the crowd to give way, that a narrow path was cleared to allow her and her companions to pass.

The general sat on an iron folding-chair at the entrance of his tent; about him and at his back stood a few staff officers. Within the darker square of the passage leading to an inner compartment, still other figures were indistinctly visible.

Not more than three paces in front of the general stood the prisoner; he was unfettered and his free hands hung down beside his body. His head was bent slightly forward; the whole body was strangely distorted or twisted; the knees nearly touched, and trembled slightly — perhaps with fright, perhaps with subdued emotion; the muscular bare legs buried themselves in the sand, and stood as if petrified, without changing position for a second. The fingers of the hands were impatiently picking at the dirty shreds of his cloak. The closely shorn head was entirely uncovered, being even without the usual "tibetaika" (flat Bashkir cap). A few dirty scabs and several long scars showing signs of healing were visible upon this angular, purely Mongolian skull. The eyes looked up from beneath the brows directly upon the general. The look was calm, and almost apathetic.

In line with him stood two infantrymen with guns at their sides, and a Cossack who had removed his cap. In their immediate rear there was a little open space, but behind that, packed closely, and in perfect immobility, stood the front ranks of the spectators. Dostchak was nowhere visible.

"To be sure," said the general, in French, "the similarity is great; but there seem to be more data indicating that it is not he. If it were not for the declaration of that native — may the devil take him! — I should have done with him before this. Now we must," continued the general, with a vexed, impatient gesture — "but that can not be done! Why did that fool turn up here?"

"We might send for that Persian," advised a staff officer with gold epaulets upon his crumpled blouse. "He must know Atam Kul as he is now. He has probably seen him with Mat-Nias."

"See to it; give the necessary orders!"

"Well, surely this is Atam Kul," said somebody in the tent, in a subdued tone. "No matter how one looks at the thing, it must be he, I would be willing to lay any reasonable wager."

"All right; back your opinion, you speak so confidently."

"Let him go to the devil!"

"At the same time, that fellow Dostchak must bring some incontrovertible proofs. It is very interesting, but I think it is all nonsense."

"He seems so confident. It almost grieves me to look at the unfortunate fellow — they'll be sure to hang him! But whom are they bringing now? That must be another witness. His face seems familiar."

"That is the Persian deserter who was caught yesterday. Listen! listen!"

From behind the tent appeared the Persian, bending
over almost to the ground. He was very pale, or rather
ash-colored, and shook as if attacked with fever. He
did not know why he was called, and observing the
prisoner, hesitated and tried to back out again.

"Go on!" And he was pushed ahead vigorously by
the knee of his Cossack escort.

"Good-day!" said the general.

The Persian trembled and squatted down.

"Do you know that man?" asked the general, nodding his head in the direction of the prisoner. "He
weakens!" he continued aside to the staff officer.

The Persian remained silent, looking from side to side
with wandering eyes, evidently avoiding the point to
which his attention was directed.

"Look there!" the Cossack prompted him.

"Who is that?" The general repeated his question.
"Well, don't be afraid. What do you fear? Look well,
and tell me who it is. Interpret this for him."

An officer of small stature, with a dusky face of
foreign type, interpreted. The Persian listened attentively, looked furtively at the prisoner, and lowered his
head.

"I do not know him. He's a Khivan, that I know,
but who he is I do not know."

"You know the face of Atam Kul?" asked the interpreter; "the one who ran away from us and now serves
the Khan of Khiva?"

"Atam Kul?" repeated the Persian.

"Well, yes!"

"He who was a great commander with the Russians?
He is a great man with the Khan — Atam Kul Dakhta

[high military title]. I have seen Atam Kul; I know him. Why shouldn't 1 know Atam Kul? Three times — no, four times, exactly four times — the sun has set since Atam Kul ordered me to be beaten with a stick, but I ran away. I know Atam Kul well."

There was a general involuntary smile, and .even suppressed laughter became audible in the crowd. All seemed to feel somewhat easier. The calm voice in the tent resumed: "Well, my dear fellow, is that Atam Kul? You were so firmly convinced, would you be willing to lay two bottles and some preserved lobster?"

"Oh, the devil; it is positively all the same to me!"

"He lies, brethren, that Persian," one of the Cossacks whispered to his companion. "He is evidently putting it on thick. How can these officers believe him?"

"Shall we shoot him or hang him?" inquired a young infantryman.

"We'll cut him into slices and make straps of his hide — will that please you?"

"Be quiet — they are talking."

"Where is Atam Kul now?" the general asked the Persian.

"How can I tell where Atam Kul is now? The sun has set four times since Atam Kul was with Mat-Nias. Four thousand horsemen, four thousand footmen, and one hundred cannon were with Atam Kul. Atam Kul Dakhta is a great man with the Khan of Khiva."

"Drive the fool away!"

"Go on! get out! Be thankful that you are whole!" The Persian was led from the scene without being given a chance to make his bows in accordance with oriental etiquette.

A new witness now appeared before the prisoner — a witness who had been in the tent all this time, hidden away. The witness had heard everything, and waited. Now he went around in the prisoner's rear, altogether unexpectedly, and touched his shoulder. The man turned quickly, stepped back, and lifted his hands. He endeavored, or thus it appeared to those observing the gesture, to cover up his face, but he remembered and kept his hands half-raised.

"How are you, Atam Kul?" said Dostchak. "Well, you see we have met again. Your brother Yunus sent me to denounce you. Genderal, please hang Atam Kulka now!"

"I do not know you," came shrilly through the closed teeth of the prisoner.

"Oh, no; you know me very well!"

Dostchak drew back from the prisoner a little, looked at him long and carefully, and then turned to the general.

"Atam Kul was small — about so high," and Dostchak held his hand about three feet from the ground, "and Yunus, his brother, was still smaller. I served his father. I took them to bathe, and I bathed their father. I knew them all three, as well as their mother; I knew them all. The father had on his back, between the shoulders, about a hand's-breadth above the belt, a dark spot, like a piece of felt, of the shape of the moon when it first appears in the sky — like that," and Dostchak stooped and drew a crescent in the sand. "I speak Russian. You also speak Russian, and understand it; that is why I speak it now. You would like to eat me now, but your teeth are too short, though you are not a man, but a wolf. You are worse than a wolf!" said Dostchak, turning to the prisoner. "The oldest son, this Atam Kul, also had a dark spot on his back, in the same place. Give the order, Genderal, to take off his cloak and his shirt."

Dostchak ceased talking, went to one side and sat down quietly on the sand. He had done all he could, and waited how it would turn out.

"Take off his clothes!"

In a moment several hands seized upon the prisoner. He resisted strongly. One soldier fell; another seized him sideways.

"He is strong, the devil!"

"Throw him down at once!"

They threw him down. The poor fellow got on his knees and screamed. They tore off cloak and shirt, raised him to his feet, and turned his back. There was the black spot. The interpreter saw it at once, and put his finger upon it. The touch of his finger caused the naked back to shudder nervously.

"Well, this is positive proof," said the staff officer.

"But if it should be only an unfortunate coincidence?" said the general, in French. "The testimony of a common native evidently prejudiced against this man — whether he be Atam Kul or not — seems insufficient. It is very possible that Dostchak wants to be revenged for something. If he should be after Atam Kul's life for his own purposes only? It is strange that not a single soldier, not a single officer recognized him, though so many of us, gentlemen, know him."

At this moment Natalia Martinovna entered the circle. She held her son in her arms as she passed through the crowd. The boy was frightened by the number of people, and threw his arms around his mother's neck, looking around, with his eyes wide open.

Drawing his arms up into the sleeves of his cloak, the prisoner turned around and saw the woman.

He glanced at her. This glance was a revelation. It

expressed a burning, savage passion. The glance was instantaneous, but the lame Cossack caught it.

"Atam Kul!" he shouted.

Natalia trembled, and let her boy glide to the ground.

"Atam Kul, Atam Kul; there is no doubt of it — it is Atam Kul!" could be heard all around. All seemed to have been convinced of it, but kept silent, as if restrained by something; but this "something" vanished at once when the Cossack spoke out. It is possible that each of these men thought at the time, "I was not the first to speak, at any rate."

"Well, if it is Atam Kul, it is Atam Kul! The devil take him!" said the general, rising from his chair. "Cry as loud as you can, 'Atam Kul! Atam Kul!' As if I had not known it long ago!" he grumbled to himself as he returned to his tent. "Keep a strict watch upon him, and report to the judge-advocate to order a court-martial!" were the orders, issued in short and broken sentences.

"He is lost!" Natalia said, softly.

"Yes, he can hardly wriggle out of it now," confirmed Major Pugovitzin.

The lame Cossack stood as if stupefied, pressing his hand to his burning brow.

An unconquerable savage passion impelled the betraying glance — a glance which probably would not have been noticed by the crowd, but the very passion which instigated it made it comprehensible to the Cossack, and wrenched from him the fatal exclamation.

"The blood of Yunus will be avenged!" proudly declared Dostchak that evening.

CHAPTER XV.

THE KATA-DSHIL (SAND-STORM).

ABOUT 2 o'clock in the afternoon a strange, suffocating heat began to pervade the atmosphere. It was not the ordinary heat of the sun; it was something, also, not heretofore experienced by the white blouses. It became more and more difficult to breathe; the body broke out in profuse perspiration; the whole organism grew weak, and at the same time the blood began to circulate more rapidly, and the heart beat with increased violence. Everybody felt inclined to sleep, but sleep would not come. Thirst increased to an incredible degree — the crowd around the wells grew to heretofore unknown proportions. The heated, motionless atmosphere weighed upon everything on earth, and disposed to indolence, to inaction. .Labor was dropped by all hands. An unconquerable anxiety came over everyone, and not a man but experienced the feeling of a frightful, unbearable nightmare.

Animals evidently experienced the same feelings as the men. They were all reeking with sweat. Their colorless, deathlike eyes were immovable; the bloodshot nostrils opened wide, and ears stood up in full alarm. The horses stood at their picket-ropes without touching their feed. Their legs bent under them, but they would not lie down; all instinctively turning their backs in one direction — to the northeast.

The dogs buried themselves in the sand and whined plaintively. The camels laid themselves down, with necks extended; and, strange to say, they also turned their backs to the northeast.

If a horseman had wished to proceed in a north-easterly direction, the horse would perhaps have started, but it would have turned round as soon as ever the bridle was slackened in the least and the spurs relaxed their attack upon its foaming sides; but those who were bound in the opposite direction could scarcely restrain the ardor of their horses, who were pushing ahead in nervous excitement.

The mules gathered in troops and brayed in chorus, which, together with the sad whining of dogs, increased the general anxiety, and filled the minds of men with melancholy.

Nature was preparing for something unusual, and this unusual phenomenon was evidently coming from the northeast.

In the meantime the air was calm. The wind, which had been blowing the day before, sweeping together during the night great dunes of sand, calmed down completely, and at the present moment the flame of a candle lighted in the open air would have been motion-less, as if inclosed in a glass cylinder.

The sky had assumed a yellow, reddish tinge; the light of the sun was confined to a muddy disk, without beams, without splendor. One could freely look upon it as when protected by smoked glasses.

Thus time went on until 7 o'clock in the evening.

As the sun declined toward the west it grew more livid, and a bloody tinge spread over the ridges of sand, burying the intervening hollows in deep-blue shadows.

A threatening black wall rose up above the horizon, coming up gradually and spreading to the right and left, occupying little by little half of the sky.

When the wall came up to the sun, the livid disk sunk half behind it and then disappeared completely, dense shadows falling upon the earth immediately.

They fastened down their tents and looked after the stacks of arms. "No more fires must be built — those already lighted must be extinguished!" were the alarming orders issued.

"Kata-dshil! kata-dshil!" cried the natives, seeking a refuge among the heavy bales of the camel-train.

"Well, brethren," said the white blouses to each other, "look out for this night! There'll be such a gale! '

The first blast of the storm came about half an hour after sunset. It came as a sudden squall of great violence, but quickly subsided again. It brought with it dense clouds of fine, sandy dust, upset a few stacks of arms, and tore the fly off one of the tents. The disturbance caused in the camp by this dry squall was much increased by the darkness. There were confused cries of alarm; dark figures running about in all directions, chasing caps and hats torn away by the wind, colliding with each other and falling, rising up and rushing away again somewhere in the darkness.

The second blast came, immediately followed by another much more terrible than the preceding one. Red, fiery patches were flying across the inky sky, a muffled seemingly subterranean rumbling made itself heard, and the atmosphere was pervaded with a strong smell of sulphur.

Now the furious gale carried with it the coarse sand of the desert, burning and blistering the faces, hands, and necks — all parts of the body not protected by clothing. The horses snorted savagely and tore at their halters. "Drive down the stakes! Take care of the horses! May God preserve us from having them stampede!" the warning voices of cavalry-men and artillery-men sounded through the gloom.

The blasts of the gale were constantly increasing in power. One thought occupied all minds — to keep upon one's legs and to preserve whatever was under one's care. It was impossible to take note of what was happening elsewhere in this howling chaos. Ha! there was a shot; a second, and a third. A futile effort of a bugle to make itself heard, resulting in sounds resembling the screech of gulls in the distance. An alarm — an attack! at such a terrible time!

"Here, boys, help!" came through the uproar in a terrified, sinking voice. The voice came from the spot where Atam Kul was confined; the soldiers of the guard threw themselves in that direction. Impenetrable darkness surrounded them; the flying sand completely filled their eyes. There, straight before them loomed a massive figure as if rising from the ground, and jumped aside. "Halt! halt! What devil has hold of me? I'll not let you go!"

"Atam Kul has escaped!"

"I'm dying, brothers! Ah, death has got me — oh, the deathly sickness! O God!" some one groaned, squirming in the sand in his last convulsions.

"There were many of them — many — at least five. Three fell upon the sentry at once. I saw it with my own eyes. Send for the doctor, and bring a stretcher! What is it now?"

"O God, have mercy!"

A new blast of the wind brought with it new masses of flying, burning sand.

"We'll be buried alive! Most holy Mother of God, assist us!" exclaimed in a frightened voice a young soldier, a raw recruit, and new to the desert regions.

In good time, when it was still daylight, old Dementy had fastened down the tent of his mistress. He lashed everything with double ropes, drove down the stakes, adding some new ones for greater security, and then, inspecting his own work, declared that it would hold.

"Have no fear, matushka Natalia Martinovna," he strove to reassure his mistress, who was anxiously gazing at the threatening sky; "nothing will give way. It's quite strong. Don't mind anything during the night; I'll look out."

"I do not fear for myself, Dementy," said Natalia; "not for me."

"I know, matushka, your honor; I know. I'll make some tea for you. The orders are to build no fires, but if one knows how in a quiet fashion — in a little hole in the ground — no one will see it." The old man went away to make his arrangements "in a quiet fashion." Natalia again glanced out of her tent. It was growing dark very suddenly; the sky looked frightful indeed. A feeling of heaviness and dread took possession of her, like a foreboding of evil, of some fatal disaster.

"Petka, my darling," she addressed the child, "don't be afraid; it is nothing. There will be a big wind, but it will pass by, and then it will be nice and cool. You were very hot to-day, weren't you?"

"Hot," lisped the child, stretching himself languidly upon the bed, clad only in his little shirt with collar turned back. "Mama, I want to drink tea; mama, give me tea!"

"In a minute, sweetheart. Dementy has gone to make tea. He'll bring it, and we will drink it with lemon-drops. You like lemon-drops, don't you?"

"Lemon-dop," repeated the child.

"My dear boy!" and Natalia took her son into her

arms in a passionate embrace. A paroxysm of love and yearning for her boy seemed to have seized her; she covered him with kisses.

Suddenly the whole tent trembled, the walls swelled like the sail of a ship, and something gave way outside.

"Hold on! hold on! boys; help us!" cried the alarmed voice of old Dementy. "What a wind this is! the rope is cut as if with a knife. All right! don't be frightened, little mother; we'll make it stand." A blast of wind extinguished the candle, and in the pitchy darkness the boy began to cry. "It's the end of the world, sure!" said the old man, and then suddenly raised his voice: "Take care, you devils! Keep away! Can't you see you are on top of a man? What are you doing? What do you mean? O Lord! O Lord!"

A few mounted figures were rushing straight for the tent, and knocked down the old man. Suddenly the whole tent bent over to one side, the last ropes broke, the canvas filled, and the roof was carried straight up into the air by the wind, flapping like the wings of some gigantic specter, and quickly disappeared. At that moment Natalia, who, overcome with terror, was pressing her child to her breast, felt two strange arms stealing around her waist; a hot, offensive breath was blowing into her face. Close to her ear she heard whispered, in the Kirghiz language, "Take her away — tie her to the saddle — quick!" The voice was well known to her — she recognized the speaker, and loudly, with a wail of inexpressible despair, she cried, "Help! save me!"

She felt herself dragged over the sand; some one was lifting her up to a horse; the boy was torn from her arms. She sprang forward and, frenzied with despair, fastened her teeth to something that came in her way. Somebody groaned; a heavy fist struck her brow and bent back her head almost to her back — then she lost consciousness.

The lame Cossack, mounted on his horse, was making his way through the uproar. Around him crowded a confused mass of men, mounted and on foot, shouting to each other. He proceeded at a walk, carefully, bending over in his saddle and looking into the impenetrable mist of flying sand and dust. He was trying to make his way to the well-known little tent, but had lost his bearings, and, full of dismay, was cursing his own carelessness. How was he to find her? Where was she? He no longer knew the points of the compass. Here he ran plump against a line of infantry standing by their arms. The long rows of men were barely visible. He cried:

"What troops are there?"

"Third Battalion of Riflemen!"

"Are you on your own ground, or have you moved?"

"On our own ground!"

"Ah! that means I must go considerably more to the right," thought the Cossack. "The sappers must be close by here — ah! here they are — but where are their tool-boxes? They ought to be in front, and behind them — what is this?" Something round rolled from under the feet of his horse, which fell back upon its haunches. "God! why am I not with her at such a time!" the Cossack whispered to himself. "What is she doing now, alone, poor woman? Well, Stepniak, let us get on."

A shower of sparks was blown crackling across the road from a but partly extinguished fire of one of the company kitchens. "Now I'm all right!" the

Cossack congratulated himself. He had recognized the place.

All at once a shrill cry struck his ear; it was a woman's cry, and there was but one woman in the camp. Without stopping to pick his way, he buried the spurs in the side of his horse until it screamed, and, throwing back its head, nearly crushed its rider's face. Straight on rushed the Cossack for the voice, which seemed to proceed from the midst of the confused throng. Some horseman was being surrounded and dragged from his saddle; another, also mounted, fighting furiously, was struggling in the crowd. He also soon fell, and his horse was neighing and snorting while being seized by the bridle by a number of hands.

" Do not hit him — take him alive! " somebody shouted in a deep-bass voice. " Don't let the chief rascal escape; catch him, hold him! "

" Natalia Martinovna, where are you? " the Cossack shouted.

" Here, here! " answered several male voices.

The Cossack jumped, or rather let himself fall off his horse, allowing him to go loose. He wanted to run, but his injured leg made itself felt at once. He ground his teeth with pain, but limped in the direction whence the cries had come.

A few men were busy over something lying on the sand. The gray clothes of Natalia caught the lame officer's eye. She was lying there, prostrate, motionless, giving no signs of life.

" She's killed! " exclaimed the Cossack, and threw himself over the body.

" She's alive, God be with you! She has only fainted with fright. Have you looked for the child? No? Well, search for it — find the child! "

"And I was not here!" groaned the Cossack. "O merciful God! do not let *that* happen!"

CHAPTER XVI.

A SAD MORNING.

MORNING came, gray, misty, and sultry. The blasts of the gale were gradually decreasing in strength, but they were still scattering dense clouds of sand and dust over the whole camp. Finally the hurricane subsided into an even but fresh-blowing wind, which stirred up the accumulations of dust, blinding one's eyes, making it difficult to breathe or to see, even at a short distance.

Efforts were inaugurated to repair the damages of the night — to set up the tents that had been overthrown, and to collect such articles as the whirlwind had scattered over the steppe. Strong scouting parties of Cossacks were sent out in various directions.

The news of the disastrous occurrences of the night was already known throughout the camp. The hearts of all felt sad, from the general down to the last soldier; grief and anxiety were expressed in every glance, and occasionally a tear would be seen gliding over the sunburned faces, leaving dirty marks on the dust-covered cheeks. Not a man among them would have hesitated at any sacrifice to assuage the woman's grief, but all knew perfectly well that consolation, at least at the present moment, was out of the question.

When it became light enough to examine into the results of the nocturnal catastrophe, the state of affairs appeared as follows:

7

Natalia Martinovna's tent had been blown down by the wind; one of its walls still covered all its contents. Through the folds of the cloth could be distinguished the back of the iron bedstead, the corners of trunks, the edges of some iron-bound chest which had torn through the cloth, and various other objects belonging to the little traveling household. The roof had been carried a distance of twenty paces, and had lodged upon a sand-hill, into which the pointed poles of the structure had buried themselves. It could be seen through the dust, resembling a gigantic green parasol turned inside out in a storm. A few expiring blasts of wind — the last remnant of the gale — caused the structure to flutter and fill like a sail. The other wall of the tent, torn in halves, lay near by, and from under it protruded a pair of bare limbs, partly covered with rough leather leggings. They pulled them out, and found a dead body with a deep bayonet-wound in the side and the marks of violent blows about the head. On examination it was found to be one of the pretended servants of a Bokhara merchant, from the plundered caravan.

A little farther on a crowd of soldiers surrounded another prostrate body. This was old Dementy, with a deep cut in his head, giving no signs of life. In his convulsively clinched fist he held a piece of camel's-hair cloth, nearly the whole side of a native "khalat." Three soldiers were dragging over the sand, upon a felt-mat, still another corpse; a torn cloak, begrimed with dust and blood, had been thrown carelessly over the body.

" It's the Persian — the dog! — he's gone! " said one of the carriers. " He evidently did not die here — he crawled away; we found him near the picket-line."

"Just outside the line there lies a horse," remarked a Cossack who accompanied the small procession; "it is none of ours. You know the devils must have escaped to Adam Krilgan, but no tracks could be found except this carrion; the whole country has been swept clean by the hurricane."

In the guard-house where Atam Kul had been confined was found the body of the sentry, but the prisoner had left no trace behind, except two or three impressions of bare feet, which, God knows how, had remained undisturbed. It was very clear who were the perpetrators of the whole outrage. Atam Kul, not satisfied with the opportunity offered for his own escape, had attempted to take with him a very precious, much-coveted prize. By accident he failed to gain his real object. Little Petka was nowhere to be found, dead or alive.

Natalia returned to consciousness. She did not weep or complain, she never spoke, but her very silence told of so much suffering, such grief, that not one of those surrounding her dared to console her in words, or even look at her. They all kept silence; the officers merely stood around her with downcast eyes.

"If you only —" began one of them, but only sobbed like a child, and hurried away, in order not to grieve her still more with his untimely tears.

The woman sat as if petrified — like a statue — on one of the trunks; her eyes were lifeless, glassy; a thick strand of her auburn hair hung down from her forehead over the face; a white shoulder shone through rents in her garments, torn during her struggle; the shoulder was shivering slightly, but evidently not with cold.

Kustikof took off his overcoat and laid it gently over

Natalia's shoulders; she did not even notice it. The soldiers set up her tent, talking in whispers. The stout doctor was bathing Dementy's head; the hospital steward was deftly arranging the instruments for blood-letting, asking in a whisper for a towel and cup.

They set up the tent, repaired damages, and put everything in its usual order.

"Now, my little dove," the doctor addressed Natalia. "Come on, my daughter. Lie down upon the bed and rest. I'll give you a drop of something, and you must take it. Come, now!"

"Where?" Natalia inquired in a hoarse whisper, half unconsciously.

"Gentlemen, please assist in lifting her. Take hold of her thus, under the arms. Now, this is nice," continued the doctor; "but easily, gently. With God's help you will get better and strong. You are young, you know. Everything may turn out well yet. We may find —"

Natalia gave vent to a loud, unearthly scream, and again relapsed into unconsciousness.

"Oh, what a beast I am!" said the doctor, striking himself on the forehead. "It was that unlucky word 'find' that did it. Old fool that I am!"

A horse stopped before the tent, snorted, and began to paw the sand with its foreleg. From its saddle alighted the general, who threw the reins to a Cossack, and entered the tent.

"Well, how is it?" he began, then glanced around, looked at Natalia Martinovna lying upon the bed, wrung his hands, and walked out.

The scouting parties had not yet returned. The lame Cossack was with one of them, having set out before dawn with his platoon, and two reports from him had already reached the camp. One was brought by a Cossack, with a request that some reinforcements be sent after him, to provide for an emergency; the other report was brought by a native, and this last one fanned into life in the breasts of all in the camp a small spark of hope.

"I am on the trail," he had written with a pencil upon a torn piece of newspaper.

From all these happenings the most dire consequences resulted.

CHAPTER XVII.

IN PURSUIT.

THE Cossacks pursued at a full gallop, the platoon being spread over a considerable distance. The riders, bending from their saddles, carefully noted every track in the sand, every suspicious indentation or cavity. They looked ahead and to either side, but always pushing on without interruption, belaboring with their whips their shaggy, stumpy, poorly fed and ill-groomed, but obedient and enduring little beasts.

The lame Cossack was in the lead. Near him, lifting himself in his stirrups, rode a young Yunker Cossack (cadet), and an old sergeant, with thin red beard, sprinkled with gray, on whose homespun shirt dangled two crosses.

All listened intently, ceaselessly using their eyes, and rarely exchanging a few brief remarks.

The detachment resembled a pack of hounds in full cry. The abrupt, broken conversation reminded one somewhat of the yelping of dogs who have picked up the scent.

"Nothing!" exclaimed the sergeant, shaking his head and whipping his white-legged animal.

"Have we not been drawing to the right a litttle too much, Esaul?" the Yunker inquired, somewhat hesitatingly.

"We've got to go straight ahead, all the same," the sergeant replied, authoritatively. "We are gaining on them, and we must keep on. The "esaul" * never answered at all, but looked searchingly straight ahead where a wavy dark line was clearly defined in the brightening dawn.

"If they depend on the horses they stole from our camp," said the sergeant, "they'll not go far, but if they had fresh horses ready for them, then — shoot me in the beard! — it's a nasty business. To chase the wind over the field or the Turkoman over the steppe is all the same!"

"Halt!"

One of the Cossacks went head over heels, landing square upon the sand.

"What is it, brethren?"

They all halted.

"Are these tracks of shod hoofs?"

"Our shoes — Orenburg shoeing — they're ours."

"We've found them!"

A sandy level occupying the interval between two dunes here cut across the trail, and at its farther edge there was a piece of ground swept clean by the winds. Here a few horse-tracks had been preserved, and at

---

* "Esaul," non-commissioned officer of Cossacks — of corporal's rank.— TRANSLATOR.

these the Cossacks were looking carefully after coming to a halt.

"It must be theirs; there's nobody else."

Dostchak and another native were with this party, both of them keeping considerably in advance of the platoon, as leaders keep ahead of the pack. They galloped up to the top of the ridges, looking, sniffing, and listening, and again disappeared in the hollows, remaining invisible for a time, appearing again at the very spot where nobody expected to see them.

"Dostchak is working hard!" said the Cossacks, shaking their heads and following the nimble horseman with their eyes.

"Well, tura [master], what is this?" he asked, as he galloped up to the lame Cossack, holding in his hand a soiled red ribbon. "Behind that hill over there I stopped a little to let my horse breathe. The sand is moist there, and this was lying right there."

"Petka's belt!" groaned the Cossack. His eyes filled with moisture, and red spots appeared upon his cheeks.

Profiting by the brief halt, the Cossacks' horses also gathered breath, and a few succeeded in having a roll on the sand (a habit of the horse of the steppe), and then shook themselves and galloped on again. From here the lame Cossack dispatched the native to the camp with his brief, laconic epistle.

The direction taken in the pursuit had now been fully justified. They went on to the spot described by Dostchak, and halted again. Yes, there the others had halted also. There were tracks of three horses only. With Atam Kul there had been five men — he was the sixth. Two dead bodies remained in camp and the carcass of one horse was found; that meant that there were four riders for three horses — one of them was carrying two. No fresh horse had been waiting for them, in the sergeant's opinion. In accordance with these considerations, the fugitives could not be far off; their horses must be tired — especially the one with two men on his back. There were no other tracks in sight; that pointed to the absence of any hostile force in the neighborhood. And even if they were to encounter a small band of horsemen, a hundred or so, they could not prove very formidable antagonists to a platoon of well-armed Cossacks. The only thing was, to lose no time — and they lost none.

Encouraged by their first success, the Cossacks resumed the chase. Something looms up in front — a fallen horse, with legs extended, the body swelled like a barrel and eyes glassy and staring; on one side of the carcass quite a pile of sand had accumulated.

"This must have lain here for some time," remarked one of the Cossacks, pointing at the sand-heap.

"It is still warm," said the sergeant. "As to the sand, it doesn't take long to pile up when the wind blows strong. That horse may have lain here half an hour — no more. The legs are still limber, don't you see?"

Other tracks were found, and among the hoof-tracks there were impressions of naked feet; the steps were long, the toes pressed deeply into the ground, the heels hardly touched at all. "The rascal is running, holding onto the stirrup; that is why he steps so far. Now they must be close by — they can't go far in that fashion."

The face of the lame Cossack was illuminated with hope. "In a few minutes," he thought; "perhaps behind those very hills."

"Hey!" A general cry arose almost simultaneously

—a cry of triumph. They ran against Dostchak and nearly overthrew him. Not more than a hundred paces ahead of them a horseman emerged from a depression of the ground at a feeble, tired gait. All recognized at once the broad, round-shouldered back. The rider held with one hand some small object wrapped in a fold of his cloak; with the other hand, armed with a whip, he was persistently lashing the unfortunate animal which bore him, on the head, on the croup, on the belly, wherever he could reach. Behind this horseman, clinging closely to the sand, two men on foot climbed out of the hollow, clad in their shirts alone. They looked around like wolves at bay, and hastened on after the other to get hold of his stirrups again. Another rider came in sight, but his animal could proceed only at a walk, and staggered under the saddle, ready to fall.

The Cossacks gave a yell and broke into a full run; but a moment later another yell, much louder, resounded from the sand-hills and hollows all around them. The sands became dotted with high black caps and dirty red cloaks. The steppe thundered under the hoofs of numberless horses.

The platoon at once rallied in a group, and the Cossacks instinctively slid from their saddles. A party of Turkomans, numbering several hundred, began to form a wide circle around the platoon, flanking the men from the Ural, to the right and left, in front and rear.

"Ah! shoot them in the beard!" shouted the old sergeant, and toppled over from his saddle.

"He's killed, brethren, he's killed!" And like a bag another Cossack fell from his saddle.

"Keep straight, close together! Guard the horses;

don't let go of your bridles!" roared the lame Cossack. "Don't be afraid; we'll get out of this!"

The first shots were scarcely heard by the Cossacks.

CHAPTER XVIII.

THE RESCUE.

THE reinforcements left the camp. The detachment was dispatched to meet an emergency, but those composing it did not know that the emergency had already arisen.

It was supposed that the Cossacks had advanced about twelve versts, perhaps more. At a distance of five versts shots could be easily heard, especially with the wind fair. The expedition had already marched that distance and heard nothing, consequently everything must be all right ahead of them.

That was the general opinion of the small expedition, and therefore they advanced steadily without hurrying in the least, saving the strength of both horses and men — all the more because marching in the deep sand, in hot weather, is very laborious.

A squadron of Cossacks was in advance, followed by a company of infantry, the latter keeping at a considerable distance. The infantry does not fraternize much with the horsemen.

"At any rate," said Major Pugovitzin, who led the expedition, "as a reconnaissance it is not altogether useless — they have to be made; but altogether it seems a piece of foolishness to me — we are going for nothing. They talk of a night attack — the plague take them!—

of a demonstration, supported by a strong force in reserve. It's all stuff and nonsense. The whole uproar was caused by Atam Kul and his companions. That Persian was a cunning beast! "

"He's got his reward! " remarked Kustikof.

"Got his reward? Yes; but that was, after all, only a lucky accident — a bullet fired at random when it was as dark as pitch. It was lucky we did not hit our own men! "

"Golovin went in pursuit at once. He may catch up with them, capture Atam Kul, rescue Petka. O God! what would I not give to have that chance! "

"Would you give a quarter's salary? " Pugovitzin asked, with a smile.

"All right! You are always joking, but, by God! I do not take it that way. It is nice to be a Cossack, a cavalryman! "

"Why? "

"I should have set out at once, together with Golovin. I should have searched every corner, examined everything, and caught them. But when you are hampered with infantry at two versts an hour! The Cossacks will have finished everything without us before we get up with them."

"Oh, no; they can't do much without us! "

"It's beastly luck! "

"Well, boy, we must have patience. What are you stopping there for? Why is the fourth platoon lagging behind? What are the non-commissioned officers doing? " The captain halted his shaggy horse and looked back at the rear of the column.

The tired soldiers hurried forward and closed up with those in front.

"Eh, Proshka, you bandy-legged devil! " growled

Corporal Bubnof, "can't you keep your pipe going while marching along?"

"I spilled my tobacco, uncle. In a minute I'll be up with them."

"It is insupportable!" Kustikof muttered to himself.

"Wouldn't it be nice, you know," Pugovitzin resumed the conversation a little later — "wouldn't it be nice? Natalia Martinovna is sitting there, killing herself — it is no joke, such a grief; not every mother could stand it. She's lost all hope — is in despair. All at once a horseman on a tired, dusty horse rides up to the tent, dismounts, and delivers to her the lost son. 'Take him — here he is, alive and well!' Do you know, it would be well if there was some slight wound to show, in the hand or on the shoulder — not too dangerous and not too painful — plenty of blood — that would serve as decoration. Wouldn't it be nice?" And the captain bent over from his horse and slapped the younger officer on the shoulder, laughing joyously through the dense clouds of tobacco-smoke from his cheap cigar.

"You are always joking — it is very serious to me. I grieve when I remember —"

"You're sorry; and do you think I am happy? Only, all of you who were sitting around her there could scarcely keep from whimpering, and making long faces — that did not help her. I know the little lady. I knew her long ago. She can bear grief — she has had experience. She is stronger than any of you. Of course, she was taken unawares by a terrible shock — but only wait; she will get over it. She will discover more quickly than you what it is necessary to do and how to proceed. She has no need of consoling words or commiserative tears, and your long faces can do her no good."

Pugovitzin ceased talking, took several strong pulls at his cigar, and flung the stump away into the sand.

"What is keeping our Cossacks back? They are going very slowly," he continued, looking ahead attentively from under the long visor of his cap. "Yes, it's a foolish business; they'll not catch Atam Kul; he did not start out to fall into our hands again. I know the wolf; you'll not see the boy again. It was lucky the mother was rescued in time!"

"Is there no hope?" Kustikof asked, or rather remarked mechanically.

"Oh, I don't say that — anything may happen," said Pugovitzin, shrugging his shoulders. "Look! Isn't somebody coming back at a full gallop?"

"Yes; two men. What has happened? Do you hear anything?" An alarmed expression overspread the young officer's face. The soldiers had quickened their steps; they were almost running. All weariness was forgotten; they forgot they were wading ankle-deep in sand. The whole company was now moving at a double-quick, and many of them were looking to their guns while running.

"Firing!" said Pugovitzin.

"They are shooting, boys; they are shooting. Our Cossacks are hurrying up. What can it be? Now our Cossacks are beginning to fire."

"That's a bad habit! Easy, brethren; there is somebody tumbling — he is off his horse!"

"Get along, get along! How heavy the firing is!"

"A falconet [native howitzer], I suppose."

While exchanging these remarks the soldiers had regained their breath, and were now setting their accouterments to rights and getting at their cartridge-boxes.

Kustikof gave his horse the whip and hurried forward, stirring up the unfortunate animal with his heels
and sword-scabbard at the same time. He did not see
or hear anything beyond the distant reports of gun-
shots fired by the squadron of Cossacks belonging to
the detachment, who had now halted along the summit
of a sandy ridge. The Cossacks could be seen to dismount and then mount again, some moving a little to
the right and then back again, and once more forward
over the ridge. They were evidently undecided, and
waiting for the infantry to come up — the favorite bulwark of the Cossack, when any affair seems to be too
much for him.

This bulwark, a handful of white blouses, numbering
about seventy, was rapidly approaching, and in this
movement, in contrast to those of the Cossacks, there
was nothing indecisive, nothing indicative of any doubt.
The white blouses knew where to go and what they
had to do.

"Don't get excited — easy; we'll get there, if they
don't run away!" could be heard in the calm, reassuring bass voice of Major Pugovitzin, who was just
lighting a new cigar, and, having no knife handy, carefully bit off the pointed end. At last the white blouses
reached the sandy ridge and could see everything. All
the hills before them were dotted with horsemen;
they were uniformly dressed in dark-red cloaks and
high black caps. Now they would gather in groups,
and then again deploy in skirmish-line, spurring their
long-legged horses, covered with blankets. There a
larger group gathered, and galloped along, with two
triangular ensigns fluttering above their heads. These
horsemen came forward at a full run, then, after violently pulling up their horses, retreated again faster

than they had come. Whenever a horseman halted, a
little white cloud of smoke puffed up, and the sharp
report of a gun could be heard. Here and there the
little white clouds are constantly puffing up, rising in
the wind and forming into long strips of mist, which
ranged themselves along the sandy ridges, gradually
rising higher and higher.

The natives all seemed to swarm in one direction;
they were fighting somebody there, but who it was
could not be seen. Beyond those hills their unseen
enemy must be hidden.

"Golovin is there with his platoon," said the Cossack
officer. "They are pressing him hard."

"We must drive them away from there at once!"

"It's dangerous — there is such a crowd of them.
However, let us wait for the infantry. Those fellows
scatter so much, we can't hit anybody."

"Never fear — just wait a moment."

The Cossacks were thus talking and consulting, without any definite result, when the company came; then
they picked up courage and got into their saddles
again. The leader of the squadron accosted Pugovitzin:

"Good-day, Major!" bringing all five fingers to the
visor of his cap, and bowing not ungracefully from his
saddle. "The enemy is in very formidable numbers —
some in sight and others still hidden. In view of this
inequality of forces, caution will have to be employed
in our movements; and furthermore I would suggest —"

"Bugler, sound the attack!" said Pugovitzin, without
paying any attention to the Cossack officer's flow of
fine words.

The bugler put the instrument to his mouth, but no
sound issued; it was choked up with sand. He blew
into the other end, coughed, and finally succeeded in

sounding the charge, which was repeated by the drums. The attack began.

A few skirmishers, in pairs, ran ahead. It was a strange sight, this handful of infantry advancing so confidently against an enemy exceeding them tenfold in strength. They formed into a small column at the sound of some indistinct word of command, and encouraged by two drums and the cracked bugle, the white blouses went forward.

"Fire!" said Pugovitzin without removing his cigar. Some of the soldiers in line stepped forward, one even sat down in the sand; they took aim, and with a sharp report the first shot went forth from the "Berdankas" (Berdan rifles); a second followed. The bullets were whistling dismally through the air.

The squadron also moved, advancing at a walk, without getting ahead of the infantry line.

"At the word of command from me, start off at a gallop, but keep a sharp lookout," exclaimed the Cossack commander, prancing showily in front of his line. "If the command is 'Halt!' you will at once fall back upon our infantry support."

"He's in a sweat, brother," an infantryman whispered to his neighbor. "He should wring out his shirt. What is the use of giving instructions for running away?"

The small detachment advanced farther and farther, without stopping, unswervingly and irresistibly, making straight for the center of the enemy now rallying along the ridges; straight to where their masses were densest, and where the two triangular ensigns were waving. Behind this center lay the hills surrounded by the Turkomans, and upon which thus far their principal efforts had been directed.

From behind these hills a small number of men were now making their appearance; they were leading their horses by the bridles — three and four to a man; the others surrounded the horse-keepers in an open skirmish line, keeping up a constant fire from their small carbines. The lame Cossack had heard the firing of his rescuers, and had resolved to lead forth his platoon from its defensive position.

At the sound of the first shots from the infantry the Turkomans began to waver and to contract their wide circle. Only occasionally their small bullets came whistling along, striking the sand with a dull splash not far from the column. A few wounded horses lay struggling here and there, some of them striving to get upon their legs, staggering along a few steps, and falling again; a few bodies of men, some flat on their backs, some drawn up as in pain, were dyeing red the yellow sand beneath them. Some horsemen galloped up to these bodies, and bending from their saddles without alighting, they snatched them up, throwing them on the horses' croups, and then followed at a run their already retreating companions. Riderless horses, with saddles and trappings askew, were scattered over the sand-hills, neighing loudly. A few men were sent in pursuit of them, to catch them by the bridle, or simply drive them after the others.

"Ah! if one might catch a couple of pairs of these racers!" sighed one of the Cossacks. They looked after them enviously, but did not venture to break from their line for the purpose. Where would the Cossack be with his shaggy little gelding, if he were to match horse against horse with the Turkomans on their fiery, marvelously trained racers that can jump a fourteen-foot ditch or a wall the height of a man — jump them as

8

easily as if these formidable obstacles did not exist at
all. Fighting in organized bodies they were a match
for them, but singly the Cossacks stood no chance, and
they were fully justified in being careful.

" They worried you somewhat!" exclaimed Pugovitzin
on meeting Golovin, extending his hand to him.

" Yes, brother; thanks — you have rescued me," said
the Cossack. " It looked squally for a time; our cartridges were giving out — we thought the end was
near."

" Did you lose many? "

" Six, and ten horses; some killed, and some ran off. I
caught up with that cursed fellow. I had him almost
in my hands. I could have rescued Petka. Ah! fate!
fate!" And Golovin turned aside and wiped his eyes
with the sleeve of his blouse.

"I had already written hopefully," he continued; "and
now — well, how is she?"

"Come back and you will see!" said Pugovitzin,
gruffly.

"In what order will the return march be made?
Have you any orders to give on that subject, Major?"

" You must furnish horses to carry the dead and the
wounded. What orders should there be?" the major
added, angrily, and then gave his command:

"With God, boys! "

The small detachment moved off in the direction of
the camp. The Turkomans did not pursue. They saw
the white blouses; they knew them of old, and concluded to salute them only from a distance, sending a
few random bullets into the air.

CHAPTER XIX.

WAITING.

No sooner had Golovin's brief note been received in the camp than it was shown to Natalia.

"He's found — saved!" she exclaimed, breathing with difficulty. "Had they carried him away? Tell me — why don't you speak?" She was seized by a nervous tremor, her cheeks reddened, her eyes shone with a vivid brilliancy; apparently beside herself, she rushed for the entrance of the tent.

The doctor intercepted her. "Where are you going, Natalia Martinovna? Wait, matushka; stop! What —"

"I am going myself. My horse — for the love of God, the horse! Saddle him, Dementy — quick, quick!" Natalia rushed about in the tent as if searching for something. Her reason seemed to have left her, and she was mechanically repeating, "The horse — oh, quick! quick!" The tone of her voice grew lower and lower — at last it was only a faint whisper; she staggered — the doctor supported her falling form and led her to the bed.

Once more Natalia Martinovna had sunk into insensibility. The terrible shock to her nerves caused by the letter had provoked this violent outbreak; after the excitement followed a complete collapse. When she opened her eyes again, gazing stupidly about, the doctor began to ply her with a flow of small talk which he intended to be soothing.

"That was very good!" he said, patting her hand. "You wanted to go yourself, of course; you ordered

Dementy to saddle up, but your poor Dementy —" The
doctor did not go on; it struck him that to tell her at
that moment of the fate of the poor old man would be
altogether out of place.

"Golovin has only just got onto the trail," he continued. " Thanks be to God, he is chasing them now —
and all will be well. At night they will return and
bring your Petka. How we shall watch you after this,
truly! There'll be an officer's guard before your tent;
it will be completely surrounded. But you must be
quiet now, our little dove — lie still. I'll moisten
your head with vinegar again — that does you good.
That's it! Karpof, have you got ready what I told
you to prepare? Bring it in, if it's ready."

" This minute, your honor; it will be ready in a
second," answered, from behind the tent, Karpof, the
soldier who had sprained himself at the wells, and who
had been detailed in old Dementy's place.

"You must drink a cup of hot tea with some red
wine in it. Here, I'll put it to your lips. That is well,
that's excellent! But now, what's this — the eyes wet
again? It's a shame! Wait, I'll dry them." The doctor
drew from his pocket a dirty, frayed handkerchief,
looked at it, and hid it again in his pocket. That
wouldn't do; then he grasped the skirt of his blouse —
that was still worse. "Ah!" he groaned, looking around
despairingly until he found a towel "comparatively"
clean, and gently passed a corner of it over the woman's
eyes, going on with his chattering: " The whole camp
is so sorry for you! The soldiers are quite melancholy,
and some of them quite furious. Nobody thinks of
anything but your misfortune. The general has sent
six times to inquire, and came twice himself. When I
passed Gorlastoi's tent I saw they were not playing

cards — what a convincing sign of sympathy! Quietly,
now, my boy, quietly!" the doctor continued in a
whisper to Karpof, who came in a with a tray containing
a small copper teakettle and a glass with silver holder.
"'Sh! don't wake her, God bless her! Go, boy, and
tell them all around to keep perfectly quiet — tell them
she has fallen asleep."

The doctor rose heavily from the bed, walked on his
tiptoes to the corner of the tent, let himself down cautiously upon a folding-chair, threw a glance at his
patient, and with the greatest caution, in order to avoid
all rustling of the paper, he drew from his pocket and
unfolded a much-used, crumpled copy of the "Russian
Invalid," issued only seven months ago.

The whole camp was waiting with the greatest impatience for the return of Golovin with his platoon.
Every sand-hill the top of which afforded a wider view
was crowded with people — on foot and mounted —
and all kept their eyes fixed in the direction from
which the Cossacks must first come within the scope
of vision.

The sun was mercilessly pouring down its hottest
rays, but no attention was paid to that — no one thought
of seeking the shade of the tents. On the small bastions which had been completed, on the parapets of the
new fortification — everywhere the white blouses of
the soldiers and tunics of the officers could be seen, and
from minute to minute new watchers joined the various
groups.

"Well, how is it?" they asked, blinking their eyes
and shading them from the sun with their hands, while
glancing at the undulating horizon. "Do you see
nothing?"

"There's nothing to be seen."

" They must have gone far —"

" Will they get him, or not? "

" Oh, heavenly Queen! wouldn't it —"

" If they bring him — there would be such a thanks-giving service! "

" But how is she herself?   Have you seen her, boys? "

" Look, look!   That is dust — it is moving; don't you see? "

" Captain, lend me your field-glass for a minute — I just want one glance, for just one second! "

" They are coming! "

" No — it's nothing.   The wind is stirring up the sand. See — it has subsided again, and there is nothing in sight! "

" They'll not turn back before night — that is sure."

Thus desultory conversation went on upon the sand-hills of Khala-at, and on the parapets of the newly erected fort of St. George. The whole day was con-sumed in this wearisome, impatient expectation. The sun was again preparing to take its final plunge beyond the western horizon when the wind began to blow, and the distance became obscured with clouds of dust. It was growing dark, and still Golovin, with his platoon, had not returned. From Pugovitzin, also, there had been no news.

" They must have gone far, indeed! " was the general opinion in the camp. Everybody was getting uneasy. Could anything serious have happened to them?

Fires began to glimmer here and there, when the sound of snorting horses was borne faintly upon the wind — evoking an answer from the picket-ropes in camp. " Ours " were coming at last. But no singing could be heard. It was not customary with the Tur-kestan battalions to return from an expedition without

song and beating of drums — if they had been successful.

"It's evident that they have failed — they're not up
to singing." That was the opinion formed by the
camp. All became sad, voices were lowered, the
crowds stood waiting, looking out into the darkness.

Yonder, between the sand-hills, somber masses were
moving slowly; some low — the infantry; and the
others looming up higher — the cavalry. Smaller
particles were separating from the mass and approaching more rapidly. The challenge of the outer pickets
was heard, and all rushed from the camp to meet the
returning column.

First came Major Pugovitzin with his company, then
came the Cossacks who had accompanied him, and last
came Golovin with his platoon, and he proceeded
directly to the general's headquarters.

CHAPTER XX.

THE NEW YORK HERALD CORRESPONDENT.

THE round bastions of the new fort loomed up lonely,
melancholy, and uninviting. Surrounded with dunes of
deadly drifting sand, Khala-at resembled some vast
ruined monument or burial-place.

The handful of people left in the fort were looking
dejectedly, from the top of the ramparts, into the
desert — into the endless distance, where the haze
now hid the last stragglers in the rear of the advancing
column.

All was sad and quiet within the fortification; the

faces of all were clouded — frowning. The greatest disgust, burning anger, and discontent with a blind fate were expressed in the dark sunburned faces of these men who thus far had not been subjected to any special physical hardship; but they had suffered the greatest moral hardship, in their eyes, by being compelled to "remain" while the others "went on."

And where had the others gone? It was possible that all those who had marched would find their graves in the sandy deserts stretching away to the southwest, in that terrible region to which that ominous name of "Man's Perdition" had been given; it was possible that those graves would be preceded by long days and weeks of cruel privation and suffering — all that was possible. Nevertheless, those who departed were happy, looking ahead full of confidence, brimming over with life, energy sparkling in their eyes. Those who remained looked upon themselves as already buried alive.

The traces of the vast camp, which the sand had not yet obliterated, only added to the general picture of loneliness.

There were the well-beaten squares where the tents had stood; there on that long streak, where the remnants of horse-feed and droppings are scattered about, were the picket-ropes of the cavalry; there were the wheel-tracks of the cannon. In the hollows the soil was blackened with cinders and smoke-begrimed fragments of broken-down ovens upon which the soldiers' uninviting food had been cooked. Shreds and pieces of felt and straw mats, ends of rope, pieces of paper, and colored rags strewed the sand. Parts of broken dishes shone in the sunlight like diamonds. Two or three ragged natives roamed about over the vast space like jackals, bending over and picking up what seemed still useful to them, glancing once in awhile furtively at the fort like thieves, and then resuming their search.

About twenty camels, left behind on account of their feebleness, could be seen on the sand-hills, seeking in vain for food, be it only a few solitary dry blades of grass. All the immediate vicinity of the fort has long since been browsed by their predecessors — nothing more can be found. To go farther afield is dangerous. Packs of wolves, equally hungry and with scent sharpened by fasting, are roving there, attracted by the odors arising from carcasses of camels and horses lying about in the sand. Not a few of the latter fell victims to hunger and over-exertion, and now inclosed the fort at Khala-at with a circle of fetid, tainted air.

This was the third day since the white blouses went away, the third day since the pillars of dust long visible along the horizon had subsided. There was no news from any direction, only isolation and discontent. The days were provokingly long; it seemed as if a whole week could be made of one of them.

This day was over at last. Darkness settled down upon the dismal surroundings; fires were lighted in the fort. Sleep would be welcome now, to pass away the slowly creeping time unconsciously, but there is no sleep. Gloom weighs upon every heart and drives away refreshing slumber. It is the same as in daylight — on the ramparts still linger the silent, restless shadows.

There was no meat — the last was issued long ago. Of hard bread there was still enough, but it began to look less and less appetizing. But all this would be considered no great trouble, or something to laugh at, if only the longed-for relief force would hurry up — if they could only hear the gloriously welcome order to follow up the expedition.

"Isn't it dark?" said one of the sentries, as he came face to face with his neighbor on the adjoining beat, at the corner where the cannon was planted.

"Very dark!" the other assented. Each turned his back to the other.and again paced along the ramparts. When they met again the first one remarked, "Listen! brother; do you hear nothing?"

"Let's look," said the other. They did not separate again, but stood still in silence, listening intently. One of them sat down in order to bring the nearest sand-hills into relief against the sky.

"Hoof-beats on the sand," said one.

"Three horses running — they are coming this way. What can it be, coming from that side?"

"Some roving band —'

"No! They are heading straight for the fort. It must be the mail, or some courier."

"Look!"

Not far away three dark shadows could be distinguished; two looming up high, the third lower. The first were horsemen, the other a led-animal loaded with something. The muzzles of carbines stood out from the shoulders of the riders. It was impossible to distinguish their costumes in the darkness.

"Who goes there?" came the loud challenge from the top of the corner bastion. "Who goes there?" was repeated from the parapet, upon which, in addition to the sentries, a crowd of curious spectators appeared, brought to their feet by the noise of the challenge.

The riders halted at a distance of about twenty paces. One of them dismounted; the other remained in the saddle.

"We your men — ours — good men. Hold on; don't
shoot, please!" hurriedly shouted the one who had dismounted.

"*Nous sommes vos amis!*" came in a loud, determined
voice from the rider on the horse. "*Eh bien! Ou est
monsieur le chef du camp?* Sharip!"—he turned to his
companion, now speaking Russian—"fire, tea—the
bottle and the blankets!" Having given these orders,
the horseman deliberately dismounted, stretched his
legs, and sat down on the sand. With slow, precise, and
measured movements he extracted a cigar, and with a
knife taken from a pocket-case cut off the end, lighted a
match that flamed up in the darkness, and for a moment
illuminated the end of a nose, a reddish mustache, and
a closely cropped, neatly trimmed beard, and then
began to smoke, sending forth into the nocturnal air
the aromatic perfume of a costly Havana.

The soldiers wondered, "What funny creature have
we here? What was he jabbering about? It must have
been German."

"Didn't you understand, Vaska?"

"To the devil with him!" said Vaska, shaking his
head. "Such balderdash that nobody can understand!
However, boys, this must be reported to the colonel,
all the same."

But there was no necessity for a report. Several
officers had already emerged from the fort, and now
gathered around the new arrivals.

"What is going on there?" exclaimed the colonel's
voice; and the soldiers respectfully made way for him.

A half-hour later the new-comer was seated upon a
carpet in one of the officers' tents, a little roomier than
the others. The bright blaze of a camp-fire fell full
upon him as he sat there with a glass in his hand, tell-

ing his adventures, laughing and joking merrily with
the officers gathered around him. The conversation
was carried on in French and German; of Russian he
knew only such words as he used in giving orders to
his servant — a native Kirghiz from Perovsk. In addition to these words he knew "How many versts?"
"Eat," and "Wake early," and only very lately his command of the Russian language had been strengthened
by the acquisition of the sentence, "Oh, it's hot!"
Beyond these phrases he declined to extend his studies.

He was dressed in a suit of light gray, and wore a
hat of American pattern, with a wide neck-shield; high,
thick-soled top-boots, fastened with straps above the
knees, completed his costume. Over one shoulder hung
a short carbine (said to shoot about forty times per
minute); a pair of revolvers showed from his belt, and
over the other shoulder he carried a case with field-
glasses and a small note-book, also with case and strap.

His low, broad-shouldered form bespake uncommon
agility, endurance, and strength; his gray eyes looked
about him calmly and pleasantly; the cut of his mustache and beard proclaimed him a "real Yankee."

In answer to a question from the colonel commanding the fort at Khala-at, he introduced himself as "Mr.
Henry Blake, correspondent of the New York *Herald.*"
He related how he alone, with his Kirghiz servant, had
traversed more than a thousand miles of the steppe,
guided only by his map and compass, reposing but little
confidence in the local knowledge of his guide; how he
had finally succeeded in reaching Khala-at, hoping to
find there the whole Russian expedition and its commander. He was very sorry indeed that the column
had already set out upon its march; but it did not
matter—he felt sure of overtaking them before long. In

the morning at daylight he would set out in pursuit by the same means which had carried him thus far.

"Well, no, brother," said the colonel, in Russian, but under his breath; "we will not let you go from here all by yourself. Who knows him, and who wants to be held responsible for such a goose?"

"To your health!" said Mr. Henry Blake, smiling as if in answer to the colonel's suppressed remark, and, with a polite bow, swallowed a dram of rum from his silver traveling-cup.

The decision of the commanding officer that the correspondent must be detained at the fort until the commander of the expedition could be communicated with, and an answer received with instructions, was made known to the traveler, with many conciliatory phrases to sweeten the bitter pill; and he was asked to accept the hospitality of the fort, where everything that might add to his comfort would be at his service.

Mr. Henry Blake seemed slightly disconcerted when first learning this decision, and his brows contracted into a frown, but he soon brightened up and regained his former joyousness, continuing to relate episodes from his trying and adventurous journeys.

It was time to go to bed. The American firmly declined the offer of a tent and folding-bed, saying . that he had become accustomed to his blanket. After talking to his native servant, he stretched himself upon the sand, smoked a final cigar, made entries in his note-book, and was soon soundly asleep, breaking the stillness of the night with a healthy, resounding snore.

In the morning there was no correspondent of the New York *Herald* in the fort. He had departed an hour before dawn in the direction of the advancing expedition. For the commander of the fort he left a brief but very cordial note, saying that he wished to express his thanks for the attention and hospitality shown him at the fort, and hoping to see his Khala-at friends again before long; if not sooner, then surely at Khiva.

" He is the devil ! " declared the colonel, after reading the note.

"Smart!" remarked one of the officers.

" Free as a bird, the lucky fellow!" enviously sighed another.

" If they catch him on the road they will impale him, or do something worse with him!" gloomily prophesied a third. But the colonel decided that there could be nothing worse than to be impaled. To this they all consented. They conversed wearily for a little while longer, and then surrendered themselves to their customary occupation — to fret, to chafe, to gaze into the distance, and to wait for the relieving-force.

CHAPTER XXI.

THE WHITE BLOUSES.

FOR many days now the white blouses have been marching through the drifting sands. Ahead goes the advance-guard, mostly Cossacks, and a few infantrymen. They are marching briskly, with no perceptible signs of weariness, but closer observation will reveal the haggard faces, the emaciated horses, through whose sides the ribs are so plainly visible — the effect of insufficiency of both food and water. Behind the advance-guard the main body of the column drags itself along. The dust hangs over it in clouds. It is a silent march — one hears no tramp of steed or step of man, nor clatter of wheels, as the cannon are dragged along. The fine, friable sand absorbs all sounds, and only the heavy breathing and the tired snort of weary horses are heard in this moving mass of dust.

The soldier, small of stature, but hard as flint, marches firmly, though it is soft underfoot; with his back a little bent, for upon this back he carries his knapsack — containing his baggage, bread for three days, spare boots, an overcoat rolled tightly, the whole weighing between fifty and sixty pounds — and in addition he has two cartridge-boxes at his belt, the Berdan rifle in his hands, a shelter-tent, and a tin canteen covered with felt and filled with water. But it is nothing! Their backs have long since grown as accustomed to such a burden as the camel to its pack. How many thousand versts have not the white blouses measured under this load! They never count the versts — how many they have covered or how many are still before them.

At night he gets no sleep — it's all right! There is very little to eat — that's nothing! There is no water — that's nasty; but, well, one gets over it!

When the soldier's strength gives out he dies without a murmur. The others bury him, and go on. From their mouths comes not a single reproach; not a single regret, not a single complaint is heard.

With the Cossack it is quite a different affair. He is always fretting for his family, his fireside, or his home station. Say to a Cossack, "Would you rather go home than go on this march? Stay behind, brother; go home!" and the Cossack will shine all over with gladness; a broad smile will spread all over his face. He will hurry his preparations as if everything was burning under his fingers.

Say the same to a white blouse; tell him, "You'll be left behind," and the poor fellow will look as miserable as if cold water had been thrown over him. He will not eat nor drink, but only fret and look with burning envy upon the fortunate ones who are preparing for a long march.

Such are our white blouses.

CHAPTER XXII.

TRACKS.

A SMALL band of rovers of the steppe, consisting of about twenty horses and ten riders, so that each person had two animals, had found its way to a position between the fort at Khala-at and the Russian column, and was now following in its tracks.

These were no dangerous antagonists; they were simply cowardly wolves, ready to swerve from their road at the least sign of danger to themselves.

They were following the tracks, reckoning that some kind of booty must certainly fall to their share. A camel may be left behind or fall from exhaustion, and a bale may be thrown away, or something may be lost — or, better still, a straggling man may lose his way and afford them a chance to throw the noose of their long ropes over his head.

The band moved along at a trot, in open order; they

did not hurry much, not wishing to overtake the column, nor did they linger, for fear of being caught up with by somebody else.

They looked sharply ahead and to either side, but most frequently to the rear. They saw before them the trail of the marching column, covering a wide track. There had been no desert-winds to cover this terrible trail with sand, and an appalling picture of human suffering and endurance thus unrolled itself before the eyes of these robbers.

In dark, putrescent heaps the carcasses of fallen camels dotted the reddish sand. They came upon horses barely able to keep upon their legs, but standing motionless, ready from minute to minute to sink down into the burning sand never to rise again. The eyes of these unfortunate animals had already lost their living luster; they gazed dumbly into the distance. They never moved their heads nor pricked up their ears when the robbers rode up to them in the hope of profiting by something that was left upon them. Frequently the first touch of the robber would cause the animal to sink to the earth.

The plunderers also found traces of what must have been gigantic fires. They could see large black patches from afar, and the wind drove before it ashes and charred particles. It was evident that these fires were never built for warming the men or cooking their food. Sometimes the material had not been entirely consumed, and then they saw shreds of burned blankets, ends of rope, shapeless, half-melted pieces of iron. The white blouses burned, without exception, all that the surviving camels could not carry — all that ought to have been thrown away. They were told that every little thing, every trifle falling into the hands of the

9

enemy would be considered a trophy, and the white blouses never leave trophies to the enemy.

"Ah! the devils, the dogs!" exclaimed one of the robbers. "They have burned everything, so as to leave us nothing!" And he flung to the ground a worthless rag of half-burned cloth he had just picked up.

"How many camels have fallen! Allah, Allah!" remarked another. "Yesterday I went ahead a little, to the top of a hill, where I could see the caravans marching. How many there were!"

"Yes," said a third, coming up. "For three hours long the road is covered with them. If only half of them get to the Amu Daria, a hundred boats would not set them across the river."

"They will not get to the water!" gruffly observed an old man in a ragged cloak, and a high shaggy cap upon his head. "They can't get there. At the wells there is water for a hundred stomachs, but they number thousands. They don't even know where the wells are."

"I'm not sure of that," another broke in, shaking his head incredulously. "They drove Sadik and all of our men from the first wells — they must have known all about them. I have heard they have hollow tubes through which everything can be seen for a thousand versts; and they have books in which everything is written down."

"Behind us is Allah, behind them is Satan!" said the old man. "Allah is stronger than Satan. He knows that we are now finding plenty of fallen camels and horses, and soon we shall meet fallen men."

"I see new tracks here!" exclaimed one of the band who had been searching more to the right than any of them and was now galloping up. He pointed at the sand. "See there; those passed by long ago, yesterday, but these went only to-day. There are many of the others—you can't count them; of these there are only twelve tracks—three horses passed here, two under saddle and one led by the bridle. There are their feet. There are only two of them, and they are by themselves, not with the others; we are ten."

"We are ten," was repeated by several other voices. The bandits understood perfectly well what their companion meant when he said, "We are ten!"

"We'll not catch up with them!" said the old man. "Our horses are poor, but theirs run well; look at their long steps!"

"Ah! if we had only seen them sooner!"

"Ten wolves to one tiger is not enough!" the old man again remarked.

"In the evening you will know what the day has been!" sententiously observed he who had first discovered the new tracks.

"Let's follow them!" And the whole band crowded together and much increased their speed.

The wolves were following in the tracks of the tiger. The tracks were made by three horses of the correspondent of the New York *Herald* and his servant. Mr. Henry Blake did not at that moment suspect that the pack of wolves was chasing him.

CHAPTER XXIII.

ADAM KRILGAN.

THE white blouses had reached Adam Krilgan. At this place the sand-hills inclosed some wells scattered over a wide basin in their midst.

A stifling, dry heat, like that of a burning oven, simmered in this basin. At its very bottom could be seen, like black dots, the small apertures of the wells. There were not many of them and they were deep and narrow. The water could be obtained only by lowering buckets down into their deep cavity with long ropes — a tedious and tiresome method.

A thousand thirsting beings had come to these wells. Drink, drink was the one prevailing thought of all. "Water" was the only word pronounced by these dry, withered tongues. But the water was obtained only drop by drop.

The wells were guarded like sanctuaries; a strong watch was set over them. The regular turn in drinking, once established, was never changed for anybody or anything. The general and the meanest soldier stood equals in their turn. If anybody's life had depended upon a hair, if it had depended upon a single drop of water given out of his regular turn, it would not have been given, because the lives of all were in the same position.

But, in spite of all, these precious weighed and measured drops were not sufficient; the wells contained less water than had been anticipated.

It was difficult to recognize as water the fluid that

came out of these wells. Dark yellow, thick, and with an offensive putrid flavor, the water was consumed with eagerness, and even the moisture adhering to the bottoms of the vessels was carefully licked up. In one of the water-holes a dead dog had been found. The disgusting putrescent, swollen carcass of the animal when thrown upon the sand tainted the air around. Instinctively the men turned away from the well thus defiled; but thirst soon conquered their disgust, and they drank the fetid water. For a full glass of that water they would have given all they possessed. In a long, faltering line the men stood like shadows for more than ten hours about the wells, waiting their turn. They knew that they could not lose their turn. Officers with lists of names in their hands regulated the issue, and whoever was sleeping when his time came was sure to be called. But still there prevailed an unconscious dread, because they all knew that these wells were their only sources of life; without them there was only inevitable death — they were no longer strong enough to go back.

These exhausted men, tortured by a thirst of two days, could not retrace the road over which they had come, and whoever would drop by the way would never again rise upon his feet. They all knew this very well.

The whole expedition had not advanced to Adam Krilgan at once. Only the infantry was there. The Cossacks with their horses were left temporarily at the first wells, and were to follow only when the infantry column was ready to push on farther. If both had come here together the place would once more have earned its terrible name of Adam Krilgan (Man's Perdition).

Suddenly a cry arose — a cry full of despair, before the terror of which the eyes of all grew dark.

"The cavalry is coming! There they are in the sand-hills!"

Another thousand thirsty people, and as many horses barely able to keep their legs for want of water. These new-comers depended upon these wells of Adam Krilgan — they must drink themselves, they must water their horses, while those who had come here two days before had not yet all been supplied!

The unexpected arrival of the cavalry was somebody's fatal blunder.

A panic quickly began to spread in the camp — a panic which might result in general demoralization.

Driven by the instinct of self-preservation, with arms in their hands, the men might fall upon each other to obtain water. The strong would have slain the weak, the subordinate would in such a death-struggle refuse to recognize his superior — all discipline would have vanished like smoke in the air, and the precincts of Adam Krilgan would have presented so dreadful a picture of human delirious fury that all legends of disasters happening there in the past would have paled into insignificance before the present.

All this might have occurred if the people concerned had been different; but these were battalions of white blouses — they knew how to perish without losing their human dignity.

An extraordinary council of war was called. An old gray-haired man, whose name now graces the most glorious pages of the history of Russian arms, was at the head of this council.

CHAPTER XXIV.

DOSTCHAK AND HIS BOTTLE.

ONCE more, as he did that other time before Atam Kul's examination, Dostchak passed through the whole bivouac, and directed his steps to the general's headquarters.

In making out the lists for the turns at the wells the poor natives accompanying the column had been forgotten. With baked lips and sunken eyes, bereft of all strength, and voiceless, many of them had already sunk into the sand in their death-agony. "Su, su!" (water) in the shrillest whisper was all that could be heard of their struggle.

Staggering, and falling more than once, Dostchak went on to the general to address him in behalf of his unfortunate countrymen.

"Back!" shouted the sentry, standing in his way.

"Let me go, please, let me go!" begged Dostchak, striving to turn aside the gun of the man guarding the approach.

"Back!" the sentry said again — only not quite so emphatically and crossly as the first time.

"You let me go — man lives; you no let go — man dies!" said the native, seating himself in the sand at the very feet of the sentry. In this movement there was so much resolution expressed to wait until his object was gained, in the glance of his old eyes there was such a sparkle of life, such persuasion as to the necessity of his seeing whom he came to see, that the soldier put by his gun and asked, "What do you want?"

Another soldier came out of the tent. Some one
questioned Dostchak, and the general stepped forward.

"To the northward from here — over there," Dostchak told the general — "with a good horse one hour's
ride — there are other wells. You do not know them,
but I know. I remember. I recognize this place.
Long, long ago I was here. That is true — there must
be other wells. Tell, Genderal, tell your soldiers to
come after me. I'll go first. I lead them to the water.
Here there is little water — many men. Some people
here, other people there — enough water for all. Listen
to me! Tell your soldiers to follow old Dostchak. But
now give water to my people — they die. Only give
orders to rub their lips with a wet cloth. Genderal,
take pity on them!" Thus spoke the old man, now rising from his knees and then getting down again; and at
the same time two others of the natives crawled up
from behind — the strongest among them — and, raising
themselves upon their elbows, they looked at the
general as hungry, perishing dogs look at their master.

"I have not yet drank myself," calmly spoke the
general. "I will give you my portion when my turn
comes; I can get no other water for you."

The soldier on guard suddenly staggered; the gun
fell from his hands — he took another step and fell to
the ground. He had been attacked by sunstroke.

"Water, quick! water!" shouted one of the officers,
running up. "On his temples and into his mouth!"

Where was there any water to be got? A strange
demand, indeed, which was made mechanically, unconsciously, under the impulse of the moment. The
speaker himself became confused at his mistake and
turned away. Then Natalia Martinovna appeared, God
only knew whence, entirely unexpected to all, and

stooped over the fallen man. She held in her hand a
small round-bottomed bottle.* From it she moistened
a handkerchief and laid it upon the soldier's head.
Then she forced open his clinched teeth and poured a
few drops from the bottle. The dying natives close
by saw the water sparkling as the sunlight struck the
greenish glass. Gathering their last strength, they
wriggled up to the sister of mercy and convulsively
seized her dress. Some soldiers rushed up to release
her.

"Hold on!" Natalia said, calmly. "There is a drop
left for them; they do not need much — only hold their
hands so that they can not grasp the bottle. That's it!"
The soldiers kept a firm hold of the natives' hands until
Natalia had poured into their mouths what was left in
the bottle. Left to themselves they would have been
ready to crush the neck of the saving vessel with their
teeth, or to tear the bottle from her hands.

The natives wept, and kissed the tracks left in the
sand by the woman's feet. The soldiers crossed themselves reverently.

The ends of the thin muslin kerchief which covered
Natalia's head fluttered in the wind, standing out
from her shoulders. In the terrible heat a trembling
mist obscured vision and gave strange outlines to
objects. It must have been from these causes that
these handkerchief-ends appeared to all those present
like a pair of shining wings.

It was impossible to ascertain on the spot the truth
or falsehood of what Dostchak had told the general
concerning some other wells. Nor was it advisable to
order at once a part of the command to proceed to

---

* Such bottles are used to keep "holy water" in. Natalia
must have carried one with her.

them. He had been there long ago. He said himself that many years had passed by since then. The wells might no longer exist though they once had been there. When the old man was informed how matters stood he exclaimed : "Give me a horse, Genderal; a good horse. See, here I have a bottle!" and he drew from the inside of his cloak a felt-covered bottle.

"You see," he continued, "this bottle is empty. Look for yourself — there is not a drop in it. Oh, if there was only a little! I will go alone; if the Turkomans do not kill me there at those other wells, I'll come back and bring you this bottle full. Then, then you will send the other men after me. Will you send them?"

It was impossible to object to such a proposition. They gave Dostchak a horse and he rode away.

CHAPTER XXV.

AT THE OTHER WELLS.

THE sandy desert lay before him in deathlike solitude when Dostchak set out from the camp. The roar and noise of the bivouac had been swallowed up completely by the sand-hills behind him. His worn-out horse, though a good one, went along slowly under his rider, not minding the kicking of heels against his thin sides, nor the strokes of the whip dealt him by the impatient native.

Carefully and anxiously Dostchak examined his surroundings — they seemed all alike. One sand-hill was followed by another, exactly alike; each wavelike ridge a repetition of its fellow — it looked as if they had all been cast in the same mold. In sharp contrast with the reddish-yellow sand, the grayish-blue cloudless sky hung over it. Desolation and emptiness on earth, and the same in the sky — not a cloud, not a bird. Why should independent creatures direct their flight to this region of death? With a scarcely perceptible rustle some large-headed lizards scurried over the sand — they do not need water. They saw the man passing by — they looked at him, but did not hide themselves. "And what brings you here?" the reptiles probably thought. "We have come across many a bone while burrowing in the sand — horses' bones, men's bones, and camels' bones; perhaps you want to add something to those bones?"

"Haïda, haïda!" Dostchak shouted to his horse. "We sha'n't get to the water very soon at this gait." The old man was not at all pleased with the looks of the country. It did not seem the same as he remembered it. Over there on that hill there used to be a large white rock. Where is it now? It must have been covered by the sand. There ought to be a trail right under that mound, but it is not there. "Why should I not find them?" the old man muttered, uneasily, and looked back. The track of his horse reached back far — far into the distance, where the haze swallowed it up. He must have traveled five versts — perhaps only half the road remained to be covered.

With nothing in sight to attract his attention, Dostchak looked for his bottle — it was there. He felt the saddle behind him — there was the rope, everything in order. He glanced down at the horse — it bore a Kirghiz saddle, the bit and bridle were of common make. As to himself—his cloak was the same as any Turkoman's; so was his sheepskin cap, and the sword sticking in his sash. "It is well that I am rigged out in this way; if I should meet any Turkomans they'll take me for one of their own people—'sh!" At that very moment two horsemen made their appearance climbing over a ridge near by. They were talking and not looking around; and there was another emerging from behind a sand-hill. Farther on still there was a group of them. Dostchak went along quietly as if he did not feel the slightest interest in the others, though he listened intently.

"We went to look at the Russians," said one of the horsemen, "but we didn't go very close; they have some cursed guns that carry a long distance. We could not see much."

"I saw the cannon," replied the other; "they glistened in the sun, so I could count them. They have not many of them; our Khan has more."

"Our Khan has more!" muttered Dostchak, who had come up unperceived. The Turkomans turned about and looked at him sharply.

"Is it long since you watered your horse?" one of them accosted Dostchak.

"A long time—before dawn. I thought I would water again over there, and find our people, but the Russians are there, and I had to go on without water. May Allah send every evil down upon their heads! My stallion is almost spent. Well, all right; I'll water him at Alti-Kuduk. Are you long from there?"

"Since noon. Where do you belong?"

"I belong to God's men," Dostchak replied, evasively.

They went along silently. Dostchak strove to keep up with them; he knew where they were going—just where he wanted to go. He only thought of one thing — how to get back again with water in his bottle.

"The night is dark," he concluded; "and if it's Allah's will — what is to be, will be." And he struck up in a low, cracked voice a long, monotonous chant.

A dense cloud of dust rested over the hollow where the wells were situated. A large number of people was assembled there — four hundred horses or more. The horsemen were biouvacking around the wells, their animals hobbled close at hand, and the men seated in small circles around the water-holes. They were lowering leather buckets into the apertures with long woolen ropes, and pulling them up again. The water splashed over the rim and wetted the thirsty sand. Dostchak shivered when he saw the waste; his horse snorted as if mad, opening wide its thin, bloodshot nostrils. With the greatest difficulty the old man restrained the animal, glided from the saddle, stretched his legs, and began to take the rope from his saddle. "Oh, I've lost my bucket!" he exclaimed. "What a blunder! Mullah," he addressed one of a dozen natives around the well, "give me yours, to water my horse!"

"Take it!" said the man, putting down his bucket and going away himself.

Quietly, without hurrying, Dostchak proceeded to attach the rope, scratched himself, spat in his hand, and then quickly lowered the bucket. When he pulled it up again his teeth were chattering, and his eyes were burning as he looked down into the dark, gaping aperture. "If I hurry too much they may suspect something. It is lucky these are no organized troops, but only runaways from the standard who come together to rob! They have no business to be curious about a poor roving dog — they'll take me for one of themselves."

Dostchak got his bucket full at last. He tasted a little himself, then he watered the horse, which thrust his head into the bucket with such eagerness that he nearly upset his master.

" Enough, enough, or you'll burst! " cried Dostchak, as he snatched away the bucket, pouring the remainder of the water into the sand, and laid himself down, fastening the long bridle to his arm.

The sun was about to set. The blue shadows were lengthening; it grew dark in the hollow; the atmosphere was filling with the moist exhalation from the wells.

" That's glorious! " said Dostchak to himself. " I'm in luck — but how are they over there? " and he thought of the heart-breaking scene at the other wells. " If they had all come here together," he thought, " it would have been just the same. The only hope is to divide the force — in that way they could be saved." Again he went to the well and watered his horse once more; then he drank himself, and stealthily got out his bottle — in the thickening gloom of evening his movements were less apt to excite curiosity — and began to prepare for the road.

Suddenly a word fell upon Dostchak's ear which caused him to glance around sharply, and then to listen intently to what was being said not far away.

" They do not believe him and are afraid of him," said somebody in the darkness.

" Of whom are they afraid? " asked another.

" Of Atam Kul — I've heard them tell Mat-Nias that it would be well if Satan would wring his neck."

" Much foolishness flies from their tongues! "

" That may be — but they do not all believe in him. He may be turning toward the Russians again — they do not remember injuries long. They were saying that Atam Kul had sent a letter to the Russians, and they sent him —"

" That is possible. I heard that he had been with them not long ago, and when he left them he brought somebody with him — a girl, they said, but perhaps they lied."

" No; it's a boy."

" And the Khan — does he hear nothing of all this?"

" The Khan is friendly to him, and that is what makes Mat-Nias angry. Sadik also hates him on account of that old affair. They made peace before the Khan, but Sadik remembers — he never forgave a wrong in his life."

" That is true. Where shall we go from here?"

" To Sardiba-Kul, they say."

" They say that at Sardiba-Kul —"

The voices became less audible, but they continued to talk. As soon as Dostchak could hear no more he took his horse by the bridle and quietly led him away from the wells. Nobody had paid any attention to him when he came, and now not a head was turned when he mounted his horse and rode away from the bivouac.

The night air was fresh, and the horse, having been amply watered, made good speed, and before long patches of dusky red — the reflection of the camp-fires — looming up above the horizon showed Dostchak where his road lay.

CHAPTER XXVI.

SARDIBA-KUL AND UTCH-CHUCHAK.

THE white blouses were once more advancing from their camp at the wells of Adam Krilgan and Alti-Kuduk, where they suffered such frightful privations and hardships. If they had broken down under those privations they would not have advanced, and must have perished at that fatal spot, but they still had strength and energy enough to march.

The road back to where they came from was well known to them. They would soon find water there — such as it was. The road ahead of them was as dark and unknown as the future. There was water ahead; that they all knew — the Amu Daria, the objective point of their march. But where was it — far or near? That nobody knew. Between the wells from which the expedition started and the Amu there was a vast extent of deadly sands, and that region must be crossed.

Some said it was but a day's march ahead; some said it was three days'. Others, again, maintained that it was more than à hundred versts, or nearly a week's marching. If it was two days' march, the men would get through, and perhaps the camels and horses; if it was more, nobody would get through, and all these questions would be decided at once.

To remain where they were was death; to go back was dishonor; to go ahead was to place all upon a single card, and wait. The white blouses preferred the last; to play the single critical, fatal card — so they went ahead.

WATER AT LAST!

The following night was passed, without water, in the sand. A deathlike stillness reigned in the camp; strange sounds came over the steppe from all directions, sounds which caused the experienced soldiers to keep on the alert. Frequently a number of them would press their ears to the ground, and then they could clearly distinguish the tramp of horses — the movements of whole masses of horsemen. The heretofore silent waste, quiet as the grave, seemed to be quickening into life. Faint but audible sounds came through the air also, but nothing could be seen; it was very dark.

"Do you hear that racket?" one soldier whispered into the ear of his comrade.

"I hear it. There's many people —'sh!"

"A horse snorted — over there on that side."

"The whole horde seems to be promenading."

"Did you notice how the sun set last evening?"

"Why?"

"All our fellows saw it. The captain took off his cap and crossed himself, and said, 'Boys, the Amu Daria is near. Let's pray, boys, to God."

"What did they see?"

"An eagle in the sky. We only saw him for a minute; then he went up, God's bird, ever so high, and soared, and at last he turned away over the sand-hills there. They say where eagles are water is near."

"Thirty versts — an eagle will go no farther from the water; that is true!"

"Yes, thirty versts — it may be nearer. Now you can hear that noise again — back of the rearguard!"

"I hear it."

"They, also, can't go far from the water; there are so many of them. A few of them may do it — but such crowds, not for anything."

10

"They seem to be everywhere — all around the camp; there must be many!"

"With daylight our eyes will see what our ears hear now. Look! the grand round is coming. Who goes there?"

"The round!" comes in reply out of the darkness, and a group of men on foot approaches along the picket-line. The old general himself, walking heavily in the deep sand, was inspecting in person the outer line of pickets, familiarly touching the visor of his cap when the men came to attention on recognizing the well-known figure of their commander-in-chief. The old man, observing the watchful care, the energy and animation displayed by his men, said to himself, with a feeling of pride, "Happy the general to whom it is given to command such men!"

Long before dawn the expedition was on the march again. Myriads of stars still sparkled in the dark heavens, but they only sparkled, and gave no light. Beneath them it was dark, and it was difficult to distinguish the still darker mass of the long line of hump-backed camels led out in close column. A somewhat brighter line — the infantry — surrounded the vast column of pack-animals.

The whole force marched in strictest order, ready for battle. The enemy was close at hand, and no precaution must be neglected. The movement scarcely reminded one of a desperate march of worn-out troops through a deadly desert. It had more the air of a well-ordered, often-rehearsed maneuver.

Daylight came; the wavy outlines of hills became more clearly defined, and the horizon widened more and more. This line was watched closely by every one, from the general down to the humblest "loutch" employed in the camel-train. It was now seen to be dotted with black moving objects. The enemy was aware at last that the deadly desert that was to have been the grave of the "giaours" had proved but an unreliable ally of the "faithful." The Russians did not yet know that the desert was already crossed, that they stood upon the threshold of a cultivated, irrigated, rich section of the Khivan Khan's dominions; but the others knew it, and knew also that now they must depend only upon their own strength to stem the impending influx of white blouses. They gathered from all sides in dense masses to arrest their powerful enemy in his hitherto uninterrupted progress.

Ahead of the moving column, still far distant, but perfectly clear, rose three slight elevations. These were the Utch-Chuchak (three hills), and beyond them lay the Amu — the end of all suffering and anxiety.

Without any orders, as if under the influence of one common idea, all quickened their steps; the horses pulled at their bridles; the camels extended their long necks, snorted with their torn nostrils, and bellowed.

"Water!" was reported from the advance-guard. "Water, water!" resounded throughout the length of the column. A shining streak, reflecting in its bosom the purple and golden tint of the morning dawn, stretched away to the left of Utch-Chuchak. It was as if an electric spark had run through the whole force from the first man to the last.

On the sandy heights, on either side, small white clouds of smoke were puffing up with increasing frequency — these were the Turkomans trying to arrest the advance of the expedition, yelling and shouting, and galloping over the hills, to the right, to the left, in front and in rear. They were not replied to with a single shot.

The water that had been sighted was not the Amu, as was subsequently ascertained. To the great river of this unknown country it was still a good day's march. This was the lake of Sardiba-Kul, lying in a shining semicircle in a small valley at the foot of the Utch-Chuchak. A green border of rushes served as a frame to this glistening, transparent mirror. How delicious appeared to inflamed eyes the vivid green — the sign of life! It was so long since the Russians had seen any green that they hardly remembered its beauty.

With the greatest difficulty the horses were prevented from rushing into the water, where the majority would have become foundered after their prolonged compulsory abstinence.

A lively bivouac soon encircled the banks of the Sardiba-Kul. Fires were burning merrily, and everywhere sounds of singing and music could be heard. The faces of all shone with pride and triumph. At this time the fate of the Khanate of Khiva was decided. The principal and most powerful enemy — nature — had been conquered. There now remained only trifling obstacles to overcome, such as the white blouses were accustomed to look upon with contempt.

"Well, boys, thanks be to God, we got there!" exclaimed a soldier, as he was hurriedly divesting himself of his shirt.

"Ah, friend, water is free now — not measured; drink your fill!"

"Is it very deep here?"

"Very."

"Don't go there — it's a deep hole. Bless you!"

"It is three months since we have done any washing."

"They say we will stay here a day—we can wash shirts and drawers."

"The captain's horse killed itself. The bugler, Demka, did not watch him, and he ran into the lake. He drank and drank until he bursted!"

"Some men, also, have taken too much—it's not the beasts only that are crazy. Look there—look! How the Cossacks are driving those red devils!"

And while soldiers were quietly and merrily bathing and washing, enjoying the abundance of unmeasured water, a lively fusillade was going on all around the lake. Great masses of the enemy's cavalry emerged from beyond the Utch-Chuchak, and retreated again, pursued by the Cossacks and some infantry. Among the continuous rattle of musketry the louder reports of field-pieces could be heard occasionally.

By noon the enemy had retreated, and all returned to the camp and to rest—a rest well earned by so much privation and suffering. At headquarters a band of music was playing. All sorrow and trouble were forgotten. The terrible desert lay behind them; before them a wide and well-beaten road. The gigantic undertaking of a few Turkestan battalions had been accomplished—a feat which caused the world to look upon them with admiration and say, "Yes, those are soldiers!"

CHAPTER XXVII.

NEWS.

A STRANGE morning!

The steep, broken banks of the Amu Daria are almost perpendicular. During freshets the water rises nearly to the level of these banks, washing and undermining them, and forming long parallel furrows on either side, the bottoms of which are filled with a sediment of mud, sand, and organic débris. When the water falls and recedes from these abrupt rocky walls, it leaves behind low, damp bars extending along the foot of the cliffs. These bars, or second shore-line — called "tugas" by the natives — are the favorite resort of gulls, king-fishers, snipe, and other aquatic birds. Worms of various kinds, insects, and sometimes small fish, are found in vast multitudes on these bars by the birds, and the abundance of food attracts the feathered inhabitants from the whole river valley.

The dark-yellow, muddy water flows along noiselessly — not a single boat is visible on its surface; but at times huge fish jump up with a splash, and disappear again, slightly ruffling the gently flowing waters, and leaving behind them ever-widening circles.

It is hot. The gulls have grown tired of flying and are sitting motionless upon the sand-bars, resting from their early exertions — the dense flocks of birds appearing like patches of snow upon the reddish sand. Here and there, between the bars, small bodies of standing water are glistening and shining in the sunlight.

A thin layer of fog conceals the distant, opposite

shore — a few hills only, streaked with blue shadows, can be discerned rising above the fog.

The expedition had gone into camp upon the heights of the river-bank, whence innumerable narrow and crooked, well-trodden paths were leading down. Over these paths an almost continuous chain of soldiers was always passing, going and coming. They descended with empty vessels, ascending afterward with kettles, tubs, and buckets filled to overflowing. The kitchens were located at the water's edge; huge pillars of thick, black smoke were rising from under the huge kettles. Here also, not far away, the small boats, resembling pontoons, which had been carried in pieces across the desert by the camel-train, were being put together and launched; sailors and infantry soldiers getting into them with evident delight, trying their qualities, and working hard at the short but strong oars.

All the native boats had long since been carried away by the Turkomans to the other shore, and therefore these pontoons were only intended as preliminary means for beginning the crossing of troops. With their help, and chiefly through the daring and enterprise of some companies of sailors from the Caspian fleet, it was expected to recover a goodly number of boats, somehow, from the opposite shore; the only way being, of course, to take them out of the hands of the enemy.

All hostile opponents had long since been driven from the right bank of the Amu and forced to cross the river, the wide channel of which now lay between the Russians and their enemies. Consequently the camp was quiet, and considered safe, and many of the customary precautions were no longer enforced. It would not do to tire out uselessly the soldiers who were so much in need of complete rest and recuperation.

Joy and pride at the accomplishment of their task filled the breasts of all those who were well, and also had its beneficial effect upon the sick. Every day saw more and more of the hospital-cots losing their occupants, and the physicians' labors grew less arduous with every hour.

Increased labor and cares had thus far to a certain extent deadened the anguish consuming Natalia Martinovna's heart, but now, in comparative idleness, her grief began to resume its first crushing weight. It was sad to look at the woman. Formerly, though thoughtful and always serious, she showed every sign of blooming health and unimpaired strength. Now, pale and thin, with eyes ever cast down, as if guilty of some crime, she was the personification of grief and anguish.

People came and spoke to her, trying to interest her in something, but all these attempts appeared to be in vain; and the least incautious word falling from a careless tongue, the slightest hint at her misfortune, brought forth abundant noiseless tears. At such times the greatest anguish was expressed in her face, which had always borne the traces of much suffering, and the careless chatterer would curse himself and his tongue, and for a long time after would not dare to speak, or even go near the unfortunate mother.

Golovin alone never forgot himself in her presence, and could lead her on to talk on general subjects, occasionally even succeeding in rousing her to some attention and interest. But, on the other hand, the lame Cossack was changing nearly as much as Natalia. He looked more like a walking corpse than a living man. The fierce struggle began to tell even upon his iron constitution; and frequently, on returning to his Cossack bivouac and throwing himself upon his blanket, pressing his head upon the hard leather pillow, he would groan, and even weep, and then, quickly removing all traces of weakness from his face, go back again to the woman for one drop of whose blood he was ready to sacrifice all his own.

The Cossack had lost all hope of saving the son and returning him to his mother, but naturally he did not let Natalia know it. Natalia felt confident that sooner or later her son would be returned to her arms; but she, also, never whispered a word of this hope. It was as if she feared to find some people ready with one word to shatter this hope into fragments, and therefore she guarded it jealously, hiding it carefully from everybody's eye or ear. This hope upheld her in her minutes of severest trial, but it also at times caused her the most bitter anguish.

"He is alive, but where is he? How is he treated? In what rough and cruel hands is the boy? What frightful hardships is he undergoing. What is the poor boy suffering now?" Sometimes it appeared to Natalia that she could more easily bear to see her child's corpse than to continue in this exasperating uncertainty.

She would have sacrificed anything for news of him. Oh, if it would only come from somewhere — in a puff of that scorching desert-wind, or on the wings of that silvery gull sweeping in graceful flight across the river! And, led by some indefinable instinctive feeling, Natalia was constantly expecting this blessed news. And she waited.

Once, toward evening, when it was growing cooler and the rosy light of the setting sun gave grateful relief to burning eyes, weary of the monotonous landscape, Natalia walked slowly along the shore, admiring the glints of light shooting across the water as the gulls darted hither and thither in pursuit of their prey. She was alone; even the lame Cossack did not accompany her. The large dog " Kutzec " ran after her, energetically wagging his short stump of a tail, but when Natalia stroked the kind animal's head his ambition seemed to be fully satisfied, for after giving vent to a few expressive barks he turned around and ran back to his station about the company kitchen.

Close to the water's edge a few native laborers and militiamen were lounging, and a few minutes later the little assembly was joined by a dozen or so of roving beggars coming from God knows where. Nearly all of them pretended to be Persian slaves escaped from their masters to seek Russian protection, and our soldiers willingly gave them an asylum, dividing cheerfully with these new-comers their own frugal and scanty meals. Of late the number of these unknown and apparently helpless people in the Russian camp had increased considerably, but, as formerly, no special attention was paid to them.

Natalia Martinovna was walking past one of the many groups of these people, when a black-faced, ragged, and half-naked native approached her; glancing at her inquisitively with his bleared, rascally eyes, he extended toward her his hand, which was wrapped up in a cloth. The unfortunate seemed to have been wounded, as dark stains of oozing blood were easily perceptible upon the dirty rag. He muttered something in a language unknown to Natalia, always keeping his hand extended, and after keeping at her side for a few steps he fell upon his knees. Natalia turned toward him and stooped down. The native at once began to unwrap the cloth, when suddenly Natalia

Martinovna drew back and trembled. She felt in her hand a piece of folded paper. "Take it and read it," said the man in Russian, "then you will know all!"

Natalia wanted to cry out, but could not; she wanted to raise her hand to summon somebody to her assistance, but her strength failed her. The ground seemed to revolve under feet — she staggered, but the paper which had found its way into her possession thus mysteriously was convulsively clutched in her thin, slender fingers. The man in rags had vanished as if he had never been there. He had probably succeeded in losing himself in the crowd of other natives, just as black, just as ragged, and just as dirty as he was.

The cool wind from the river had a reviving effect upon Natalia's nerves. She roused herself and walked quickly through the whole camp to her tent. Some secret presentiment told her that in this scrap of paper was contained the solution of the problem, the news she had so long and anxiously expected.

"Your son is with me — it is well with him. Come yourself, and it will be well with you. If you do not come it will be bad for him, and bad for you also. After a few days the Russians will cross the river; ours will not prevent them. On that day people will come to you — go with them! If my men perish, and if you do not come, I can not answer for your son.

"MULLAH ATAM KUL."

That was what the note contained.

"Natalia Martinovna, may I enter?" asked from without the voice of the lame Cossack.

Natalia could not answer. She trembled as if in a violent fever. She stood in the middle of her tent, one hand pressing upon the table, while the other deftly, but with convulsive haste, concealed the fatal note in her bosom.

"Natalia Martinovna!" the voice could again be heard outside of the tent.

CHAPTER XXVIII.

DOSTCHAK CONCEIVES A PLAN.

THE white blouses had gained the other shore. They did not cross where the camp was established on first reaching the water. For a few days the expedition skirted the river on its right bank, moving downward; the principal force ascended the cliffs, apparently moving away from the water and once more heading for the desert, but they soon changed direction again and regained the river, on the bank of which their camp was made each night. A smaller force, lightly equipped, moved along the sand-bars in the river, being often obliged to wade for long distances. This force served as convoy for the small fleet of boats proceeding by water, and being reinforced day by day by acquisitions of native boats, which were seized wherever the nimble sailors could lay their hands upon them — sometimes with fighting and sometimes without, as luck would have it.

In this way the means of transportation had increased to such an extent that when the crossing-place was reached it was considered feasible to take the decisive step — and the step was taken. The Russian battalions penetrated into the very heart of the Khanate of Khiva.

The camp was pitched in gardens under the shade of gigantic plantain-trees, in the vicinity of Khagar-Asp, a Khivan fortified town. Reports had been received to the effect that other expeditions, coming from the Caucasus and from Orenburg, were on the march to Khiva, and that they were already near, and these rumors instigated the Turkestan column to greater haste in order to reach the walls of Khiva and not let the palm of first success fall into other hands. It was even said that the steamers of our Aral fleet had ascended from Kazalinsk to the delta of the Amu Daria, and that they would push farther up that stream. The Khivan drama was entering upon its last act — the dismemberment.

Dostchak was celebrating a great holiday. He had attired himself in his very best red cloak, the same that had been presented to him by the commander-in-chief only last week. He also put on his yellow trousers embroidered with silk; these trousers Dostchak had bought of a soldier after a foraging expedition. Many excellent articles were sold cheap on that occasion, and for these trousers, to which the otherwise poor fellow could never have aspired in his wildest dreams, he paid altogether two "kokans" (about 20 cents). Over his small oily tybeteika (Bashkir cap) he wore a large striped woolen turban.

"You are like the Mulla of Samarkand!" said Sharip, raising his hands in astonishment on seeing Dostchak in his full dress.

"He's a warrior!" said Karim, shaking his head and smacking his lips.

"Oho!" cried the general's native servant, Uzen. "You look a greater man now than mine. Truly, you are greater — your ribbon is so much redder. Let me

see! and there are two little yellow roads on the sides
— one is the road by which you went to the wells, and
on the other you came back again; there they are,
both the roads.

The servant, who had come to the place of meeting
on horseback, alighted, and walking up to Dostchak
looked long and earnestly at his breast, on the left side
of his cloak; then, stepping back a pace, he. looked
again, bending his head a little aside, and, winking,
again cried, "Oho!" He then went to tie up his sorrel
stallion, covering him from ears to tail with a warm
horse-cloth.

On old Dostchak's breast there twinkled in the sun a
large gold medal suspended by a red gold-edged ribbon. It shone like the sun, which was reflected in its
disk, and the same bright reflection was thrown upon
the old man's face. It shone brightly on this aged
countenance, marked with scars and wrinkles, and it
reflected the greatest satisfaction, joy, and full and
unlimited happiness.

Dostchak had received this medal from the general
only to-day — he received it for his bold journey to the
wells at Alti-Kuduk; and now he was gathering his
friends to rejoice with him over his good fortune. His
companions were as much pleased as he was himself.
They had clubbed together and purchased a sheep from
the Cossacks — it did not come high — cut it up, procured some rice, and then proceeded to cook a grand
"pilaf," such as they had not seen for six months at
least.

Soldiers passing by and happening to stop were
asked at once to sit down, the simple natives rejoicing
over every new guest added to the feast. And why
should they care how many came, since Sharip had

emptied a whole sack of rice into the huge kettle? That kettleful would have been amply sufficient for half a company.

The natives had selected a pleasant place for their festivities. Three plantain-trees were growing close together in a row on the bank of an irrigating ditch. These trees cast such a dense, cool shade! It extended over the water, and spread so far that even Uzen's horse, which was tethered ten paces away, enjoyed its shelter. Behind the plantain-trees rose a high wall lined with a row of tall poplars, and through the interstices between them could be seen the dark-green branches of more plantain-trees, with ripe yellow fruit shining like amber here and there in the sunlight. There must have been vast quantities of this fruit when any of it could be preserved in the immediate vicinity of a hungry, populous camp.

The semi-spherical cupola of a mosque rose beyond the poplars, and upon its top a clumsy stork's-nest loomed up darkly. The long-legged bird, white, with black wings and a long red bill, stood upon its nest without any fear of the people camped below, though probably it had never in its life seen such crowds before. Somewhere in the distance music was playing, just near enough to allow the feasting natives to enjoy it.

"That's just what we like!" said Uzen, looking complacently first at his own person and then all around; and all his companions agreed with him.

"You've spoken truly," said Dostchak, adjusting his new turban upon his head; "that's true."

Encouraged by the applause evoked by his profound remark, Uzen ventured to dish up some news. "The Khan," he said, "has written a letter to the genderal asking him to stay awhile where he is, and not go any

farther. 'You,' he writes, 'wait until I drive those others
away — to fight all at once is very hard for me.'"

"Well?"

"'What,' he says, 'do you want of Khiva? You don't
need Khiva, but I,' he says, 'I need it. You,' he says,
'wait, please, and I will send you forty cloaks, forty
camels, forty sheep, forty horses, and forty women —
good Khivan and Persian women; only stay where you
are, please!'"

"Who has told you all that, old fellow?" inquired an
infantry soldier who was puffing at his short pipe.

"Who told me — me?"

"Yes, you!"

"Don't the genderal smoke small pipe made of
paper?"

"Cigarettes? Yes, he smokes them."

"Don't the Cossack Demianka bring fire to the genderal?"

"Yes."

"The genderal smokes, and Cossack Demianka gives
him fire — there is only a small table between the Cossack and the genderal;" and the native showed with his
hands that only about half a yard separated one from
the other.

"I suppose so," consented the soldier.

"Over such a short road one can hear everything,
can't he?"

"Very likely."

"Well, that same Cossack Demianka told me that the
Khan wrote to the genderal, and I tell it to you."

"You are right," Dostchak again consented. "I
should like to see that letter. The Khan's name must
be written with gold paint."

"Can you read their lingo, or yours — or is it all the

same?" asked the company clerk, Kuska, who had
come up staggering and was now holding onto a
branch of a tree to steady himself upon his legs.

" Say, Brother Kuska," said the infantryman, " where
did you get it?" explaining his meaning by inserting
two fingers between his throat and the collar of his
shirt.

" I?—do you mean me? Oh, I can't always remember. I am the company clerk—I'm an official. Hey,
tamir [my friend], what is your name? Shaltai-Boltai
something. Do you know how to carry your gun on
guard?"

" What do I want with a gun on guard?" replied the
native. " I don't have to stand guard."

" I can read a little," said Dostchak; "the Mullah
at Almatakh taught me. " But I can not write — I
never learned. It's hard to write; very difficult
indeed!"

" Yes, it's hard."

" But which is more difficult — to write Russian or to
write Tartarsky?"

" In Tartarsky it is much harder," Clerk Kuska gave
his opinion. " I manage to get away pretty slick with
ours, but of yours I can't make anything, even when
I'm drunk. The devil himself could not decipher your
loops and pothooks; and it's all upside down, and reads
backward!"

" But you can write Russian well?" tentatively questioned Dostchak, twirling his fingers.

" Like print!"

" Can you write like the genderal?"

" Not only like the general — I write good enough for
the minister. I take a sheet of paper and with one —
two strokes like this the sheet is half-covered! In a

11

week I've got away with fourteen report-books. That's
what you may call real, thorough education!"

"Sit down, please; sit down there! *Plov ashat —
makhan ashat* [eat pilaf, eat mutton]. Sit down, please!"
urged Dostchak, hurriedly clearing a place next to himself for his guest.

The pilaf was ready, and they began dishing it out in
large shallow saucers. They spread a horse-cloth and
placed the smoking dishes before the guests, who with
naked fingers were soon diving into the hot compound
of rice, meat, and melted fat. They ate with enjoyment and appetite; they ate as if to repay themselves,
with interest, for past privations. Such pilaf did not
fall to their lot many times in their simple, frugal lives!

They ate all day, and in the evening it was as if the
two-year-old sheep had never existed, and but little of
the rice remained in Sharip's kettle.

During all this time old Dostchak was doing the
honors chiefly to Clerk Kuska. He flattered him with
the titles of Mullah and Mirza; selected for him the
choicest morsels, and even placed them in his mouth
with his own fingers. Before long Kuska succumbed,
drunk as he already was, and now gorged to repletion.
Dostchak gently and carefully removed him to the
wall, and placed a cloth over his head to prevent his
being recognized from the road.

"Why are you bothering yourself so much about
him?" Uzen, the general's servant, asked the old man.
"Don't you see he's been feeding like a pig, and he is
drunk? You might have treated some better man!"

"That man is very necessary to me," muttered
Dostchak. "Oh, how necessary! He can write like
the genderal himself!"

"What good does that do you?"

"That man," began Dostchak, and stopped, listening intently in the direction of his hut; then, probably finding everything satisfactory, he continued: "That man can do a great thing for me — Dostchak; and from that thing good will come to the good and evil to the bad."

"You are talking riddles!"

"Yes, riddles! Dostchak has been thinking a long time. When I went to the other wells — for these — do you see?" pointing with his finger to his medal and ribbon, making it clear what wells he referred to — "at that time Dostchak was already thinking, and he is thinking now, and will think to-morrow, and he tells nobody what he is thinking; but in due time all the people will know, and they will say, 'Well, old Dostchak, if he is old, his mind has not left him on account of his age!'"

The last guests went away. The night was dark and quiet; not a light was visible anywhere. The moon had not yet risen and the stars gave but little light. Especially under the trees it was so dark that a cat could not have seen anything, not even the white blouse of Clerk Kuska as he lay there filling the neighborhood with his snoring.

In the distance the officers' tents shone like gigantic many-colored lanterns, and here and there glimmered like sparks the burning ends of cigars. In the direction of Khazar-Asp a reddish reflection appeared on the sky above the horizon — it did not look like the moon, nor like a conflagration, though it might be either; and not far away two officers were discussing the point. Their voices fell clearly upon the ears of Dostchak, who was guarding the nocturnal slumbers of his guest — the man who was so "very necessary" to him.

CHAPTER XXIX.

"I AM A MOTHER."

"What does that mean?" muttered Golovin, who was seated upon a folding-chair in his tent. "What can it mean? Not to come near her for a whole day! H'm! nor at night — in the morning you will know why. I can't understand it." And he read over again a note which Natalia had handed him in person an hour ago, when she was closing the door of her tent in his face, pushing out from within this little squarely folded piece of paper, covered with her feminine but somewhat resolute handwriting. In this note he was requested not to look in upon her at her tent during the whole day, and not to make any inquiries in the evening, but that in the morning, early, he might come, and then he would know the reason of this strange prohibition.

When the lame Cossack had read the note for the twentieth time, he placed his forefinger against his forehead and again inquired:

"What can this mean?" Was it only he whom Natalia Martinovna did not wish to see for a whole day, or all in general — and had all of them received such messages? No; evidently not. She would have neither paper nor time enough to prepare so many notes. It must be meant only for him. Anyhow, the others did not trouble her so much with their society as he did. He was there most of the day, from morning to evening, and even at night he often guarded her tent from a distance. Certainly, the prohibition could only refer to him alone. But what did it mean?

Golovin tried to remember whether he had offended her in some way, or thoughtlessly given vent to some expression deserving such punishment. He rehearsed every trifling occurrence — he remembered all — every smallest step, every motion, the most insignificant word — it all came to him with such perfect clearness, as if it had only happened a minute ago. No; there was nothing of the kind. She had been kind to him yesterday, and more kind to-day, kinder than she had been for some time. Yes, that was it. He had kissed her hand, and she had touched his brow with her lips, holding his head between her hands in a kind of embrace. "Good-by, my friend," she had said on that last occasion. Why good-by? She had usually said *da svidania (au revoir)*, or "until to-morrow," or something of that kind, but this time it was "good-by." Golovin began to feel uneasy over this good-by. He rose, adjusted his tunic, threw his saber over his shoulder, reached with his hand for his cap, and again sat down.

"No! she has forbidden it, and I must not do it. To-morrow! to-morrow! I'll not have to suffer long — only one night. I will go to sleep and never know how the night goes by, and to-morrow, early in the morning — I might look over there from a distance — she may go out for something and I may see her. No! that would be taking a mean advantage. I'll suffer. What must be must be. She has asked it, and that is enough!" And with renewed resolution the lame Cossack doffed his tunic and saber, threw himself upon his bed, and smoked his cigar.

It was getting dark, stars began to twinkle in the sky, and the last ray of golden light was extinguished in the west; the noise and clatter of the camp subsided.

Night came, the same night which the lame Cossack proposed to pass away in sleep; but this blissful sleep would not come, and Golovin felt sure that it wouldn't. His head was burning, his heart was beating with increased violence, and his heaving chest demanded air. He must get out of his tent — out from under this confining roof of cloth, which, though ever so light, now appeared to him like the heavy vault of a grave.

Out in the air it was all the same — there was no sleep for Golovin. He staggered about in the darkness, stumbling occasionally over tent-ropes and stakes. "What relief is this?" he asks the nearest sentry. "The first!" comes the answer. "A long time yet!" sighs Golovin, and again walks about without picking his way, and lighting one cigar after another.

"Ah!" he said, with a deprecating gesture. "I will go ahead." He passed through the Cossack camp, by the train and by the general's headquarters, and there he was, quite near. "There she is — there is her tent!" The Cossack stood still — he was ashamed. He turned abruptly and walked back quietly. "There was no light," he thought. "She must be asleep. Oh, will not morning come soon! It is only a brief summer night, but how it drags along!"

With a weary, oppressed heart Golovin was watching how at last the faint streak of dawn grew wider and wider, lighter and lighter; how the crimson spots began to blaze up from the horizon; how the tops of the poplar and plantain trees, and the mosque and its stork's-nest shone in golden light, and how the vast, quiet bivouac once more broke out into life and action.

"It's time — no, it is early yet," he considered. "But she always rises with daylight. I may go now, I am sure! She will understand how I have suffered during this night; she will pardon my haste." Golovin proceeded to Natalia's tent. Karpof was up and pottering about attending to the samovar. In the tent all was quiet.

"She is still sleeping. Good-morning, Karpof!" Golovin accosted the orderly, and seated himself upon an overturned bucket.

"I wish you good health!" replied the soldier. "The mistress wanted a lemon, and I got a couple yesterday at the sutler's; they are such nice ones; one is a little dry, to be sure, but the other is splendid!"

"You got the lemons?" asked Golovin; that was not what he wished to say at all, but no other words seemed to come to his tongue.

"It is time to get up," said the orderly. "Would it not be better to waken her?"

"Did she go to bed late last night?"

"I do not know. I was away for an hour or two. When I came back the tent was already closed from the inside — that means that she was asleep. Is it 6 o'clock yet?"

"Half-past."

"Would it not be better to call her? The samovar has boiled long since."

"H'm, h'm!" coughed the Cossack.

"It's all right; it's time," the servant encouraged him.

"Natalia Martinovna!" called Golovin. There was no answer.

"A little louder," advised Karpof.

"Natalia Martinovna!" Perfect silence reigned in the tent. Golovin laid his ear against the cloth and listened. Not the slightest rustle could be heard. The walls of a tent are not thick enough to prevent

the breathing of a sleeping person from being heard.
Golovin turned pale. "What can this be?" he whispered.

Karpof was busy about his samovar and did not hear
the question. Carefully Golovin parted the folds of
the tent and looked in. Natalia Martinovna's bed was
vacant — there was not a soul in the tent. On the
small table there lay two letters, their white squares
staring right into his eyes — they seemed to tell him,
"Take us up and read." And Golovin read them. One
of these notes was the same piece of paper which the
ragged Persian had thrust into Natalia's hand; the
other was in her own writing, and contained but a few
words.

"I am a mother. Forgive me, all of you. Good-by.
God grant that it be not forever!"

That was all the note contained.

"Here is the samovar," said Karpof, entering the
tent with the tray in his hands.

PART SECOND.

CHAPTER XXX.

THE FLIGHT.

NATALIA had resolved to go. From the moment that all hesitation gave way to this resolution her whole mind, all her faculties, were directed upon the accomplishment of her flight. It was certainly flight. Could Natalia have communicated her resolve to anybody? Could she have consulted anybody? Certainly not. If she had merely hinted a word of her purpose, she would have been overwhelmed with protests from all sides, and such measures would have been taken as would have completely paralyzed her own will in the matter. She would have been detained by force.

In the meantime the day appointed in Atam Kul's letter was approaching. The Russians accomplished the crossing of the river, and she could expect from minute to minute the arrival of the men for whose lives the head of her own son must answer. These men would assist her in escaping from the camp and guide her to him — to her son — and at the same time to Atam Kul. But Natalia put away from herself the last name altogether. She avoided all thought of him. Her ideas, her expectations all centered in the first, beside which, for the moment, nothing else existed. She already felt like a stranger in the camp. She seemed to have broken all ties that had attached her to it thus far. She passed through some terrible moments of struggle, but after that nothing appeared terrible to her; she saw not a step she was not willing to take.

The previous night those men had come. One of them had already been in her tent. It was again a Persian, who had crawled in stealthily from under the side of her tent — a thing easily accomplished, since the tent stood next to the wall, and close to it grew two plantain-trees with wide branches interlaced with grape-vines. The Persian climbed over the wall, and stretching himself upon one of the lower branches of the trees, he waited until Natalia herself unfastened the lower edge of the tent and showed him where to get in. Half an hour before this she had written the note to Golovin and called the orderly.

" Karpof! "

" What, matushka, your honor? "

" Did you wish to visit anybody to-day? "

" Yes, your honor; there is a towny of mine, you know — from my village—"

" All right; go! You can come back as late as you like."

" I thank you most humbly, your honor! " And Karpof went away to his " towny " at the other end of the camp, and never dreamed that on returning he would not find his mistress, and perhaps never see her again.

Holding his breath, drawn up into the smallest compass, and trembling slightly, like a wolf in the trap, sat the Persian, between a trunk and the table, covering himself in case of emergencies with a horse-cloth. The ragged fellow knew well that he risked his head if he was betrayed; but he also knew that if he returned alone to Atam Kul he would only fall from the frying-pan into the fire. His black roving eyes gleamed forth uneasily from under his cloth. At the very minute when Natalia was talking with Karpof he was shutting his eyes, muttering to himself some passages from the Koran — mixing up all that he knew by heart of the sacred book. However, he understood all Natalia said, and grew calm again.

Natalia Martinovna quickly began her preparations. She gathered a small bundle and thoughtfully tied it up in a black handkerchief — a white one would have attracted the eyes of the sentries, and drawn their attention upon her. This was all her baggage. She then carefully tied the straps of the entrance-flap from within, in order not to alarm the returning Karpof, and to make him believe that she slept. Having accomplished this, she sat down upon her bed, placed her head between her hands, and thought.

"It is time! It is already dark!" whispered the ragged one.

Natalia shivered as the whisper struck her ear, and looked about her as if frightened. "It is time!" she also said, and rose from the bed.

The Persian emerged from his horse-cloth, and glided out of the tent by the same way by which he had entered, Natalia following him.

"If it were light," whispered the Persian, "we could not go this way; but it's night now and dark, and we can risk it. Follow after me — don't get behind. Here! hold onto this vine!" And Natalia went without hesitation, taking no thought of herself and leaving everything to her guide. She did not move like a living being, but like a machine. After advancing about twenty paces along the wall, the Persian came to a break where an irrigating ditch half-full of water passed through. The opening was scarcely large enough for a dog.

"Lie down!" said the Persian. Natalia's clothes were suddenly drenched, and as she felt her body immersed in the cold water, she began to tremble, and her teeth chattered nervously. "Crawl along!" the voice before her said. "It is like a grave!" passed through Natalia's head as she felt the mud walls over and close beside her, so near that she hurt her elbows, hands, and head as she moved along. At last she saw a star twinkling ahead of her, and then another, and a third, and they rose from the tunnel and could stand upright once more. Dirty water was dripping from the Persian's rags; Natalia's garment's clung to her body, heavy as lead.

"This here is dry," said the Persian, showing her the bundle. "I held it with my teeth — that's why it is dry. Now we must go here — over there are your soldiers." It was true; she could hear Russian conversation not more than ten paces away, and she could see the glimmer of the soldiers' pipes.

"They say the Orenburg expedition has already reached Khiva?"

"I've heard they have."

"They got there before us, the devils!"

"That's nothing. They are not ahead of us. Without us they could not have undertaken it at all."

"May the will of Allah be done!" whispered the Persian. "We must go here."

The dense foliage of grape-vines rustled about Natalia's person; she frequently stubbed her feet against the knotty roots and tangled vines, while her feet sank into the soft mold of a cultivated vineyard. For a long time they passed through vineyards. At times they would sink to the earth, lie down, and wait and listen to the voices of sentries, now on one side, now on the other, sometimes at some distance, and then again close by. A hobbled horse pricked up his ears and snorted in fright, probably scenting the fugitives.

"This way is farther — much farther," whispered the guide, " but there are no dogs here. A man you can always fool, but a dog never. If a dog should see us or hear us it would be all up with the poor Persian. Here, this way!"

The fugitives again passed through some opening and entered the court of an empty dwelling. The traces of a terrible struggle were everywhere visible here. Broken dishes and furniture and torn clothing were lying about.

"Wait here — I go to find out how the Russians have placed their sentries to-night. They change their places every night. I know how it was last night, but I don't know to-day. Sit here and wait." He pushed her into a corner of the dark dwelling, and added: " Wait; I come soon. If you hear noise over there," pointing with his finger —" if you hear shooting, or if I cry loud — I shall cry, without fail — then go home by yourself; you understand?"

"I understand," whispered Natalia, and sat down to wait.

How dark it was in the building, and how sultry! How slowly the time seemed to drag! An invisible hand seized her dress. "Come!" whispered the well-known voice at her very ear. "Glory be to Allah!" said the Persian. " On that side are the Cossacks — we can easily pass them. If the infantry was there, our business would be finished, but these fellows sleep; they see nothing and hear but very little. Let us go!

Do you know," suddenly asked her guide, "where the last Russian sentries are now?" He spoke no longer in a whisper, but in his natural voice, causing Natalia to shiver and to turn her face toward him. "They are over there; and you know how far their bullets carry — now they could hardly reach us. Allah has been merciful to us this night!"

CHAPTER XXXI.

BEYOND THE RUSSIAN CAMP.

"WE'LL go a little farther, where our people are waiting, and there we'll find horses. We shall not go on foot the whole way." These explanations were made to Natalia by the Persian while he kept a strong hold of her dress. He probably still feared that she would change her mind and run away.

"We must go a long way yet to-night. Atam Kul is now at Khazar-Asp. Mat-Nias has gone to Khiva; Mat Murad is not far from Atam Kul, and all the others are over there to the westward fighting with the Russians who came from the sea." The Persian now began to whistle occasionally. At first there was no answer, but after proceeding for about half a verst there came an answering whistle from the right of the road, where the dark outlines of a staff ornamented with horse-tails loomed up above some saint's grave.

"Here!" commanded the Persian, drawing Natalia closer to himself. In a second they were surrounded by six armed natives. "I brought her," said the Persian, in a self-satisfied tone. " I brought a fine woman. Atam Kul will give me many thanks, and make me a present of a cloak, a horse, and a hundred kokans, as he promised."

" Perhaps he'll give them to you, perhaps not," one of the natives said, doubtingly.

" He'll give them! " replied another, with more confidence.

" Let us have the horses!" the Persian interrupted them.

"She is all wet!" remarked one of the men, feeling Natalia. " See — she is shivering. You are chilled through — yes?"

" She is not fat at all!" added another, also examining her.

" Hey! you must take them off — that will not do. I have two cloaks; I will give her one, and she'll be warmer. Take them off!"

Awkward hands began to roughly divest Natalia of her garments; hooks were broken and flew off, strings were torn. " How she is bundled up! Our women know better how to dress," said one of the men who were acting as " maids " to Natalia Martinovna. " Take it off! What are you holding back for? Take hold of her hand!"

Natalia mechanically protested against the unwelcome assistance, but she was only half-conscious. It seemed as if all that was happening to her was not reality, but a dream. They divested her of everything but her chemise, and then threw over her shoulders a wadded and quilted cloak. This garment gave forth a very disagreeable odor, but it was warm, and the warmth acted gratefully upon the woman's shivering limbs.

"Give her your cap!" said the Persian to somebody;
"you can get along with your turban. Now — now you
are just like a 'dshigit,' and not like a woman at all.
Ha! ha! We can go along in daylight and nobody
will know you. Well, now, to horse! Take her and
lift her up. That's right. Hold the bridle — you need
no whip. You go ahead and you two at her side; we
will keep behind. Go on!"

The tall Turkoman racer carried Natalia quietly
enough. The soft cushion of the saddle and high stirrups allowed her to sit quite comfortably, as in an arm-
chair. She let the bridle drop and took hold of the
horn of the saddle. Her head was going around and a
rushing sound was in her ears, and the voices of the
horsemen surrounding her seemed to reach her from
some great distance.

The Turkoman horses know no gait except a bold,
long walk or a full run. At present the whole cavalcade proceeded at a walk, but they were making as
rapid progress as ordinary horses would have accomplished at a short gallop.

"We must go far before daylight," the natives were
saying. "We have to fear both the Russians and our
people. If the Tekkemen — may Allah preserve us
from them! — should see us, they'll kill us. The Cho-
dori also will give us no peace. If the Yomuds see us,
it will be no use to say anything!"

"We are having terrible times now! They are not
even afraid of the Khan. Everybody does as he pleases.
Go on, you, in front; let us make a little more speed!"

The cavalcade was now passing over a narrow road
between walled gardens. On both sides could be seen
dark groups of trees and water glistened in places.
They frequently crossed rickety bridges spanning the

irrigating canals. All around was dark and silent. So
much cultivated ground, so many dwellings, and a total
absence of people! All had fled or hidden themselves
on hearing that the Russians had crossed the Amu,
leaving their houses and gardens to destruction and
plunder at the hands of the conquerors. Later, when
the fugitives returned to their settlements, they would
not believe their eyes until they felt with their hands
each article of household furniture and utensil. They
had not expected to find anything whole or untouched.

By daylight the party was at least forty versts from
the Russian camp. Around the fortified town of Khazar-Asp they described a wide circuit, but it was necessary to halt and rest the horses. This was, however, not
the principal reason for the halt; the horses could have
proceeded farther without resting, but with the morning came daylight, and of that these natives were
afraid, even though they were already beyond the reach
of pursuit.

They selected a convenient spot, well concealed from
the road, and prepared for a bivouac. The place they
chose was the courtyard of an old mosque, inclosed by
a high wall. In the center of the court was a small
square pond, or "khauss," filled with not very inviting
standing water. Over the pond hung the inevitable
plantains, covering with their deep shade nearly the
whole inclosure; along the outer wall, which was
pierced by a wide gate, extended a half-ruined shed for
horses, with troughs let into the wall. Quantities of
dry dung and cinders bore evidence that the place was
frequently used as a camping-ground. A great deal of
alarmed talk and consultation was caused among the
men of the party by the circumstance that one small
heap of cinders was not quite cool; but there was no

12

choice—it was safest to remain where they were, and finally they hastened their preparations for a day-camp.

They led Natalia into one of the buildings at the rear of the court, spread a horse-cloth, gave her a saddle-cushion, and posted a guard at the entrance.

"I'll make you some tea directly, and bring it in," said the Persian. "I have a kettle, and I'll make a fire — the tea will soon be ready. I'm only sorry I did not take the sugar that was on your table in the tent. I left also the bread that was in a bag — hanging up. Well, we have something, and it may be enough. Until it's ready you must sleep." But Natalia did not need the last injunction. She had hardly descended from the horse when her limbs refused to support her. Somehow she dragged herself into the place pointed out to her, fell upon the cloth, and immediately sank into a deathlike sleep. It was a sound sleep — a sleep which could not be broken by any noise — the sleep of total exhaustion.

The nervous excitement which had given her strength to survive the night with all its alarming incidents now yielded to complete physical collapse. When the Persian brought his little kettle with tea, half of a dry maize-cake, and a small green cup, he could not awaken his voluntary prisoner. He did not trouble himself much about it, but placed what he had brought near her head, coughed and expectorated, and then laid himself down at her feet like a dog, and was soon filling the building with his snore.

CHAPTER XXXII.

ATAM KUL'S MOB.

BEFORE night they continued their journey. Natalia was aroused with great difficulty, and after they had awakened her it was long before she really came to herself, apparently not recognizing the place or the people, and sitting with wild, wide-open eyes staring at her surroundings. It seemed as if she had forgotten all that had occurred the previous evening and night. She did not understand what they were doing with her. Her whole body was stiff, and she was as weak as a child; they had to carry her out of the building on their hands and place her in the saddle. The freshness of the evening air, however, and the moisture permeating the atmosphere from the evaporation going on in the numerous irrigating ditches, now running full and frequently overflowing the road, acted beneficially upon her nerves, and she gradually gained control of herself.

The party once more turned into the main road, which henceforward had been intentionally obstructed or destroyed in expectation of a Russian advance. The bridges were torn up; in the roadway there were pools of standing water and mud, into which horses would sink above their knees. In other places the road was obstructed by barricades of carts broken up and thrown together in heaps; whole trees had been felled across the highway — all these measures having been adopted to impede the movements of our troops and to gain time for negotiations. Here and there behind the walls and buildings frightened heads appeared,

generally clad in the tall sheepskin cap, and more
rarely in turbans. These heads all disappeared when the
cavalcade came up, only to pop out again after it had
passed, and to look after it with curiosity and fear.
Disorder was already beginning to arise in the Khanate, which made it impossible for the settled population, the owners of houses and tillers of the soil, to
clearly distinguish friend from enemy, and countryman
from stranger. It was beginning to be a question with
them whether fire and sword were carried into their
country by the white blouses or by the black-capped
Turkomans. The fanatical hatred of all Russians began
to yield to fear of the plundering Turkomans of the
steppe, who had fallen upon the oasis of the Khanate
like wolves upon an expiring camel.

The part played by the Turkomans during the late
occurrences in Khiva resembles that played by the
Ukraine and other border freebooters during the troub-
lous times of our " Interregnum." The Turkomans, the
" beloved army of Allah," which threatened the whole
world, the "rampart of the greatness and power of
the Khan of Khiva," as they were called by several
so-called authorities, had proved themselves unreliable
in face of the white blouses, yielding the field to the
latter. Feeling convinced that they could no longer
count upon booty from that quarter, and unwilling to
return homeward to their desert strongholds with
empty hands, they fell upon the settled population of the
Khanate. The Khan's troops — his regular infantry,
artillery, and armed levies — were massed in protection of Klitch-Nias-Bayu, which was threatened by
the Caucasian and Orenburg expeditions. From the
east another much-dreaded enemy was advancing, the
Turkestan battalions. Whom could he oppose to them?

What was he to do? There was only one course of action left — to guard the road and to postpone, if only for one single day, the fatal minute.

Mat Nias and Mat Murad were already losing their heads, moving hither and thither with their half-demoralized forces, while Atam Kul with his volunteers and Sadik with his Kirghiz from Kizil-Kum were already concocting plans for retreating to the Turkoman steppes, to Merv, leaving the Khan to his fate.

Louder and louder grew in Khiva proper the voice for peace and submission.

"Allah is turning away from our Khan," said one of the men escorting Natalia Martinovna.

The cavalcade was now proceeding slowly, the increasing darkness making the passage over the roads of this pillaged and obstructed section of country much more difficult. They were frequently compelled to halt and dismount in order to remove with their hands the broken and piled-up carts, and to make a passage sufficient for letting a saddle-horse through. On many such occasions they lost an hour's time or more.

At times strange sounds fell upon their ears. Something between a cracked bugle and a flute — a singular, doleful quaver — trembled and thrilled through the nocturnal air. That was the music of the chebizga, a primitive instrument made of a reed perforated with a row of holes like the flute. At other times these sounds subsided, and then they could hear the beating of drums and the monotonous chant resembling a continuous whine. It reminded one of the howling of a pack of wolves who are looking at some coveted prey inaccessible to them.

"Those are our people," said one of the natives, pointing with the whip in his hand.

"Hey!" they were unexpectedly challenged from the right of the road. The horses trembled and rose on their hind legs; the riders instinctively looked to their weapons.

"Who is on the road?" the challenge was repeated.

"That is Dost-Mahomet," said the Persian; "that is his voice!"

"We are friends — friends!" cried the "dshigits."

Several horsemen emerged from the gloom and rode up. In spite of the darkness they looked closely at Natalia Martinovna, and in spite of her cloak and cap one of them asked, "A woman?"

"Yes, a woman, but not yours!" the Persian replied, gruffly.

"Where did you get her?"

"There, where she is not now! Eh, friend? Go on farther — go!"

"Ah, she is young! Easy; what are you doing? My knife is handy enough — what are you afraid of?"

"This is Atam Kul's wife," said the Persian. "He will give it to you if I tell him. Just wait; he'll show you. What do you want to look at other people's women for?"

"Well, we only look. We have not touched her, have we?"

"Where is he?"

"At Rustem's house. He is sitting in the garden. But do not go .to see him. He is in such humor nobody can go near him. He had some trouble with Mat Nias."

"I'm not afraid of him. Go on!"

The cavalcade passed through a gate between two low bastions with castellated tops. The horses' hoofs clattered upon the flags with which the court was paved.

Again the horsemen traversed a narrow, steep, covered passage, and then, in single file, passed over a
narrow path meandering between apricot-trees and
grape-vines Before them a dark, massive building
was visible, with feeble reflections of camp-fires upon
its walls. Voices became audible. The Persian alighted
from his horse, gave the bridle to one of his men,
passed his hands over Natalia's form as if to assure
himself that she was there, and then entered Rustem's
villa, or fort.

The other riders, remaining behind, also began to
alight from their tired steeds. Farther on shone the
white and red squares of paper lanterns. Some one
came hurriedly forth to meet them.

"Allah has been merciful to us," said the voice of the
Persian.

CHAPTER XXXIII.

MAT MURAD'S HEADQUARTERS.

About twenty versts from Khiva, on the Khazar-Asp
road, the hamlet of Chaganak lies concealed between
luxuriant gardens. It is a small hamlet, consisting of
only eight dwelling-houses. These buildings stand
four on either side of the road. From roof to roof of
the houses thus confronting each other long poles have
been laid, piled with brushwood, and the whole again
covered with zinc plates. This shed protects the whole
street, making it dark and cool, and the inhabitants of
Chaganak sit here the whole day, from morning till
night, in front of their shops, enjoying the shade and

trying to entice each passing traveler to tarry, to take a smoke from the ever-ready kalyan, to drink tea and in the meantime to give his horse a breathing-spell.

The Chaganak people are all traders; they keep kalyan-pipes, samovars, and deal in anything a traveler may need. They make their living altogether off the wayfarers, and therefore each passer-by who lingers under their arcade-like street means some profit to them, however small. Long trains of carts are especially profitable to these people. As soon as the squeak of their ungreased axles is heard on the road, they hasten to rekindle the charcoal under the samovars, and to throw brushwood upon the fires in the cold winter-time. Then they look out from under their shed and wait. They do not crowd each other to invite the travelers to their own shop — knowing well that there is business enough for all, as there are only eight little shops, or rather eight "caravanseraïs," as they love to call them.

At the present time a large number of strangers were occupying Chaganak; the whole street was blocked with horses and there was no space to walk along the road, nor was there any room left in the shops, and even the courtyards from the gates to the back walls were crowded to overflowing with people. At this time, however, the wonderful influx of strangers brought with it no profit to the inhabitants. The proprietors were not present, having run away and hidden themselves, and leaving behind only two gray-haired old men who were too feeble to walk, not to speak of running away. The strange people had arrived only the day before, and had now occupied the hamlet for a whole day without making any signs of taking their departure. All the horse-feed on hand had been fed to the animals; all the tobacco had been smoked by the men, and all the tea had gone down their thirsty throats; they had consumed more than would have lasted the owners a year.

The visitors were Mat Murad with his force of cavalry and infantry. Not many were left to him of either, owing to the spreading demoralization, which caused numbers of them to depart for other fields where the prospect was more encouraging. He still had an armed mob numbering about five hundred — too few to oppose the Russians, but by far too many for the poor people of Chaganak; but nobody troubled himself about them.

The noise and talking under the sheds of Chaganak could be heard far afield; and in addition there was the clatter of weapons, the neighing and snorting of the vicious Turkoman stallions, the whining and yelping of dogs. Beyond the walls the smoke was rising in thick pillars, blackening and smirching the sides and bottoms of iron and copper kettles; a band of sheep was being driven together for slaughter, and the snapping of whips by the men bringing them up could be heard beyond the last house in the row.

From a safe distance the rightful residents of Chaganak were looking on, and praying, "Allah! Allah! take these bands away, quickly!" But Allah probably did not hear their fervent prayers. Mat Murad did not go, nor did he take away his "bands."

The "Datkha" (a military rank equal to a colonelcy) occupied the second dwelling, belonging to Mullah Amandshula. This house was more roomy than the others; the courtyard contained a pond, and around it grew four shady plantains. Under these trees Mat Murad had established himself upon some costly car-

pets and rugs. Near by, along the wall, stood his
horses and those of his immediate suite. At the
entrance-gate sat two guards, dressed in dark-red
cloaks, armed with long muskets with thin wooden
" rests" or forks attached to the barrels. Nobody was
admitted through the gate without special order or
permission from the Datkha himself. There had been
so many two-faced and double-tongued people about of
late that one could never know whether he had to do
with good or evil persons, therefore no unknown individual was admitted without the strictest examination
and fullest identification.

Mat Murad did not, however, occupy his position
under the plantains alone; before daylight he had been
joined by Mullah Sadik and his Kirghiz. This well-
known agitator of the nomad tribes brought with him
two hundred horsemen, easily distinguished by their
outward appearance from Mat Murad's body-guard.
A majority of Sadik's men were Kirghiz from Kuzil-
Kum; they rode their small Kirghiz horses, and were
mostly clad in yellow cloaks of camel's-hair cloth. On
their heads they wore summer hats of thin whitish
felt. They kept aloof from the Turkomans and Murad's
guards, and conducted themselves just as they did in
the steppe. They hobbled their horses and left them
to feed at will on the grass and herbage around the
hamlet, while ten men in turn stood guard over the
browsing herd, the remainder sitting around in circles
in the full glare of the sun. They were beginning to
light fires and to disembowel the sheep they had
driven up.

Mullah Sadik was attired just like the lowest of his
Kirghiz; in the same camel's-hair cloak, the same felt
hat, in red trousers embroidered with colored silks, but

much worn and faded. He was lying upon a carpet, squinting about with his narrow, slanting Kirghiz eyes, and noisily propelling through his teeth dense clouds from his " kalyan."

Mat Murad sat full of dignity, continually stroking his thick black beard, and frowning angrily with his shaggy gray brows. He was evidently in bad humor, and spoke sharply in a scolding tone. Sadik, however, carried on his share in the conversation with perfect equanimity, and did not seem to care about the subject under discussion. Only his prominently developed cheek-bones trembled slightly, and upon his thin lips there appeared at times, not a smile, but a grimace as of pain. It was probably the latter, since an old wound received five years before, under Khatin-Cham, had never properly healed, and often opened anew, especially in hot weather.

Besides these chiefs who were averse to the party favoring further resistance to the Russians, a few other individuals had joined in the consultation, among them Ata Nazr Khan, a tall Turkoman of the Yomud tribe, who subsequently went over to the Russians and rendered them no little service against his countrymen. An envoy from Mat Nias, Karim Khodsha, was also seated among the others, dressed in a large turban and a light-green silken cloak — an insignia of his clerical dignity. In spite of this dignity he was armed from head to foot, and kept near to his hand a double-barreled gun from Tula, with a fine carved stock embellished with gilding.

One of the attendants had just set down before the chief a dish of pilas; two boys in red jackets and gold-laced caps were serving the guests, handing them the pipes, and moving about between the sitting men with great agility. The hair of these boys was not shorn in accordance with Mussulman custom, but plaited in strands which hung down from under their caps, giving their faces a pleasing but feminine appearance, and reminding one more of girls than of boys. These were Min and Balta Nias, the favorite pages of Mat Murad.

"They have surrendered Khazar-Asp without a fight," said Mat Murad — "the old women! They could not detain the Russians on the road until I could come! They are women, not warriors!"

"But you would have lingered still longer with the Khan, suing for his favor," remarked Sadik, biting his lips.

"What is the Khan's favor to me — pshaw!" said Mat Murad, spitting out viciously. "The Khan is now upheld only by me, and lives by my favor."

"You are not the Khan's only servant and helper," muttered the envoy of Mat Nias as if talking to himself.

"You may well talk!" exclaimed Murad, turning upon him. "You and yours would long ago have kissed the 'giaour's' tail, or surrendered your guns to them, ready for use. You need not talk!"

"Time will show whose eyes could see better into the distance!" Karim Khodsha replied, quietly.

"If it were not for our dissensions, — if we acted more in unison, — if there were no double-tongued dogs among us, the Russians would never have reached the Amu. Who let them come to Sardiba-Kul? What cowards ran away into the steppe like hares and wolves? All of you, you hirelings! And you were with them; you were doing it all upon Mat Nias' advice."

"I had but few men — the Turkomans were much

stronger, but left before me. Sadik went after them.
What could I do alone?"

"I left when Atam Kul turned his back," said Sadik,
smiling. "I do not intend to fall into the claws of the
Russians. You know all about my affairs. The wolf
does not invade a pasture when the shepherds are the
strongest."

"And therefore you ran away at the first cry! You
did not even collect the boats on this shore, but left
them to the Russians."

"Some manage in one way and some in another,"
said Sadik, looking around. "You should find out if
somebody else was not to blame. It may be that somebody found it to his advantage to yield to the Russians."

"Whom do you mean?" asked Mat Murad, contracting his brows.

"Not you — where are your eyes? The Russians have
paid no money to you — or have they tried, perhaps?"
And Sadik gazed straight into the commander's eyes,
which were quickly lowered.

"I would have him skinned alive," shouted Mat Murad,
"if I knew it for certain. There will always be rumors
current, but you can not believe them all."

"Where is he now?"

"When he first joined us he camped at Sheik-Arik;
then he came this way by the Merv road. Now he is
close by."

"Does he not come here? It is long since he has
shown himself."

"A long time — it almost seems as if he was purposely
hiding and did not wish to come under our eyes. I have
sent to summon him."

"It is evident that his conscience is not clear," broke
in Sadik. "That is why he hides."

"I shall catch him if it be true what people are saying. I'd impale him without troubling the Khan about
a trial. I sent him word the other day, and he answered
snappishly. It was lucky for him that I had but few
people with me then and he a great many, or he should
have spoken to me in another tone!"

"It is just for this reason," said Karim Khodsha, sententiously, "because you are all trying to have each
other impaled, that we must now sue the Russians for
peace. You are all guilty together. You yourselves
let your passions and whims hinder us from accomplish-
ing our purpose. Some show their teeth on account of
old quarrels," said he, glancing at Sadik. "You can't
agree with him, and you threaten him with the stake.
That is told to him, and draws his mind from the common cause. Believe me, believe the word of Mat Nias,
any kind of peace with the Russians is better than final
destruction and demoralization!"

"That is an old song; it has been sung to us before,
and resulted not in our way but in their way."

"Let us see—"

"It is all right for you," said Sadik; "you have got
yourself into no special trouble with anybody—it is all
right for you. If we make peace with the Russians,
they will not touch you; they will not take your lands,
your gardens, and your dwellings from you—you will
not be beggared. You will live as you did before, in
comfort and quiet—only your power will not be as
great as before. It is all right for you. But you would
make me lose my skin. *I* am their sworn enemy, and
have been always. If I fall into their hands I'll not
live long. Of my wealth not a single crumb remains.
Peace with the Russians is not to my mind; it is all the
same to me what happens. When I have lost my troops,

and I am alive, I shall go to Merv, to the Tekke, to wait and watch when fortune will again come our way. That is what I shall do — I have spoken truly!"

"Atam Kul does not think the same as you," said Mat Murad. "The white blouses will probably not do him any further injury; they do not seem to remember a fault very long."

"He has been working in that direction for a long time; but he is cunning, he does not show the bent of his mind. I am watching him, though, the runaway dog!"

"And what is your last word for Mat Nias?" said Karim Khodsha, rising to his feet.

"The same as ever." Mat Murad turned to him without rising. "But tell the Khan that I am his servant no longer, since he has become a Russian slave. Tell him that. Do not change or soften a word of my message. Do you hear?"

"Lunatic!" said Karim Khodsha, shrugging his shoulders, and walked toward the gate. There his attendants had already brought his horse, a tall racer, covered with cloths of brilliant colors, and with bit and bridle richly ornamented with tassels. When Karim Khodsha mounted, one of his guards held his stirrup while another assisted the old man. Adjusting himself in his saddle, he pulled back the bridle until the horse rose upon its haunches, and then looked again at Mat Murad, as if to request of him by a glance another last decisive word.

"May Allah bless your road!" said Murad, not without irony, raising his hand.

Karim Khodsha emerged from the courtyard surrounded by his suite. The horsemen made their way with difficulty through the crowded street, but when they reached the highway they proceeded at a rapid gait in the direction of the gardens of Khiva, which were rising darkly above the horizon.

"It is time for me also!" said Sadik, rising with difficulty; and placing a finger against his lips he whistled loudly.

Thus whistle the horse-herders when they wish to make the whole drove start at once. When this whistle resounds over the steppe the horses tremble, prick up their ears, and begin to gather in groups, as if fearing some hidden danger. This is a premonitory whistle. Sadik's whistle, however, was answered by another just without the gate, then by another farther away, and again another barely audible in the distance. The Kirghiz guarding the herd began to contract their circle. The bivouac of the warriors of the steppe was breaking up.

"Are you going to Merv?" Mat Murad inquired, with a sneer.

"No; I shall yet remain," Sadik replied, impudently. "It will not do to go to a strange land with empty hands. I still hope to pick up something."

"Something of ours?"

"Whatever turns up. Ask Ata Nazr Khan where he loaded up forty-four camels, and where he sent them to. Perhaps something may be left for me in that neighborhood."

"Did you see them?" angrily asked the Turkoman. "And if you did, do not tell anybody else — I will do as much for you."

"All my affairs you may proclaim to the world. I shall go to Atam Kul and consult with him. We are friends now." Sadik's reply was tinged with bitter irony.

LED FORTH TO TESTIFY.

"And must I alone await the Russians?" shouted Mat Murad, his eyes burning with rage and his glossy beard trembling with strong emotion.

"Dispute with them the road, keep them at bay, and we will strike them in the rear. Haïda!" Sadik bowed in his saddle, plied his whip, and bounded out of the gate.

"It would be better to go to Khiva than to stay here," was Ata Nazr Khan's advice to Mat Murad.

"Let us consider a little," said the Datkha, rising from his seat. "See there! the sun is setting in clouds and fog, but do you know how it will rise to-morrow? It is all according to Allah's will, and to his wrath there will be an end sometime." Mat Murad considered long, gazing at the crimson evening sky. Blue shadows were spreading from walls and trees, and the flames of the fires under the shed grew brighter. The noise of the bivouac was subsiding, and the freshness of the night air penetrated the double wadded and quilted cloak of the commander, causing him to shiver slightly.

Suddenly two shots were heard, and then voices full of alarm shouted, "Who is this?" "Catch him! stop him!" "Cut him off from the road!" "He can't get away!" "Hold him!"

These were the cries of some pursuers. They were coming nearer and nearer.

CHAPTER XXXIV.

THE HAREM OF MULLAH ATAM KUL.

"Good-day," said Atam Kul, seizing Natalia Martinovna around the neck.

She did not return the greeting, but stood like a stone.

One of the natives held up an oiled paper lantern, pushing it almost against the face of the unfortunate woman.

"She is dead!" cried the renegade, staggering back.

Natalia's face was as white as a sheet, the eyes were dumb and motionless, the mouth stood half-open like that of a corpse, with the lower jaw pendent as if the muscles of the face had lost all control over its movements.

Her breath seemed to be suspended. It was a real corpse, but an uncanny kind of a corpse, standing upon its feet without prop or assistance.

A terrible fear fell upon the superstitious savage. Atam Kul retreated two more steps. Natalia began to sway as soon as he removed his hand from her shoulder.

"That is nothing," fawned the Persian; "that will pass away. It is only exhaustion. We have traveled too far. She is all right; she is a strong woman — just like a native. That is nothing!"

God only knows what took place in the soul of Atam Kul at that moment. He retreated still farther into the darkness, where the light of the lantern did not fall, and turned away. "Take her into the house — there, with the others," he said, hoarsely; "the women are there — take her to them."

The dull thud of a falling body forced from Atam Kul's breast a hoarse, savage cry, but he did not stir from his position, trembling, and afraid to look at the fallen one.

"Take her away! Carry her on your hands!" he cried, and rushed away through the garden in the direction of the building occupied by his native followers, who were contentedly gorging themselves with a stew of fat meat.

The Persian and one other man lifted Natalia up and carried her away. In the darkness it was difficult to distinguish anything ahead of them, but the Persian soon struck against the rough surface of a wall, and moving his hand along it until he felt the bolt of a wicket, drew it and passed through, after which the three found themselves surrounded by still more impenetrable darkness — even the stars which twinkled faintly in the sky had disappeared. They were under a roof.

"Eh, you old crow, make a light! Why are you hiding?" shouted the Persian. "Quick! Do you hear?"

A frightened feminine whisper and a slight rustling could be heard in a corner.

"I'll bring a lantern," said one of the men, letting down Natalia's limbs carefully to the floor. "You'll not get them to move in a hurry!"

A reddish spot at last began to glimmer in the darkness, and above it, not very clearly defined, appeared the outlines of dry lips, a toothless mouth, and the end of an old woman's nose. The spark began to grow — a dry splinter of wood began to smoke and crackle, and at last blazed up brightly, throwing a flickering, fantastic light upon the surroundings. It was the interior of a dwelling, somewhat richly decorated, according to the local ideas of luxury. The walls were smoothly plastered with alabaster and painted in fresco patterns of flowers and fanciful leaves. On the square-beamed ceiling some rough gilding glistened in the uncertain light. A soft felt-mat covered the floor of the dwelling, and around the walls bright-colored carpets and wadded quilts were piled up. In the center a small circular space was left bare, upon which a few cinders were visible, and beside it lay a bundle of twigs and wisps of straw. Various domestic utensils were also lying about, with remnants of a supper, and a tinned copper kettle with tea. The mat around the hearth was strewn with well-gnawed melon-rinds and the husks of pistachio-nuts. Some unfinished needlework on red cloth was also lying there, and a young kitten, partly entangled in it, was peeping out from under its folds and looking at the intruder, blinking its greenish eyes.

There were three women in the building — two still young, who drew their grayish-blue burnouses over their heads, and huddling together in a corner, looked out from there with a more frightened expression than the kitten; and an old woman, homely, with yellow complexion and a face disfigured by smallpox and much wrinkled, who was hurriedly placing a piece of tallow candle into a copper candlestick. She did not progress very satisfactorily with this undertaking; the splinter of wood, being nearly consumed, burned her fingers, while the candle was gliding through her trembling hand.

"Well, here is the lantern!" said one of the natives, entering the house and glancing furtively in the direction where the young women were sitting. "Ah!

they are hiding," he continued, as he hung the lantern
to a hook near the door.

"Go away, go away!" snarled the old woman; "what
are you looking at? It is against the law for you to
come here. Go! What do these strange men come
here for? What did you bring? Who gave you permission?"

"Wait; let me look a little!" said the native, jokingly.

"No looking here; I'll tell the master to-morrow.
He'll show you—get out!"

"Why should I go? You might as well give those to
us. We brought a new one for him, and such a one
that after this he will not look at such carrion as
those!"

"You are carrion yourself, you dead dog!" replied
one of the women in a loud and somewhat shrill voice.

"Where did you bring her from?" inquired the
other.

"She is a Russian. We did not take her—she came
herself; but she was taken ill on the road. Ah! she lies
there like a clod. We had so much trouble with her on
the road!"

"You've done a great deal, indeed!" grumbled the
Persian. "Go away! I can arrange matters here without you. It may be that he will come back. What has
become of him? He was waiting, and then wouldn't
wait, but rushed off without even looking at her."

"She is young!" muttered the old woman, who had
squatted down on her heels and was looking at the prostrate form. She unceremoniously turned Natalia's
face to the light and began feeling her breast, shoulders,
and arms with her claw-like fingers. "She is young—
not old at all. These Russians do not get old very
quickly. We had one that remained a good-looking

woman until she was forty years of age — always good
and fresh, while ours were no longer worth looking at.
They almost killed her from envy."

"You attend to her properly," said the Persian.
"You see that I have delivered her to you alive — look!
she is breathing; you can see for yourself. To-morrow
she must be all right. Wash her and dress her nicely,
and see that she meets Atam Kul properly when he
comes. Keep her quiet, and cover her with something
warm, and bathe her head — that helps. I'm sorry we
have no Russian whisky; it would do her much good, I
know. Rub her heels with pepper — that may —"

"Go away! go away! We know without you what
should be done. I have not lived sixty years in this
world for nothing! Go away, and tell them all not to
touch our door again; they give us no rest, the hungry
dogs! I shall bolt the door from the inside, but tell
them, anyhow. Go away now!"

"Well, I only want you to see that I gave her to you
alive. Remember that!" the Persian repeated once
more. "Good health to you! Good-by!"

"Go!"

The Persian retreated to the door, threw one more
glance at his voluntary captive, and left the building,
slamming the narrow, heavy door, studded with flat-
headed iron nails without any regard for symmetry or
pattern.

The women now remained alone.

The men had scarcely left the building, and the old
woman had barely closed and bolted the door behind
them, when curiosity — the ruling passion of women,
and of Asiatic women especially — seized upon both
wives of Mullah Atam Kul.

Cat-like, with a single bound, they sprang to Natalia's side and began to examine her. The women had thrown off their wide cloaks and remained in long silken shirts alone. The light of the lantern fell brightly upon their somewhat peculiar features. One of them, who had exchanged courtesies with the native, was a Persian, tall in stature, with a fine, bold physiognomy. The large black eyes, with bluish "whites" and fringed with long lashes, had a somewhat savage and repelling look. In her glance two prevailing expressions were always interchanging — viciousness and slavish fear. It was the glance of a dog when he is being punished by his master's hand — always ready to bite that hand, and only awaiting the proper minute, while fear of this same hand remains uppermost and paralyzes the desire to resist. Traces of this internal struggle, this hesitation between rage and fear, can be discerned in his whining, in his bark — now fawning, now threatening.

The border of her red cap, strung with metallic pendants, fell low over her forehead, almost to the thick black brows, giving to the whole face a still more uninviting aspect. The large long nose, with finely cut, trembling nostrils, spoke of slyness and cunning, even while a pleasant and sympathetic smile played around the mouth. Even the blackened teeth did not disfigure this mouth, in nowise spoiling its graceful lines. Her black hair hung down from under her cap, covered with metallic chain ornaments and jingling at every motion made by the woman. Massive pendants, reaching to her shoulders, were inserted in her ears, and around her neck shone and sparkled several rows of glass beads. The whole bosom of her red shirt was ornamented with gold and silver coins, arranged in an original and rather tasteful pattern. Her long slender

fingers were studded with rings, set chiefly with turquoises and carnelians; the finger-nails were dyed as
well as the teeth, not black, however, but a bright
blood-red.

The Persian girl was still young; perhaps seventeen,
no more. Her shirt, or blouse, unconfined by any belt,
displayed a firm and elastic figure. She was the favorite wife of Mullah Atam Kul; hence it will be easily
understood with what feelings of fear and jealousy she
now looked upon her new rival lying there prostrate
before her. She was drawing comparisons between
herself and the new arrival, examining every feature
and endeavoring to discover something that might be
counted in her favor. Evidently she was not very well
satisfied with the result of this comparison. Above all,
displeased her the long, silky, light-auburn hair of
Natalia, which shone in the lantern's light with a peculiar luster. She let the hair pass through her fingers,
weighed it in her hand and measured its length, but
suddenly she broke into a disdainful laugh. The sharp
eyes of a jealous rival had discovered a gray hair
among these shining locks, and this discovery had
aroused her to an open expression of her joy.

"Now, what is that Persian mare snorting about?"
snarled the old woman. "Be still! I'll give it to
you!"

"I'll strike you! Look here!" the Persian replied,
with flashing eyes, but retreating a little and saying
not another word.

"'Sh! you noisy one!" scolded the old woman, pouring some water out of a jar into a shallow dish. "Hang
a mat before the door. Somebody might come around
spying again. I thought I heard a step just now."

The other wife of Mullah Atam Kul was a Kirghiz

woman. It was only necessary to glance at her prominent cheek-bones, at those narrow, furtive, oblique eyes and the strong yellow teeth, to dispel all doubts as to her origin. The head of this daughter of the steppe was covered with a huge white turban (djavluk), the ends of which, hanging down over her shoulders, were embroidered with gold thread. She was a stout, robust woman, and her thin tunic fitted closely to her massive rotund figure.

Having satisfied her curiosity, the Kirghiz woman cheerfully began to assist the old hag in attending to the patient. She wetted the end of a towel in water and vinegar, loosened Natalia's belt, drew the heavy man's boots from her feet, and raised her head, placing under it a long cylindrical pillow. During these kindly ministrations she impressed several kisses upon the unconscious form, and moved the kettle nearer to the fire, in order to let Natalia have some hot tea when she recovered from her swoon. Only she and the old hag did anything for the Russian woman; the Persian in the meantime, having completed her inspection, seated herself once more against the wall, folding her arms around her knees and resting her chin upon the latter.

In the soul of the Kirghiz woman jealousy had been ignited only for a moment, and quickly subsided as soon as she looked upon the features of the new wife of Mullah Atam Kul — features, though then lifeless, so full of weariness, sadness, and the profoundest misery.

They disrobed Natalia completely, bathing her whole body with tepid water and vinegar, and then covered her up with a wadded quilt.

"She has some life in her now!" chattered the old woman. "She is no longer dead. Death has gone out and sleep has come in his place. See how nicely she breathes. She sleeps. Well, let her sleep; later on I will wake her and dress her. I know when that must be. To-morrow she will be quite well, and the Mullah will make me a present — and to you also, Aïbulgan, but not to you over there, who did nothing, but only sat and looked at us two working!" The old woman glanced angrily in the direction where the Persian was seated.

"Djellie worked also," said the Kirghiz woman in defense of her companion. "She bathed her head; I saw it myself."

"But I heard what she whispered while she was doing it. If I were to hint a word of it to our master he would not let her live; he would order her to be killed. I heard her."

"What did you hear?" calmly asked the Persian.

"I heard what I heard."

"What did I say?"

"'Her throat ought to be squeezed so tightly that she would not come to again!' that is what you said. Isn't that it? I am old, but I can still hear."

"And what of that! I tell Atam Kul himself anything that comes into my head. He loves me; he told me only yesterday that there is not a better woman in the world than I am. Let us see who will be on top, I or she. We'll see. Aïbulgan is all right — he only looks upon her once in awhile; it is all the same to her."

"Silence, you long-nosed crow — you slave!" Aïbulgan turned upon the Persian.

"You are without nose — it is set in the middle of your face like a button; there is nothing to be seen but cheek-bones and teeth."

"Look out that those teeth don't fasten upon you!" shrieked the Kirghiz woman.

"Quiet there!" cried the old woman; "what are you bawling about? Are you going to fight again as you did in the morning? Your last scratches are not healed yet. Silence!"

This exhortation somewhat quieted the enraged women and prevented for this time a fight such as are of common occurrence in harem life.

Natalia Martinovna stirred and groaned in her sleep. "What! have you awakened her, you vermin? It is necessary that she should sleep now, and you are making a noise. Be quiet—she may go to sleep again —sitstill!"

"Tell us a story," proposed Aïbulgan, who at once quieted down, "and we will sit and listen."

"You just wait!" threatened the willful and vicious Djellie.

"Well, then, listen!" said the old woman, bending once more over the face of the sleeper and listening; then she coughed, expectorated, and began in a low voice, almost a whisper. Both the listeners drew nearer. The old woman went on, in a monotonous, droning tone. Aïbulgan, having already forgotten her quarrel, laid her head upon the Persian's knee; the latter lowered her eyes and sat motionless, winding the ends of her tresses around her fingers. The coins upon her bosom scarcely rose with her breath. A few nocturnal flies and moths circled around the lantern, occasionally striking against its oiled paper sides.

In a corner of the room something was breathing calmly, invisible behind the piled carpets and large silken cushions.

The old woman began her tale. The story was a

long one, describing the doings and intrigues of a community of women governed by a female Khan. The
plot hinged upon a conflict between ambition and a
mother's love, in which the latter conquered.

"Yes, that is what it means to be a mother!" added
the aged story-teller, not in the monotonous, sing-song
tone she employed for the tale, but in her natural
voice. "Well, I have finished my story. How did you
like it? 'Sh — be quiet; I believe our patient is awake."

Natalia Martinovna had opened her eyes some time
before, looking at her unfamiliar surroundings. At this
moment she was leaning upon her elbow, pushing the
strands of hair away from her forehead, and sighing
deeply. All at once, over there in the corner where
the fringed carpets and cushions were piled up, some
small creature also sighed, opened wide its eyes, and
gave vent to the plaintive and soul-stirring cry of a
child.

"Mama, mama!" Nobody knew at first what was
happening. Natalia sprang to her feet, trembling all
over, then rushed into the corner. Small arms clasped
her around the neck, a small flushed face was caress-
ingly rubbing against her own — the mother had found
her son.

Then Djellie, the Persian, and Aïbulgan, and the old
story-teller understood what was happening in their
dwelling. The old woman's mouth broadened into a
good-natured, toothless smile. As she looked at the
Russian woman, her tongue almost unconsciously
repeated the closing words of her story, "That is
what it means to be a mother!"

Djellie bent over into the corner and leaned her face
against the wall, without once turning around; her
shoulders and arms down to the elbows were shaking

convulsively, and at every tremor the coins sewed upon her shirt gave forth a silvery jingle.

Aïbulgan fell at Natalia's feet, embracing them ardently, and pressing her thick lips upon them, the noisy kisses of the soft-hearted Kirghiz woman resounding through the room.

Dawn was breaking. The golden light of morning invaded the dwelling through the cracks of the door, and through the panes of oiled paper with which the upper window-frames were fitted.

People were moving and tramping about in court-yard and gardens. The vicious stallions neighed and snorted as they were led to the morning watering.

"Eh! you women — get ready!" came through the door of the harem in the Persian's voice. "Mullah Atam Kul is coming — withdraw the bolts, quickly!"

CHAPTER XXXV.

PROVIDENCE.

THE door of the women's house opened wide. The morning sun illuminated brightly with its golden rays the garden adjoining the harem. The emerald-green foliage of the grape-vines was gorgeously hung with trembling drops of dew, which the young sun had not yet succeeded in drinking up. From behind the grape-vines and beyond the dense screen of green arose the gray pillars of poplars, and behind these again darker masses of luxuriant plantains could be seen, giving a view of the opposite wall only here and there through breaks in the foliage.

A brisk morning breeze was blowing in through the door, freshening the close, sultry atmosphere in the interior of the building. At first the inmates with undisguised delight inhaled the fresh air into their lungs, and Natalia also became aware of its beneficial effect upon her debilitated system. She felt renewed courage and strength — qualities most necessary to her at the present moment.

All shut their dazzled eyes before the shining square of light caused by the open door, when the black shadow of a colossal round-shouldered figure suddenly appeared in bold relief upon the illuminated surface. A huge turban and a wide cloak, unconfined by belt or girdle, apparently enlarged still more the visitor's dimensions. Behind him two or three other dark countenances were visible, and the bright barrels of flint-lock muskets, provided with "rests," loomed up among them, together with the high black sheepskin caps of the Turkomans set upon close-cropped heads at various angles. The sound of conversation could be heard through the door.

But the door was closed again, and all was dark and quiet once more within the female apartments of the dwelling — the darkness appearing much denser and more impenetrable after the brief flash of light caused by the opening of the door.

Atam Kul himself closed the door behind him and bolted it; leaving his suite and even his most devoted follower, the Persian, in the courtyard, he entered the building alone. For a few moments he was unable to distinguish anything, and stood upon the threshold, but soon his eye became accustomed to the red, somber light which filtered through the oiled paper window over the door, and from a smoke-obscured opening in one corner, under the roof, and he was enabled to distinguish the figures of women present in the building. At the first sound of men's voices Aïbulgan had fled to the farthest corner of the room, turned away her face and covered it with her cloak, drawing it up even over her turban and leaving nothing of herself to be seen but an indistinct, unshapely mass.

Djellie, with a rapid but graceful movement, stretched herself out at full length, designedly tearing the front of her shirt so as to expose half of her bosom, and thus lay upon the carpet with both hands under her head. The pose thus assumed was both effective and beautiful, and worthy of the trained coquette of an Asiatic harem.

The old woman sat down in half-concealment beside the door, trembling like a dog under the stick suspended threateningly over its head, and blinking her tearful eyes, looked straight into Atam Kul's face. Her timid, slavish air betrayed her anxiety not only to obey but to anticipate the slightest wish or hint of her dreaded master. The woman's whole soul was animated by the one instinct of ascertaining his wishes and whims and to see to their immediate execution.

Natalia, raising her head, perceived the dark massive figure towering in the lighted square of the door, and instinctively pressed the boy, who was crying and trembling nervously, to her breast with firmer pressure. At that moment she experienced within herself such a revival of moral power, such courage, that she felt equal for a struggle no matter how great the disparity of forces. She even looked down with the contempt of the stronger for the weaker upon the man

who was the cause of her sufferings and grief, and in
whose full power she now found herself.

"You all go away!" said Mullah Atam Kul, stepping
forward.   He placed his hand upon Natalia Martinovna's shoulder, and even set one foot upon her trail-
ing cloak, as if to indicate by these motions that his
command did not refer to her, but only to the other
three women.

The old story-teller slipped across to the opposite
wall and began to hurriedly unfasten a little door leading to the second and inner court of the women's
apartments.   Aïbulgan crept along the wall without
raising her face, and was the first to run out when the
door was opened.   Djellie did not stir from her position.
She stretched herself indolently and yawned, casting
upon Atam Kul a long look expressive of the most
naïve want of comprehension as to what was going on
before her.   She even smiled, and was about to say
something, probably to ask for an explanation, when
the renegade repeated, sternly:

"You also must go!"

The Persian again smiled, and emphatically shook her
head.

"Well?" repeated Atam Kul.

Djellie rose slowly to her feet, and after stretching
herself again while standing up, and by this pose dis-
playing the beautiful proportions of her young body,
and causing her metal ornaments to tinkle melodiously,
she advanced toward Atam Kul, who receded a few
paces.

"What! Do you want to replace me by *that* one?"
inquired Djellie, pointing at the Russian woman.

"Away!" shouted the renegade, snatching a whip
from his girdle and raising it threateningly.

JUDGMENT AND PUNISHMENT.

Behind the interior door a slight exclamation burst from the lips of Aïbulgan, who had been listening. The Persian did not tremble, but quickly raised her hands before her face, to protect it against the impending stroke.·

"It is well!" she said; "but remember, when you come to me — and I know it will be soon, perhaps to-day — then I shall say to you, 'Away!' You may order me to be cut down — I know that is in your power, but while I am alive Djellie will no longer be your wife unless she is tied hand and foot. And you remember, also," she continued, addressing Natalia Martinovna, "though you may not be his by your own will, I shall never forgive you. Remember that!" The Persian slowly glided to the door, and stopping for a moment upon the threshold, she. laughed loudly, and then slammed the door behind her and latched it.

Atam Kul and Natalia remained — not altogether alone, however; the little boy was between them. The two-legged wolf now stood before her without speaking. He did not know what to say, how to begin, or how to proceed in this affair. The savage was nonplused for the moment, and only mechanically pressed in his hands the heavy handle of his whip, scowling in the meantime from under his brows, now at the door through which Djellie had disappeared, now at his voluntary captive.

Petka glanced at Atam Kul through his outspread fingers. He had accommodated himself to a certain extent to his new circumstances, and become familiar with the new face of this pirate of the steppes, who had caressed him so often, especially during the last few days, and not fully understanding what had just occurred before his eyes, he had thus far looked on with perfect equanimity. The moment, however, the whip

14

was raised the boy's whole body began to tremble, and
he nestled more closely into his mother's bosom. He
speedily discovered that the stroke was not intended for
him and became reassured.

"Good-day!" Atam Kul began once more.

"I have come," Natalia replied, in a faint, scarcely
audible voice.

The renegade seated himself heavily upon the carpet,
his hands almost touching the dress of Natalia, who
withdrew her garments from his reach.

"Why?" he asked, in a hoarse voice, throwing a furtive glance at her. Atam Kul's eyes gleamed like live
coals; a nervous excitement seized him. He quickly
moved nearer to Natalia and seized her with both
hands. At that moment he felt only a burning, insatia-
ble passion. If a knife had then been thrust into his
breast he would not have felt it — he would not have
heeded the sharp point piercing his vitals. The child
was between them; Atam Kul thrust him aside with
one powerful hand, and Petka rolled like a ball over the
carpet, terror preventing him from making an outcry.

"You cursed beast!" Natalia cried, savagely, rushing forward to pick up the boy. Behind the door the
loud laugh of the Persian was heard again.

"Hey!" yelled the renegade, and the old woman,
thinking that the shout must be intended for her,
entered the room. She knew what kind of services her
master would demand of her.

"Take her away, take her!" cried Atam Kul; "but
place this puppy in a sack and throw it into the water."

The old woman sprang across the floor with the
agility of a cat and caught hold of Natalia Martinovna.
She seized her elbows from behind, and endeavored to
place her upon her back.

"I have come to you," gasped the unfortunate woman, full of terror and desperation. "I came to you of my own will — why will you use violence? You called me to give me back my son. Drown him? You would drown Petka? I will suffer death before you touch him! He is not yours; he is mine. If you kill him, you kill me. Do you wish for my death?" She tore herself from the old woman's hands and threw herself down before Atam Kul. She even raised her arms as if about to place them around his neck.

"You just wait, you Russian slut!" came from behind the inner door. Almost simultaneously alarmed voices shouted at the opposite entrance.

"Mullah! Hey! Taksir! Mullah Atam Kul!" The snorting of horses and the stamp of iron-shod hoofs were plainly heard as if the whole garden was filled with horsemen. Atam Kul could hear the voices of his own men and those of strangers. The voice of Mat Murad sounded above them all — the commander was issuing clear and distinct orders to his followers.

"Look well over there, that he may not escape over the wall. Break in the door if he does not open. I've got you at last, you run away dog! The 'double-tongue' spoke once too often."

Atam Kul did not understand the meaning of these orders, but he scented an enemy, a terrible enemy, and felt himself in mortal danger without knowing its origin. The door began to yield before the pressure of a dozen shoulders, the hinges broke from their fastenings, and a crowd surged into the building. The renegade drew a knife and threw himself against the other door, but it had been firmly fastened on the other side. Again he heard the Persian woman's vicious laugh and her mocking voice in broken phrases. "No, you will not get through here. I am guarding this outlet. Come here, you men!" she cried, louder, "or he will break out yet."

The house now was filled with men; they snatched the knife out of Atam Kul's hand, threw him down and bound him. Then they lifted him up and carried him into the presence of Mat Murad, who was seated upon his horse in the center of the court, gazing from under his wide turban straight into his captive's eyes with an evil, triumphant smile.

No attention was at the time paid to Natalia Martinovna, who had hidden herself and her child in a corner of the room, among the cushions.

CHAPTER XXXVI.

DOSTCHAK TURNS UP AGAIN.

SADIK and his band of Kirghiz had only just taken their departure from Mat Murad's headquarters and turned into the road to Khazar-Asp, when, within a mile of the hamlet, they encountered a horseman of very suspicious appearance. He was a Kirghiz also, and was proceeding at a moderate gallop from the direction from which the Russians were expected. The man's horse was still fresh, and, to judge from its condition, the traveler must have left his last resting-place but a short time ago. The rider was clad in Kirghiz fashion, but his horse bore a Russian saddle and bridle — the former partially concealed by a striped horsecloth, which circumstance rather increased the suspicions aroused by the man's appearance.

The strange horseman no sooner caught sight of the advancing column of mounted men when he turned aside, striving to hide behind the walls of a roadside dwelling. All saw how hurriedly he endeavored to execute this maneuver and how desperately he plied the whip upon his horse's sides as he forced it to jump the wide irrigating ditch lining the road. He seemed to look full of terror upon the approaching force, and even raised one hand to the gun which was hanging over his shoulders, as if preparing to make use of his weapon.

Nobody waited for any order from Sadik, who did not have time to open his mouth before, with a yell, his men were scattering to the right and left in pursuit, taking every possible measure not to lose sight of the man who was trying to hide. The hunt for the suspicious horseman was soon in full cry.

In a few moments he made his appearance again among the trees, and then, finding himself so actively pursued, he turned and stood at bay. In a moment he was the center of a half-circle, and there remained to him only one line of retreat — back in the direction he had come from. The pursued seemed to hesitate, however, and suddenly, observing a somewhat wider interval between two of the horsemen closing in upon him, he boldly spurred his horse in that direction without seemingly paying the slightest attention to the obstacles in his way. It was at that moment that the cries of "Catch him! hold him!" were raised which alarmed the people assembled at Mat Murad's headquarters.

The horseman broke through the lines of his opponents, and, having a better animal, was leaving them behind, when Sadik brought his rifle to his shoulder, and waiting until the fugitive reached an open spot, aimed and fired. A few other bullets were sent in the same direction. The horse screamed in agony and fell with a crash, sending the rider over its head. He had not time to make an outcry or to get upon his feet before he felt himself completely enveloped in the coils of a rope. He was caught.

One of the Kirghiz, looking upon the dusty face covered with sweat, at once recognized the captive as old Dostchak from the Russian camp.

"Well, yes, I am Dostchak," the latter acknowledged at once. "Who else should I be?"

When Sadik came up an examination was at once begun.

CHAPTER XXXVII.

THE GENERAL'S LETTER.

"WHERE do you come from?" was the first question addressed by Sadik to his captive countryman.

"I? Where I come from?" repeated Dostchak, glancing around in various directions as if searching for somebody in that crowd of armed men that surrounded him in a close, impenetrable circle. A majority of the men were looking upon the prisoner only with a feeling of lively curiosity—a common quality of all Asiatics. Sadik alone inspected the native carefully from head to foot, and with special suspicion glanced at the strap of a wallet hidden in the folds of Dostchak's cloak. The strap formed a loop around his neck, and only a corner of the receptacle protruded beyond the wide border of his striped cloak of cotton cloth.

"Well, speak!" shouted the warrior of the steppe,

"or I will loosen your tongue, or tear it out by the roots!"

"Where I came from, there I am not now; and I did not come to you, but to Mullah Atam Kul. Now you know! You have seized me and detained me, and the Mullah will be angry."

"And what is that you have there?" asked Sadik, laying his hand upon the corner of the wallet, while Dostchak drew back and tried to hide it. His hands were seized, and after a brief struggle the strap around his neck was broken and the wallet taken from him.

"Oh, how savage they are!" grinned Dostchak. "Well, it was taken by force, and it's not my fault; you must let Atam Kul know that."

They tore open the wallet and abstracted from it a large paper package, and removing its wrappings began to examine the writing.

"It is in Russian; I do not understand it," said Sadik. "Mount your horses and let us go back. Mat Murad has a learned man; he'll make it out. Haïda! Keep a good hold of him; drive him on foot between two horses, that he may not get away, the dog! Whoever serves a dog will have a dog's death. Move on!"

"Just wait a little with your threats of death!" Dost-chak replied, cheerfully; "perhaps you may yet give thanks to old Dostchak, and present him with a new silk cloak and a horse."

"Oh, what a man — to talk of cloaks!" observed one of the natives, laughing. "Go on! It seems you are not accustomed to running on afoot after horses."

"Not far," the other replied, smiling.

"There is Mat Murad himself, coming to meet us. Hey there, clear the road!"

The "learned man" was found in Mat Murad's suite,

and the letter that had been concealed in Dostchak's satchel was laid before him.

"What did I say?" asked Dostchak, with a malicious smile. "I was telling the truth, but you would not believe me."

"The cursed double-souled, double-tongued dog!" exclaimed Mat Murad. "Read it again; I have not quite understood it all."

The learned man again perused the letter, and once more began to translate its contents, line for line. The listeners, concentrating their whole attention upon the reader, kept silent. Dostchak alone, it appeared, remained an entirely unconcerned witness of what was passing before his eyes. He looked about, and conversed in whispers with his captors, only working his elbows convulsively to relieve the pressure of the rope upon his arms.

"'To the brave warrior, Atam Kul,'" read the learned man; "'from the Russian general.

"'May God send him every blessing and every success, victory over his enemies, and peace in his house. For leading our men from the wells to the water he receives our thanks. We sent the promised ten cloaks and one thousand golden teels, but have received no answer as yet. Have these things been received? We also thank you for your last letter, in which you inform us of the dissensions in your Khanate and that the road to Khiva is open on your side. The other thousand teels and ten cloaks will be forwarded immediately. You promised to capture that fool Mat Murad and that bad man Mullah Sadik alive, and deliver them into our hands; for that we will agree to give you what you ask — ten thousand teels for each head. For the boats which your people delivered to us for crossing the river

the general will give you the great cross with the eagle
of the White Tsar, and the rank of colonel. May
Allah preserve thee! We will see you soon at Khiva
— only assist us as before.' "

The interpreter had finished his translation. Mat
Murad looked at Sadik, who returned his glance from
under his shaggy cap. "Before you can deliver our
heads," muttered the commander between his teeth,
"we will flay you alive. And with you we will also
finish speedily," he continued, addressing his last words
to Dostchak.

"Why would you punish a poor dshigit? What have
I done? I was sent, and, well, I brought what I was
told to bring. Did I know what was written there? I
serve the Russians unwillingly; they took me by force.
I agreed to carry this letter to Atam Kul so as to get
away from the Russians and to remain here with you.
Why do you want to kill me?"

Poor Dostchak glanced pitifully at Mat Murad, and
conducted his defense with so much apparent simplicity
that the latter smiled involuntarily.

"If I had known what was written there, I should
have brought the letter straight to you, Datkha. What
is Atam Kul to me? He is a stranger to me. If you
want me to I'll finish him with my own hands, here
before you."

The last words of Dostchak were accompanied by a
very significant gesture. A deep rage succeeded to his
assumed simplicity, suddenly and completely changing
the lines of his face. This change attracted Sadik's
attention.

"You do not know him?" he inquired, looking
straight into the old man's eyes.

"I? No, I do not know him. I saw him once when

he was serving with the Russians, and never again.
No, I do not know him!"

Mat Murad pointed with his whip. "To Rustem's
garden. Give him a horse; we shall need him yet. We
will march all night so as to surprise the renegade at
daybreak. Haïda!"

They mounted Dostchak upon a horse, tying his legs
under its belly, and to make everything safe they passed
a long rope around his neck. The whole cavalcade
then proceeded at a gallop, turning aside from the
Khazar-Asp road in the direction of Mullah Atam Kul's
quarters. Sadik, with his Kirghiz, went around by
another road, in order to cut off the retreat of their
intended victim should he become apprised in time of
the danger threatening him.

The letter, the *corpus delicti* — the work of the clerk
"who could write like the general"— Mat Murad carefully deposited in the folds of his gorgeous cloak,
richly embroidered in gold thread.

The sun had only just risen when Rustem's houses
and garden were already surrounded.

CHAPTER XXXVIII.

TRIAL AND PUNISHMENT.

MAT MURAD and Sadik dismounted from their horses.
Large Khivan carpets were spread upon the ground,
and they both seated themselves, preparing to judge
and punish the accused.

The followers of both leaders formed a circle, seating

themselves also, silently awaiting the developments
before this improvised court of justice.

Atam Kul's men kept at a distance. They were only
few, and any attempt to rescue their leader by force
was out of the question. A majority looked upon this
occurrence as a favorable opportunity for taking their
leave, and among the first to disappear was the Persian,
who, passing by the harem, gave the inmates a whispered warning to get away as quickly as possible, and
then took to the fields, across the back wall.

Atam Kul was made to sit opposite to his judges and
accusers. He gazed gloomily upon the ground, but
seemed quite unconcerned. He felt, however, that
this affair might end badly for him. He knew that his
relations with Mat Murad and Sadik had of late been
far from friendly, but had not feared them thus far,
because he knew of nothing he had done that could
give them a pretext to threaten his life. He considered
himself their companion in arms, upon an almost equal
footing, whose life they would not dare to attempt.
He was aware, of course, that at the present moment
they seemed to have assumed the right to do so. Was
there any way of extricating himself from the hands of
his enemies? He reviewed in his mind every circumstance, ever so trifling, that had occurred of late, and
involuntarily shrugged his shoulders when he could
recall nothing important. May it be the old grudge?
he thought, glancing at Sadik, but he quickly put aside
that thought and searched for new reasons. At times
he glanced furtively over the heads of the sitting men,
in the direction of his harem, and then his looks
resembled those of a dog watching a dish of food prepared for him, but out of his reach, while another dog
is gradually approaching the dish and its much-coveted

contents. A moment later he heard a woman's shriek, and it seemed to him that it was the voice of Natalia Martinovna. He trembled and sprang to his feet.

"Where are you going?" Sadik snarled between his teeth. Atam Kul's arms were pinioned and the end of the rope was fastened to his left foot, making it very difficult for him to move at all. Two of his guards easily put him back into his former position.

The compromising letter was read to him. "Of what is written there," he answered, firmly, but turning pale, "I remember nothing — I know nothing!"

"You esteem our heads very cheaply indeed," said Mat Murad. "I thank you for your appreciation. You have done us a great honor. It is no joke — ten thousand teels!"

"I would not have given a counterfeit kokan for your head," said Sadik, smiling maliciously. "I would simply throw it away as useless carrion."

"Take care — your turn may come," growled Atam Kul.

"We will take care!"

"Are you still a Mussulman?" Mat Murad inquired, shaking his head, "or have you turned renegade altogether? Have you commenced to sell your own people?"

"It is not true what is written in that letter. Show me the man who brought the paper. Where did you get it? Much may be written from ill-will. Who brought this letter?"

"Bring him here!" cried Mat Murad. Dostchak was led into the circle.

Atam Kul ground his teeth. With foam oozing from his mouth he turned upon the old man. If at that mo-

ment the ropes confining his arms had broken he would
have strangled him on the spot.

"When I was a prisoner with the Russians," hoarsely
cried the accused, "he tried to destroy me; he was preparing death for me. This is my enemy; that is a lying
paper. I'll swear upon the Koran; may lightning burn
me; may my body be covered with leprosy; may my
tongue rot in my mouth if I am lying now! That paper
is false! I am an enemy of the Russians; I do not deal
with them. That letter has been written to destroy
me!" The unfortunate was speaking excitedly, trembling all over. His face was purplish, the veins stood
out from his forehead, his eyes roved wildly from side
to side. Atam Kul seemed like one possessed.

Dostchak crossed his hands upon his heart and made
Mat Murad a deep obeisance. He moved forward, and
observing the helpless condition of Atam Kul, he
stepped to within two paces of him.

"Permit me, Datkha — permit me, a miserable worm
groveling in the dirt, your unworthy slave, to say a
word. Allow me to open your eyes that you may see
how bad a man this is. I, Dostchak, know much, and I
will tell you much that is good. Only permit me to
speak!"

"Speak!" said Mat Murad.

"This man has done much evil to your country.
Allow me to question him myself."

"He may question him," decided Sadik.

"So you received no cloaks from the Russians — you
did not — eh? Oho!" Dostchak gravely shook his head
and looked down disdainfully upon the accused. "You
really say you did not receive —"

"No; you lie, you dog!"

"Wait. And you received no money?"

" No."

" And you received no wife — a good wife that you asked of the general?"

" You lie, you cursed one!"

" Oho! what a bad, lying tongue is yours. Ask these people, Datkha, if they did not bring him the other day — it must have been yesterday — a woman, a Russian woman, from the Russian camp. And what a woman! — the best there was in the whole camp. Ask them?"

" That is so! Tura," said one of the natives. "I saw her. A Russian woman is sitting in the house there now, and she was brought yesterday, in the evening. I saw her."

" Bring her here!"

Several men rushed into the house. Atam Kul began to look alarmed, and seemed to be chafing in his bonds. A few minutes of dead silence followed. At last Natalia Martinovna appeared from behind the vineyard. They were leading her, supporting her under her arms; they were obliged to almost carry her. With the greatest difficulty she held the boy in her arms, the child trembling with fear and looking about without comprehending his position. Natalia scarcely moved of her own volition, and did not seem to see what was before her. Stupefaction seemed to have seized her whole being. She had no idea of what was expected of her or what might be demanded from her.

" I am right — don't you see? I am right!" boasted Dostchak.

" Were you brought from the Russian camp?" asked Mat Murad. She remained silent.

" Let the interpreter ask her in her own language,"

was suggested by Sadik, and the question was translated.

"Yes, I am a Russian — I am a Russian," muttered
Natalia Martinovna, addressing herself to no one in
particular. "Let me go! This is my son; it is not
yours — let us go." She spoke as if unconscious of
what she was saying; her speech resembled the mut-
terings of a person in a dream.

"Poor woman! poor woman!" said old Dostchak.
"And that is your work, you beast!" he addressed
Atam Kul. "It was to buy your fratricidal knife, to
buy your help, that they gave you this woman."

"Let us finish with him," said Sadik, yawning.
"We're only losing time. The case is clear."

Mat Murad pondered, and then ensued a few moments
of oppressive, almost unbearable silence. All kept perfectly quiet; only the horses rattled their bits and
neighed, and a flock of rose-colored sparrows played and
chirped noisily in the tops of the grove of plantains.

Atam Kul hung his head.

"Finish with him," quietly pronounced Mat Murad,
making an expressive sign with his hand, drawing his
finger around the collar of his cloak.

"Stand up, culprit!" And two gigantic Kirghiz
stepped up to the condemned man.

"Oh, great judge!" Dostchak addressed Mat Murad.
"May Allah shower many blessings upon thy wise
head! Permit me to do it — to cut the throat of this
bad man!"

"Look out for yourself — away!" the Datkha replied,
angrily, spitting upon the ground in disgust. "Make
an end of him quickly!"

"Oh, you devils!" shrieked Atam Kul at the top of
his voice. "Why do you play at justice, you robbers,

both of you? That is all you are! You have been concocting my destruction long ago. Well, take my head, taste of my innocent blood, until they weigh like millstones around your necks, until eternal damnation falls upon your heads —"

He was quickly overthrown and a cloak wrapped around his head; then he was carried bodily into the nearest building.

"Throw away that carrion!" said Mat Murad, turning his face away in disgust when they brought him the head of the two-legged wolf, Mullah Atam Kul.

"Don't throw it away!" said Sadik, and turned to old Dostchak. "Here! take this head and carry it to the Russian general as a present from me and Mat Murad! Take it!"

Dostchak seized the ghastly remnant with both his hands, threw himself down on his knees before Sadik, and fervently kissed the hem of his cloak.

Yunus — the son of his heart — was avenged.

At about the same time a group of horsemen was rapidly advancing along the road leading from Khiva to Gurlen, in the Yomud desert. In the midst of the cavalcade rode a man still young, but with a worn, pale face, with pendent, apathetic under lip. He was attired in a cloak of Cashmere shawl, and wore upon his head a high Turkoman sheepskin cap. His tall charger walked with a long easy step, while the other horses were barely keeping up with him at a short gallop. Some distance behind the cavalcade followed about forty carts in a single line, each drawn by two horses. Upon these carts heavy loads had been piled in great disorder. It was evident that the loading had been

THE KHAN OF KHIVA AND HIS SUITE.

done in a hurry. Costly carpets, iron-bound chests, bundles of clothing, and metallic vessels and implements had been thrown in promiscuously. The caravan moved rapidly, as if in flight, as if trying to escape from some dire disaster which threatened in their rear.

They were actually flying. The man was the Khan of Khiva, Saïd Rahim-Bogadur, who after a last consultation with his counselors had completely lost his head.

The Russians were already under the walls of Khiva. The Khan was flying. Where he was going he did not know himself, nor did he care. He was evidently frightened, and trembled nervously whenever certain heavy reports fell upon his ear.

The reports came from the Russian cannon.

CHAPTER XXXIX.

A FEW WORDS OF THE KHAN AND HIS SUBJECTS.

THE political changes in Central Asia were progressing, sometimes in the channels prepared by diplomacy and statesmanship, and sometimes taking new and unforeseen courses.

Everything was ready for the final development of the drama being enacted. The fall of Khiva was inevitable, and the useless shedding of blood under its walls did not in any way hasten the course of events, but only involved the sacrifice of a few unnecessary victims from the Russian ranks — ranks not very full even without those losses. Rreference is made to the attempt by

15

the Caucasian and Orenburg expeditions to take the town by storm at the very moment when the people had sent a peaceful deputation to the commander-in-chief, and opened to him the eastern gate.

The Khan of Khiva fled. This was his least excusable blunder; a stupid act, to which he was urged by fanatics, and which came very nearly causing him to lose his throne altogether.

It is probable that Saïd Rahim-Bogadur recognized his blunder in the course of time, or that the counsels of other advisers, who could see a little farther than their master, gained the upper hand over the fanatic opponents of Russian influence, for but a few days later the Khan wrote to the Russian general, expressing his readiness to submit to the will of his conqueror, and notifying him of his intention to return to the city. A joint council was established, composed of Russians and native representatives of the Khanate. This council regulated the course of further proceedings and decided the fate of the Amu Daria Oasis, and peace was thus concluded.

By this peace the Khan was returned to his city, and his control over all the tribes inhabiting the greater portion of the Khanate of Khiva was recognized; only the right bank of the Amu and its delta were incorporated with the vast domain of Russian territory.

A contribution in money was imposed upon the Khan and his subjects to cover, at least partially, the enormous expenditure caused by the various expeditions. *It only remained to collect this contribution.* This sentence is easily written, and more easily pronounced, but it was not quite so easy to carry it into effect or to comply with the most important clause of the treaty of peace.

A large number of the Khan's subjects were held

under but slight subjection; in many cases the term was but a figure of speech, and the Khan's control over them was of the feeblest. This was true of the independent Turkoman tribes settled along the left bank of the Amu, and farther southward in the heart of the open steppes which separate the Khanate from Persia and the mountain regions of the Himalayas.

Half-nomadic, half-settled brigands as they are, they had heretofore acknowledged no obligations to the Khan beyond furnishing him a certain number of armed horsemen or attendants whenever he should require them. They also delivered to their so-called ruler, in the guise of presents, a certain part of the plunder obtained by violence and robbery perpetrated upon their neighbors. This system had, in their eyes at least, legitimized or legalized their old mode of life, to which they were much attached, and which they never had the slightest intention of changing.

The Turkoman tribes made up the greater part of the population of the Khanate, and they had been the principal factors in bringing on the war, having drawn punishment and vengeance upon themselves by their plundering expeditions. It was therefore but just that the greater part of the money contribution should be laid upon their shoulders, but they flatly refused to pay their part.

The Khan Saïd Rahim possessed no power to bring the Turkomans into subjection, and openly acknowledged the fact to the Russians. To give in to these impudent robbers would have been highly injudicious — it was essential that they should be forced to submit, that their unruly spirit be broken and their customary faith in their own exemption from punishment be destroyed.

The war with the Khanate of Khiva was at an end,

but it was found unavoidable to inaugurate immediately
another war — for the subjection of unruly subjects.
With this purpose in view, various smaller but distinct
expeditions were organized by the Russians to march
against the Turkomans into the very heart of their
settlements and pasture-lands.

_____

CHAPTER XL.

AGAIN IN THE OFFICERS' CIRCLE.

A LIVELY, brilliant scene of military life was being
enacted under the dense shadows of huge plantain-trees
in the gardens and vineyards surrounding Khiva.

Since early morning the roads and the walls of the
surburban gardens had been lined with the brilliant
front of the forces belonging to the Caucasian and
Orenburg expeditions. They were all in full uniform,
and shone and sparkled as if on peaceful parade on one .
of the vast squares of the capital. The infantry in their
original " papakha " (paper helmets) and the cavalry in
their jaunty red and white "cherkeska " (caps); the
officers with shining epaulets; the sound of music,
the animated Russian language — all these combined
to cause the observer to forget that he found himself at
one of the most distant points of uncivilized Central
Asia and to imagine himself back in Europe.

In vivid contrast, though in line with this parade
front, stood the plain, campaign-stained, and almost beg-
garly looking, but formidable Turkestan battalions.
Their dusty white blouses, white caps, with linen have-

locks, yellow or almost brown from the effects of time and dust; their once-red leather trousers, boots shrunk from solar heat and smeared with grease; their knapsacks upon their shoulders — all these were in sharp contrast to the fine uniforms of the Caucasian expedition. But all this ugliness breathed a spirit of power and of strength, and inspired the fascinated beholder with a sense of invincibility — a spirit which induced the native who had looked impassively upon the other troops to lower his eyes, and, with a respect which amounted almost to a superstitious dread, to describe a wide circuit around these columns so common in appearance. The first request made by the Khan of Khiva on visiting the Russian camp was to be shown from a distance the soldiers who crossed the terrible desert. The ruler of Khiva did not believe that these were common mortals. His oriental imagination had doubtless pictured to him some kind of "Ak-Kulmak," or fabulous beings. It was interesting to see the rapt attention with which the Khan gazed upon the tanned faces of these soldiers as he passed along their front. His lips trembled, and he whispered something — perhaps a prayer; perhaps an oath.

The review was over; the troops occupied the places assigned to them for their bivouacs. The officers of the united expeditions began to gather in circles. Friends, acquaintances, and even relatives met, greeting each other more or less cordially. A merry, noisy, animated conversation was being carried on everywhere.

In Major Pugovitzin's tent about ten of his more intimate companions had assembled. The major's orderly, the bold Proshka, who had been investigating the condition of wine-cellars among the sutlers of the Caucasian expedition, had secured, to his great satisfaction, a whole half-dozen of big-bellied bottles, sealed with white wax, and with necks coated with shining tin-foil. What enjoyment awaited the guests of Major Pugovitzin after a whole series of miserable stations and months of privations! The major was still in ignorance as to whether his orderly's efforts in the adjoining camp had been crowned with success, and proceeding to the entrance of the tent that had only just been erected, he cast a questioning glance at Proshka, accompanied by a doubtful "Well?"

"I have got them," replied the orderly in a mysterious whisper, and then added in a louder tone, "They have such quantities over there; it flows everywhere like common water. The whole army could not drink it up in two days, your honor."

"Glasses!" ordered the host. "Now, gentlemen, we will ask a blessing over what God has sent us. Hey, boys, spread the carpet and trice up the sides of the tent. That's right! Be seated, gentlemen." A few soldiers hurriedly raised the walls of the tent, and thus formed a shady cover under which the breeze played fresh and cool.

"Sitting this way," began a corpulent and very bald captain, "reminds one of Dominic and Dononi" (St. Petersburg cafés). He was very fond of these comparisons, in spite of the fact that he had never been at Dominic's and Dononi's in his life, for the simple but very sufficient reason that he had never happened to have been in St. Petersburg.

"Have you a Dominic, or a what-do-you-call-him, at Cheboksarakh, where you have been stationed?" curiously inquired his neighbor.

The captain did not satisfy his neighbor's curiosity, but seemed absorbed in rapt contemplation of one of the bottles.

The lame Cossack also made his appearance, pleasantly nodding his head to the company, and, without waiting for an invitation, seated himself upon the carpet. The lively talk subsided a little upon his arrival. The sad expression of his face, though apparently calm, and even smiling, did not seem in harmony with their joyous spirits. The bald captain was continuing his abortive attempts at spelling out the French label on the wine-bottle, but he suddenly stopped, with an inquisitive "Eh?" and also subsided, returning the bottle to its place.

"Gentlemen, I will withdraw!" said the Cossack. "What is it that seems to dampen your spirits when I come? Do I trouble you in any way? I would not have come, but I felt very lonely, and hoped to overcome the feeling by listening to conversation and laughter. However, I will go —"

"Now, that is enough, old friend!" said Pugovitzin, seizing his hand. "What is the matter with you? Sit down. You are a good fellow, only you are a regular woman. Here! drink a glass of this 'fizz' that my Proshka managed to raise for us. Sit down!"

"Yesterday he was roaming about the whole camp again," whispered one officer to another, glancing at the Cossack; "he never loses hope, and keeps on searching."

"I dare say!" replied the other, shrugging his shoulders.

"But I say, what is lost is lost! Consider the time that has passed without any news whatever." And he continued to whisper into his companion's ear, holding onto a button of his coat and gesticulating with the long slender fingers of his other hand.

"Have you seen the Dutchman, gentlemen?" loudly inquired a young ensign.

"The Hussar?   He is a strange fellow!"

"You may well say strange!   He is a man, of course, only his legs are somewhat thin; but he can drink well. I saw him —"

"Would you believe it?   He poured out his brandy, then put in a piece of sugar, some extract of lemon, and then kept stirring and stirring it up, in the meantime soaking little pieces of cracker in it and eating them!   It made me sick.   Here's to your health!   Ah, if we only had some ice!   Wouldn't it be splendid?"

"A horse, a horse — a kingdom for a horse, or a piece of ice!" declaimed one of the guests.   "Only wait; we shall have all that again.   Time is passing."

"Heel-taps! gentlemen," shouted Pugovitzin.

"In expectation of future similar blessings!" Major Birnaps continued the toast.   The officers began to clink their glasses, which had been filled to the brim.

During the first moments after the catastrophe when, in Natalia Martinovna's tent, the lame Cossack had read the fatal note, he had completely lost his head. He did not know what to do or what to say.   To pursue her was the first idea to enter his head, and he rushed from the tent; but then his strength left him entirely.   He pressed both hands upon his breast, staggered ahead for a few paces, and then sat down upon the ground.   People came up and questioned him, but he made no answer.   Silently he handed the note to the first man who approached him.   The letter was read, and in fifteen minutes the news of Natalia Martinovna's flight had spread over the whole camp.   Pursuing parties were at once fitted out and inquiries instituted, but it all led to nothing.   The results of the pursuit were even less satisfactory than on the occasion when the flying Atam Kul had been pursued. At that time they had at least found tracks, and they had even seen the robber himself, but here they never discovered the faintest sign or found the slightest hint. Much time had been lost — sufficient to enable her to reach such a distance from the camp as to make the search not only difficult but dangerous for small parties. Nothing remained but to submit to fate and wait.

With what burning impatience the unfortunate Golovin watched every step of the advance, and how he fumed over the slightest obstacles, the least delay! The most frightful suggestions and apprehensions alarmed his soul and distracted his brain. At times nobody believed that his mind would withstand the strain.

She must be with Atam Kul — so much was certain. Atam Kul had gone somewhere into the heart of the Turkoman steppes — that was also known; but where was the place? The sanguinary developments at Rustem's villa were still unknown to the Russians.

The unfortunate man was wandering about the camp pale and emaciated; his hair was rapidly turning gray. He still visited the various circles and messes to listen to the cheerful conversation, but his presence always proved a damper upon the spirits of others.

Once he made up his mind to drop everything, to steal away from the camp, and to undertake the search alone. His first attempts in that direction were immediately detected, and thereafter a strict watch was kept over him without letting him know it.

The disappearance of Dostchak, which attracted much attention, seemed suspicious, and naturally it was connected with Natalia's flight. Unjust charges and accusations were heaped upon the head of the poor native.

Golovin's unrestrained grief and melancholy brooding continued to undermine his health, until his faculties as well as his whole nervous system were reduced to a condition of general numbness. His friends still came to see him, and strove to console or cheer him, but no one remained for any length of time without feeling himself repelled and anxious to get away again.

Man can not live long in such a state of mental and moral disintegration, and the Cossack's strong organization was evidently giving way under the constant pressure of an unbearable burden.

"He will end by contracting consumption," was the verdict of the physicians of the expeditionary force as they glanced at Golovin from a distance; and they immediately engaged in a learned discussion of the connection between the physical and moral life of their subject, during which they backed their assertions with numerous Latin quotations having no bearing at all upon the point at issue.

"Well, brother!" exclaimed Major Pugovitzin, as he held out his glass to touch that of his melancholy guest, passing his other arm reassuringly around his waist. Golovin drank the wine in silence, at a single draught, then turned, seized a saddle-cushion lying close at hand and stretched himself out at full length, with his back toward the company.

"Do you know, gentlemen," began Lieutenant Kusti- kof, " whom I met to-day?"

"Well?"

"I went to the Caucasian camp to-day — how hot they must be with those foolish helmets! Our caps are much better. Oh! what was I talking about? Yes — I went to the camp, and I looked about. Who the devil was that? Some familiar face; I really must have seen it somewhere. I passed by again, on purpose. Yes, it was his very image! I passed once more, when the orderly, to spite me, I suppose, let down the side of the tent, and I could see no longer what was going on inside. I was so provoked!"

"But who was it?"

"Perhaps it was not he—who knows? But there certainly is a resemblance."

"Yes; but whom are you talking about?"

"Do you remember Rovitch — who was at Chiniaz?"

"It can't be!"

"Yes, upon my word! It was his seat in the saddle, too. Don't you remember he always sat a little sideways — rather affected English style? All this — yes, by God, it must be he!"

"Is he with the Orenburg troops?"

"No; his orderly was a Circassian — he must be with the Caucasian expedition. He must be on the staff — his tent stands in a garden by itself."

"We must find out about this. Gentlemen, did you hear what Kustikof has been saying? Rovitch is here!"

"Let us go to see him!"

"Oh! to the devil with him!"

"'Sh!" whispered Pugovitzin, holding up his hand, glancing at the lame Cossack. The warning came too late — he had been listening attentively.

CHAPTER XLI.

REMINISCENCES — OLD· ACQUAINTANCES.

A HORSEMAN, with officer's epaulets, clad in a short blouse, fitting closely to his well-built form, rode up to a small tent standing by itself at a little distance from the others in the large garden occupied by the staff of the Caucasian expedition. He descended from his horse in a languid, leisurely fashion, threw the bridle into the hands of the orderly just running up, and, thrusting his saber into its metallic scabbard, entered, stooping, under the canvas roof of his temporary domicile.

The officer appeared somewhat agitated and absorbed in some subject. This was noticeable in the distracted, uneasy glance which he cast over the interior of his quarters, as well as in his uncertain movements and in the gesture of his hand, altogether unintelligible to his orderly, who was looking inquiringly at his master. That gesture must mean something, express some order; it was even accompanied by the words, " Do you hear?" — only he to whom the phrase was directed could hear nothing further, and stood patiently waiting, holding the bridle of the perspiring but by no means tired horse. His master stood for a minute near the center-pole of the tent, then stepped to the folding-bed, bending his knees slightly as if about to lie down; then changed his mind, took off his cap and put it on again, and drew toward him with his foot a camp-stool, which caught in a fold of the carpet and fell with legs upward. He once more extended his leg, clad in top-boot and spur, to reach for another stool, this time with better success, and seated himself at the table, upon which he began to drum with his fingers. He took a cigar-case from his pocket, selected a cigar, bit off the end, and lighted a match, holding it until the flame scorched the ends of his fingers; he dropped it, but did not light another, and threw the cigar he had prepared under the table.

The orderly still waited patiently, looking stolidly at the horse. His master was seated now, and seemed to be gazing at the intricate shadows of branches thrown in clear outlines upon the opposite wall of his canvas tent.

"Do you wish the samovar, your honor?" The orderly at last resolved to break the silence.

" Yes; lead him well, and wait a little before water-ing him!" the officer replied, as if just awaking. It was clear that the answer did not fit the question, but the faithful and well-trained servant understood what he was to do.

"He must be drunk! Made a mistake at the general's breakfast-table!" he pondered as he was leading the horse along the wall, carefully keeping within its broad, cool shadow. "Now he will lie down and sleep for an hour and a half — then he will certainly expect to have his samovar, and call for tea and lemon the moment he opens his eyes. Some of these gentlemen get anything they want at the sutler's, and only have it put down on little cards. I must try that — maybe to-night. Be quiet, Golubok! Whoa!" The orderly stroked the neck of the fiery horse, which displayed an inclination to rise upon its hind feet. But all these reflections of the undersized, pock-marked soldier, with thin, bristling side-whiskers, narrow slits of eyes, and a good-natured expression, were far from the truth this

time.   His master did not think of lying down, but still
sat upon the camp-stool before the table, supporting
his head with both hands.   He was not drunk, and
though he had breakfasted at the general's, he had
made no " mistake."   He was not thinking of his bed
at this moment, because old reminiscences were crowding each other in his head, calling up such scenes and
pictures as would have driven sleep away most effect-
ually, even if it had been the proper time for it.

And there sat this officer gazing upon the shadows of
the branches, which must have belonged to a group of
large silvery acacias, to judge from the feather-like
shapes of leaves so distinctly traced upon the canvas.
Looking steadily before him, without removing his eyes
from those bluish, fantastic outlines, he appeared to see
within them or beyond them other lines.   A small
cloud flying by swallowed up the patterns upon the
cloth, but that did not lessen his absorption; he still
kept fixedly staring in the same direction — his steady
gaze never relaxing, his eyes only blinking slightly
when the sun again illuminated the canvas and the
familiar tracery once more appeared upon its surface.

Two straw-colored butterflies, chasing each other,
fluttered into the tent, playing about like two bright
golden spots.   They found their way to the sitting
man's shoulder and sat upon his epaulet, rising and
alighting again alternately in intertwining curves, with
an occasional longer flight to the smooth surface of the
tightly stretched canvas.

Some passer-by stumbled over a tent-rope, and swore.
The whole tent was shaking, and something seemed to
break.   A large hairy spider of a very suspicious aspect,
propelled by the vigorous movements of its shaggy legs
had gained the top of the table, and not liking the view

was preparing to let himself down again. Two horse-men passing by at a full run raised a dense cloud of dust, which invaded the interior of the tent. Again the same spider had gained the table, and was stationary, apparently considering how to proceed — whether to pass by or to enter the sleeve of the officer's coat, which appeared to him, probably, like a dark and dangerous tunnel.

Neither the butterflies, nor the awkward passer-by stumbling over the tent-ropes, nor the spider, nor the horsemen had attracted the attention of the rapt thinker, and it was owing only to an accidental motion of his hand that the nasty insect changed its intention and resolved to return by the old familiar road.

The orderly looked into the tent, and what he saw made his small eyes open wide. He looked again when almost an hour had passed by, and still it was the same. The horse Golubok had long since been taken away and unsaddled; the small traveling-samovar had boiled over several times, and the regular hour for tea had gone by, but the officer still sat and thought, still gazed at the wall of his tent, though the feathery shadows had long since disappeared and been replaced by others until now it was all solid shadow, without any tracery whatever. The bugles had sounded for "watering" in the adjoining Cossack camp, and the infantrymen in their bivouac had been called to their soup-kettles in the company kitchens. Evening was fast approaching, and still the officer sat and brooded, enveloping himself in mighty clouds of blue tobacco-smoke.

This officer had been in Central Asia a few years pre-viously — not here on the banks of the Amu, in the vicinity of Khiva, but in other parts, at Tashkent, Samarkand, and Chiniaz — and he found it impossible to

drive from his head certain memories of that time.
Scenes of a past not very remote would rise before him;
familiar faces and forms, more or less distinct, some
barely perceptible, were coming and going before his
eyes, their hazy profiles faintly outlined against the
wall of the tent. The longer the officer thought, the
clearer became to him one shape, the memory of which
had plunged him into this contemplative and retro-
spective mood. One shape was becoming more and
more distinct, throwing all others into the shade. It
stood before him as if alive, as if saying to him, " Well,
my friend, remember, try to remember — think of
everything, every trifle, every detail; neglect nothing;
weigh and consider. I shall watch you; if you should
forget, I will remind you — I shall let you skip nothing.
I, as your unsolicited, uncalled-for prompter, will recall
to you, dictate to you word for word, all your reminiscences. Do not mind it, my dear; see! there is nobody
but you and I — nobody can hear us; therefore remember. Yes, you came to Chiniaz, on the steamer Aral,
and then your adventures began.

"Ah! there is the old gunner, with his good-natured,
joyous countenance, with his long gray mustache, and
still longer pipe; and there is his stout, cross old wife,
with the smell of the kitchen about her; and there is
somebody else with them, some graceful, pleasing form
with honest, loving eyes. Do you recognize her? Look
well!

"And here is a broad, round-shouldered figure, a
little rough in appearance, in a gray shirt — well, you
can not remember names, and if they come into your
head you try to shake them out again, only you do not
always succeed. However, we have nothing to do with
names just now.

" Then there was some trouble — you were riding along on horseback and singing; you were happy and free from care, and you never suspected that a terrible deadly enemy was near. He sat there in the bush, aiming both barrels of his shotgun at you. Here the thread of your reminiscences breaks, and that is but natural; the man who is hit does not hear the report of the shot, especially if the hit is mortal and dealt from close by.

" The fog at last melts away and you see yourself upon a bed — and there, again, are the loving glances, the deft hands fluttering over your brow and bosom. You thought then that an angel was sitting by your side, fanning you with her wonderful shining wings. You worshiped that angel — why shouldn't you, if you saw in her only a messenger of God? You bent with veneration over those slender, graceful fingers. Is it not true that you remember all this perfectly? That is, you remember it now, but you have tried your best to forget it, to drive it from your memory, and to hide it with more recent brighter and stronger impressions!

" Little by little the angel lost her spiritual qualities. She descended to earth; taking to herself the attributes of earth, she was transformed into a woman — a loving woman. Do you remember what happened after that? Do you?

" Nonsense! it was nothing! What young man would not profit by his opportunities when a nice, good girl comes so willingly to his arms? Who would stop to consider and think of consequences? There was nothing very bad or unusual. The passing fancy wore itself out. Nobody loses anything by that. Even she, for instance, what did she lose? She has probably become resigned long ago and forgotten all about it. She may have

16

been married ten times, had children and nursed them, and taken care of her house, baking pies and puddings after her mother's example — and she may be perfectly happy. There were really some other aspirants; a stout, jocose major, and, again, that rough, round-shouldered man. But let me see! Did not something happen to that round-shouldered man? Yes, but that can not be laid to you. Any one insanely jealous — no, there he is, emaciated, ragged, ill, with wild, wandering eyes, wading and tottering through the swamps like a wild animal, bereft of reason and volition —" A violent shudder ran over the officer's body; he glanced about him with frightened eyes, and lifted his hand to his face as if to brush away some cobweb obstructing his vision.

"There was a child — that is another affair; there you ought to have acted differently. Ah! it is nonsense! What about that child? One can not marry every woman because she happens to be the mother of your child — that is impossible, for one reason, because we are not Turks, and polygamy has no legal standing; it is unlawful, in a measure. Why don't people understand that? Can't *you* understand it, at least, you irrepressible, unwelcome prompter? And was it his boy? Who could prove that he was the only one who —" The officer blushed up to his ears, and once more looked down and laid both hands over his face.

"What is this!" a well-known voice seemed to whisper in his ear. " Has your conscience really not become deaf altogether? It must have been aroused, you see! You seem to be ashamed of yourself. You acknowledge the hideous heartlessness of your conduct!"

It seems that even now, when all this had long since been laid aside and forgotten, a story told somewhere in one of the officers' circles and overheard by him was sufficient to overturn in a moment his carefully framed and braced structure of social morality, to arouse him from his calm self-satisfaction, and to call forth this whole chain of troublesome reminiscences. It appeared to him as if she took possession of his heart again, entering it as her rightful property, her well-known, customary home, of which she could dispose as her own, driving from it all others. But where was she? In the hands of savages, in captivity? Was she alive or dead — had the suffering mother's heart been quieted forever? And that child — his son, where was he?

A groan of anguish escaped from the officer's breast — a groan so loud that it was heard beyond the tent. The side-whiskered orderly dreaming upon his felt-mat was startled, and sprang to his feet, seized the samovar, in which the coals had long since become extinct, and ran against his master in the entrance of the tent.

The officer sallied forth with a buoyant step, inhaling with evident delight the fresh evening air scented with the tar-like odor of mulberry-trees. He stood for a few moments near the entrance, and then began slowly to pace the well-trodden path meandering between the knotty, rough trunks of the trees.

"A strange day this has been!" muttered the orderly, as he returned the samovar to its proper place.

The officer was an old acquaintance, Sergeï Nikolaïevitch Rovitch.

CHAPTER XLII.

DOSTCHAK AND HIS BAGGAGE.

DURING the same night a shot was heard on the outer picket-line of the Cossack camp. This alarming sound came near bringing the whole force to its feet, but the excitement speedily subsided when the cause of the alarm was explained.

The sentry had fired at a suspicious horseman who was riding along the picket-line. The man had made no reply, though challenged three times, and had endeavored to hide behind the walls of some building. The bullet from the Cossack's carbine prevented him from carrying out this intention. He fell from the saddle like a bag, while his horse galloped along, scattering his master's baggage over the road. The first object to fall was a large leather bag, which was immediately picked up by the men who had been alarmed by the Cossack's shot. They also raised the body of the rash rider, from which life had already fled.

In the darkness it could only be surmised that the horseman was not one of ours, and thereupon the alarm subsided. When the Cossacks looked into the satchel they spit out in disgust and flung their find away.

"That is not very nice, boys!" remarked the old sergeant, "but there must be some proceedings about this; it must be reported to the Sotnik (captain). Bring back here what you threw away, brethren; some investigation may come out of this. Put it down here, beside the body."

"Oh, what a stench!" complained the Cossack as he executed his superior's orders. "Why did that devil carry such baggage as that about with him?"

They laid out the man who had been killed, placing beside him his satchel, covered both objects with a blanket, and posted a sentry to guard them.

In the morning, at daylight, people began to gather around the scene of the night's disturbance, and among them were some who recognized the dead man, as well as the contents of his satchel. The dead man was old Dostchak. In the satchel lay the head of Atam Kul, the two-legged wolf.

"Ah! fate, fate!" sighed Major Pugovitzin a few hours later in his tent.

"Yes," answered Major Birnaps; "if he had not been killed by that shot we might have heard something of Natalia Martinovna!"

"It's fate!" repeated Pugovitzin. "Let us go to Golovin. They say the poor fellow is so much overcome with what has happened that he may not survive the excitement."

"I can not understand it," Kustikof broke in, with some heat. "Why can not something be done? We might, for instance, surround the whole Turkoman steppe, round up all the settlements, and subject every individual to the strictest examination — we should come upon her track somewhere; we should know something; but if there is no effort made —"

"You are perfectly right!" replied Pugovitzin, quite seriously. "Two months ago — I do not exactly remember where, but it was somewhere near Kuzil-Kumakh — I lost a button from my blouse. We might have surrounded the steppe, scratched the sand with our fingers or passed it through a screen, and then we should have certainly found my button."

"Ha! ha! ha!" laughed Major Birnaps, holding his shaking stomach between his hands.

" You are always making a joke of it!" complained Kustikof, and turned away. All three then proceeded to Golovin's quarters to offer what consolation they could.

The accident of the preceding night had affected him so seriously that he was confined to his bed by the doctor's orders, chiefly because he really could not keep his feet under repeated attacks of fever brought on by this new shock to his nerves.

There was but very little hope of the Cossack's final recovery. The most sanguine among the physicians belonging to the expedition expressed the opinion that only a miracle could save his life; and a miracle was scarcely to be expected in these prosaic times.

CHAPTER XLIII.

EXCITEMENT AND GATHERINGS.

THE whole camp was in a fever of excitement. "Marching orders" could be heard from one end to the other, in the messes, in the officers' tents, along the Cossack picket-ropes, and among the artillerymen camped between their guns and caissons, as well as under the low shelter-tents of the infantrymen, who were greasing their high boots, as the most important thing to be done at the first hint of a possible march.

"Who will go and who will stay behind?"

"Does your battalion go?"

"Truly, the riflemen are lucky again! The devil take them!"

"Let somebody go to headquarters to ascertain what, who, and how!"

"Ten guns are going, you say?"

"There's bad luck — my bay has fallen lame. The plague take him! It's the same every time."

Nothing but such abrupt, doubting or hopeful expressions could be heard throughout the long camp which had enfolded Khiva within its lines for the last half-month.

The Turkomans were unruly again. They had flatly refused to pay the war-indemnity imposed upon them, and the Russian spies were bringing in the most alarming news. Those in highest authority were uneasy; the subaltern officers and soldiers were boisterous, talking, and shaking each other's hands in congratulation. It was no joke to remain for a whole month for nothing, without anything to do. It would be all right at some other place, in permanent quarters — there you could occupy yourself with something; but to be stuck here in the burning sun, without stirring forward or backward — it was no wonder they were happy! The Turkomans, the dear fellows, are making trouble. Well, let us go to them, into their camps and pastures; a week or two can be passed away nicely in that way. We will see new places, and, God willing, there will be a little shooting — that is always good for the service.

"Listen, Brother Raskatof," said Pugovitzin to his sergeant-major. "In the first place, not a single boot must be found gaping in our battalion. Let that be understood! I shall look to it myself. If anybody fails

to mend his boots he'll not go to the front; he may stay
with the invalids! "

" I hear, sir, your honor," replied the red-whiskered
sergeant-major.

" There must be nothing superfluous in the baggage.
I shall inspect knapsacks on the road, and all trash will
be thrown away on the spot."

" I hear, your honor."

" Two shirts each; hard bread for five days. Full
allowance of ammunition and one-half allowance extra;
twenty rounds in the knapsack — but look to it that
there are no 'misfires.' 'Tea and sugar' money will
be issued in the evening. Send the platoon leaders to
me. Do you understand? "

" I understand, your honor."

" Well, off with you, then, and hurry up! "

" Yes, gentlemen, we can't do otherwise," remarked
the major to a group of officers, as if justifying himself
for attending to such details. " Unless we tell them
about every trifle every time, there'll always be trouble
afterward."

" You are right!" consented one of the officers. " It
is necessary to be prepared."

" They are trifles," remarked another, " only in
themselves; as a whole they may decide the fate of an
army."

" Have you seen Birnaps, gentlemen? He is almost
crazy."

" Why? "

" His battalion again remains behind. It seems an
injustice. He will not stand it."

" Well, brother, as to not standing it —"

" He is very much excited. He keeps running to

headquarters and begging. I met him to-day; he would not bow, but turned so red! "

"Now it will again be said that there has been intrigue. It is ridiculous, but, all the same, gentlemen, it seems a little hard. Just judge for yourselves."

"Oh, nonsense! Who was sent as advance-guard on the 16th? Who went to Khazar-Asp? Enough of your intrigues! We all must take our turns. Will you lend me your revolver? The cylinder of mine does not turn well."

"I'll not give it to you."

"Well, the devil take you! — I do not need it."

"May God protect you all!" shouted Major Pugovitzin, finishing up his instructions. "If a single one of you gets drunk before we march, may God have mercy on him! We'll eat him alive, and the dog will never be heard of again! God preserve you! "

"And do you know," said Lieutenant Kustikof to the lame Cossack, whom he was visiting in his tent — "do you know it is devilish hard to explain it? "

"What do you mean?" asked Golovin, listlessly. "What do you refer to? "

"Oh, I have been thinking, but really we can not count upon it with any certainty — however—"

"Your tongue seems to be all tangled up. Let it be!"

"At least," muttered Kustikof, as if talking to himself, "there is no certainty about it." And then he ran off to communicate his doubts and hopes to somebody else with better success.

"We are going into the very center of their pasturelands," he said a few minutes later to another officer. "The cavalry has received orders to move around at a

trot and take them in the flank. They may succeed in
capturing them in their houses, and unexpectedly."

"Impossible, brother; and besides —"

"Oh, yes; that is what I was going to say. We can
not count with certainty upon anything, but they may
be surrounded and captured, and not a single soul
allowed to escape. In the meantime we can search all
the by-ways, and perhaps — if one were only lucky
enough! I should refuse any rewards that might be
offered — I should want nothing; and, after all, it may
happen!" Here poor Kustikof's doubts again over-
came his hopes, and a sad expression once more overspread his features, when the man he was addressing
unexpectedly replied, "Well, don't worry. It is an
affair of state, don't you see?" His troubled heart
was much relieved when he found that some one shared
his hopes as to the rescue of Natalia Martinovna.

But if the junior lieutenant had possessed a better
knowledge of human nature he would have known that
the same hopes fluttered in every heart without exception; that this hope was not only stirring in the lame
Cossack's heart, but filled it completely, to the exclusion
of all other thoughts; that there was not a single
skeptic who dared ridicule this hope. The only sad
thing about it was that this hope was in itself so feeble
that few ventured to let their tongues express it. It
seemed as if every one thought that if he only kept
silent the disappointment would be easier to bear, and,
at any rate, the few skeptics would be deprived of the
satisfaction of saying in case of disappointment, "Well,
I told you it was impossible!"

It was interesting to observe that all conversations
relating to this secret hope were conducted in general
terms: "It is very possible that it may happen," "It

would be glorious if it were to happen," "No, that is impossible," and in such like phrases, nobody making any distinct or definite assertion, nobody daring to to pronounce the well-known, cherished name.

Only among the common soldiers one would occasionally hear a plain expression of their strong feeling on this subject:

"Oh; if we should be able to rescue her, our little gray one!"

The expedition was to march at night, long before daylight. The night was dark, without moon. The infantry began its movement with very little noise; company after company filed into the road to Kungrad. This was not the real objective point of the expedition; later, in due time, it was proposed to turn to the left, toward Chandir.

Between the walls lining the road a moving mass of somewhat lighter tint could be seen through the darkness. This was the white blouses, loaded down with their knapsacks and tents. Cannons were moving along almost without noise, leaving deep wheel-tracks in the light, dusty soil of the road. In places, where the wells had been destroyed and there were no trees, a few indistinct outlines and profiles could be distinguished against the sky, interspersed here and there with other forms and shapes — the barrels of guns, with bayonets fixed, carried at various angles. Occasionally the rugged folds of company guidons would loom up, or the shaggy knob of a gunner's sponge. Horsemen appeared like silhouettes cut from black paper, only to disappear and to be swallowed up in the solid mass of darkness. All these were moving along quietly, but uninterruptedly — there was no talking and no singing, the usual accompaniments of ordinary marches.

They went along groping their way, cautiously moving ahead. It was very dark everywhere, but the gloom was increased by the dense clouds of dust rising from under the feet of the infantrymen and the wheels of the cannons. It became impossible to see anything. They began to stumble against each other — the man in rear would run into the man in front; and oftener and oftener could be heard the metallic click of weapons clashing together, and warning cries, "Easy there; don't hurry so! What are you doing in front there! Carefully!"

Like small signal-fires shone here and there, higher or lower, the red glimmer of the soldier's pipe or the officer's cigarette. By these bright sparks the movement of the whole dark mass could be observed; they were evidently moving ahead, though to the casual observer it must have appeared at the first glance as if this whole chaos, though it surged, and rustled, and gave forth other more indistinct sounds, was not advancing at all, but merely tramping and stamping in one and the same spot forever.

When inclined to sleep and struggling against irresistible drowsiness, the horseman may assume various attitudes — more or less comfortable — in his saddle which will enable him to yield temporarily and trust to his horse's sagacity. When the infantryman wishes to doze he must do so walking, and he does it, waking occasionally and glancing about stupidly without, for the first moment, recognizing his surroundings or knowing who he is or where he is going. A night march, especially in the summer, when the whole atmosphere is filled with dense clouds of suffocating dust, impeding respiration, is a wearisome toil. Each verst traveled under such conditions is at least equal to five made under more favorable circumstances. As the soldiers express it graphically: "You march and march, and wonder how many versts you are making. Then comes the sun, and you see that you have advanced only two versts from your starting-point." The soldiers do not like — they very much dislike — night marches.

From the rear came the thunder of some large force approaching, and now catching up with the infantry. Precautionary words of command were heard, "To the right and left — give way! Step aside; clear the road!" But how? To the right and left are high walls, and where the walls are not, there you find deep ditches, with water glistening in the bottom, and the foot sinks deeply into the yielding mud. Somehow the infantrymen squeezed themselves against the walls, leaving a narrow space in the middle of the road, and along this space a mass of horsemen was now advancing. Horses snorted and neighed, sabers rattled in their metallic scabbards; a few figures rose in their stirrups, and hurried exclamations were exchanged in loud whispers.

"Good luck to the infantry! What battalion is this?" In answer there came from the several ranks, in a muffled roar, "We wish you good health, your Excellency!"

The commander-in-chief and his suite passed by. Looming up high into the air above the columns waved the general's flag, and the infantry closed in behind them, once more a solid mass, and again began to move.

But something is coming up in their rear; the earth fairly trembles with the stamping of numberless hoofs. Again the order, "To the right and left — give way!"

This was the cavalry force, which had marched some time after the infantry, and had received orders to catch up with them and take the head of the column.

Thicker and thicker rose the dust — adjoining files could no longer see each other; a suffocating cough seemed to rend the lungs of the tortured men; the teeth, covered with grit, were grating against each other, and all throats were drying up.

" The devil may take these Cossacks! "

" Be still, you flat-foot — make room; that's it! "

" Easy, you devil; your horse stepped on my foot, and now you knock against my eye! Don't you see? "

" May the wolves eat you! Are there many more of you? "

" Don't get mad, towney; what are you growling about? Why don't you go on? After us there are three more companies."

" Oh, for a drop of water to moisten the throat! Eh, Mitka, is there not a drop left in your canteen? "

" Here, take it ; there is just a little."

" Go on, Cossacks, go on! Why do you stop? "

" Close up your ranks! "

The Cossacks were past. The dust began to settle a little. Far away, just above the horizon, a faint streak of light appeared, the precursor of dawn. The endless confining walls began to disappear and the road became wider. A fresh breeze sprang up and a grateful moisture arose from some lake or pond to their right. The birds, awakening from their brief slumber, glanced timidly at the moving masses. A flock of sparrows rose noisily from the tops of wide-branching plantains, a stork was chattering upon his uncouth nest; somewhere in the distance the native dogs were howling.

" Halt! " came the long-expected and wished-for command. "Prepare to take breath, boys, until the rear of the column comes up!"

Joy and satisfaction again filled the hearts of the soldiers; all the tortures and miseries of the night march were forgotten.

CHAPTER XLIV.

AND WHAT IF——?

SERGEÏ NIKOLAÏEVITCH ROVITCH was on the staff, and at this moment found himself a member of the general's suite, being among those horsemen who had overtaken the infantry. Though ill, with a nervous system very much shattered, he had himself requested to be ordered on this march, in the hope of forgetting as far as possible, among the vivid and constantly changing impressions of a campaign, the anguish and remorse that weighed upon his brain and heart and pervaded his whole being ever since that moment when fate brought him in contact with some one who by a casual remark recalled to his mind a chain of memories which under ordinary conditions he would have reviewed with the self-complacent smile of a roué boasting of a successful intrigue.

But now, much to his own surprise, these very reminiscences created in him the most profound, unbearable remorse and self-reproach, and served as a grim prompter, pursuing him every minute of the day and robbing him of his sleep, completely transforming his usually careless, joyous, and self-contented disposition.

"If you are ill," the general had said to him the previous day, glancing at his pale, haggard face, "you may
stay behind."

"I thank you, your Excellency!" replied Rovitch, and
at once prepared for the march.

The universal question of "And what if —" was also
present in Sergeï Nikolaïevitch's mind, but in his case
it served to electrify his whole nature, to rouse his
energy and restore his strength, which had begun
to suffer from sleepless nights and the morbid concen-
tration of his thoughts upon one fatal subject. A certain feeling of loathing of himself grew in him with
every minute, which he fanned and strengthened as if
he found in it some consolation and relief for his moral
sufferings.

"And what if —" He resumed his mental review of
a whole chain of contingencies. Since fate had carried
him here and brought him into contact with people
whom he had forgotten long ago, though formerly they
were quite familiar to him, was it not plausible that
the very catastrophe which had overwhelmed Natalia
Martinovna was intended by fate to bring about this
moral shock, this radical revolution in his sentiments?
If fate should have reserved for him that once dear,
but neglected and disgraced being — what then? Ah!
then he would throw himself upon his knees before
her; he would describe to her all the torments he had
undergone, he would beg for her forgiveness, and she
— good-hearted and loving — would lift his heavy burden and extend to him her hand.

With what mingled rapture and contrition he would
bend over that hand and cover it with untold kisses;
how fervently would he press to his heart that other
being so well known to him! My God! if that were

really to happen! His head began to turn around; he seized the pommel of his saddle with his hand to keep from falling. This occurred just as they were passing through the open ranks of the infantry. "To the right and left—give way!" resounded Pugovitzin's rough voice almost into Rovitch's ear.

Sergeï Nikolaïevitch recognized the voice. He turned pale, and instinctively tried to hide himself. He shrank from observation and possible recognition. He did not consider how difficult it was in that chaos of dust and darkness to recognize anybody. He passed by Pugovitzin as a criminal yet undiscovered passes by a judge, imagining that he is bending upon him an ominous look—the look which precedes the still more ominous words, "Stand up, man! At last you are in the power of the law!" and Sergeï Nikolaïevitch felt provoked and angry at the streak of dawn along the horizon. He feared the sun, which prevented him from hiding, from remaining unnoticed and unnamed. Such a mental condition might result in insanity.

CHAPTER XLV.

AN UNEXPECTED AND UNDESIRED MOVE.

THE communities of the Yomud Turkomans were thoroughly alarmed. Couriers, runners, and messengers from Khiva were chasing and overtaking each other. It was impossible to analyze their hurried and conflicting reports, but one ominous sound, one warning cry was echoed by them all, "Save himself who may!"

17

One of them said, " Our people have resolved not to
submit to the Russians; why should we pay them?
Because they have beaten us, and have come to our
country and act as if they were masters?"

" The Russian general is very angry," said another.
" They are getting ready to come after us."

" Ah! I am sorry we did not succeed in harvesting
our grain. We would show them, the infidel dogs!
what it means to thrust their noses into a strange hut!
We would show them, and Allah would help us!"

" They are already on the march!" shouted another
courier. " They are coming! In two days they will be
here. Our people are gathering at Takir — mounted
men and infantry. Why are you sitting here? Move
on! Ismet gave orders to call you all."

The decision of the elders was: " Load everything
on carts, drive your cattle together in herds, and move
on farther. Let the dogs find an empty place. Let
them burn the dry dung and the cinders that we leave
behind."

" They want to capture our women and keep them as
hostages!" was the opinion of many; and they hastened,
above all, to conceal their families, to wander with them
into the very heart of the steppes, though it were far
beyond the cultivated area and in the sandy desert.
" They'll not find us there, the white blouses!"

" They are coming; they are quite near!" was
shouted by alarmed voices. " They will soon overtake us!"

" No; they are yet far. They have not passed Ulkun
Arik yet — that is not very near, and they can not be
here very soon," came from other more reassuring
messengers.

Soon after the first shouts of warning the turmoil

among the pastoral and agricultural communities became terrible. The people were crowding together, running to and fro, not knowing where and how to begin this sudden and unexpected packing up and carrying away of their portable huts and household goods.

Later reports restored quiet to a certain extent, and gave the elders an opportunity to consider the route to be taken in their retreat, and to start off their trains in the most convenient and promising direction. They had to abandon a fruitful settled region, abounding in water, and go into the sandy desert. This made it imperative to provide all necessaries, not only for themselves, but also for their cattle, otherwise they would fly into the desert from their dreaded enemy — the white blouses — only to find themselves confronted by other enemies no less terrible, hunger and thirst.

In the meantime the Russians were marching, always marching, without stopping or giving the Turkomans time to organize, and spreading panic and consternation before them.

Thus far the white blouses had not seen a single enemy; not a single one of the rifle-barrels cleaned so carefully in Khiva had been blackened anew by the discharge of a shot, not a cannon had been unlimbered; but among the tribes of the Yomud Turkomans, the Chodor and Solor, the people spoke of hearing distant reports of cannons; they heard them plainly, and the firing must be near, perhaps only just beyond that jagged range of sand-hills. All these sounds existed only in the disordered imagination of these nomads, who had completely lost their heads over the occurrence of the unexpected invasion, which, however, they could have easily foreseen after sending to the Russian general their peremptory refusal to submit to the new ordeɪ of things.

A large Yomud tribe settled near Zmukshir was also preparing to move, having been alarmed by these reports.   It was a very wealthy tribe, numbering over two hundred huts — all standing wide apart from each other and covering a large space.   Zmukshir was a favorite wintering-place of the Turkomans, to judge from the permanent improvements made — their large court-yards surrounded by mud walls, vast sheds, and even a few houses.   There was also a permanent bazaar, to which the people of the neighborhood resorted twice a week, bringing their produce and driving up their cattle to exchange them for wares brought by merchants from Khiva.

The settlement was encircled by bright-green fields, laid out in rectangular sections, and presenting a pleasing picture, breathing peace and plenty.   Between the fields meandered countless irrigating ditches, like silvery arteries, covering the cultivated lands with a perfect network.   Here and there sparkled square ponds, or reservoirs, their banks planted with trees.   The wheat was ripening, and exhibited a rich golden tint as it swayed gently before the breeze.   The black roofs of the huts, resembling the tops of mushrooms, loomed up among the fields; columns of smoke from kitchen-fires were rising everywhere — all was life and animation.   Herds of horned cattle and sheep were grazing in the immediate vicinity, surrounding the whole settlement with a living circle; and now all this had to be removed at once.

They took down the huts, loading the separate pieces upon carts; upon others they placed bundles of provisions and clothing, chests, rolls of carpets, and mats. They even hastily cut the yet immature wheat to keep it from falling into the hands of the "giaours."

The women were busy about the carts and the dismemberment of the huts; the men were driving up the cattle, or simply galloping about the settlement to hurry and drive the women, who were already losing their heads in the general bustle and flurry.

Not many men were left with the tribe; they ordinarily counted three hundred mounted men, but at the present moment they could scarcely collect thirty, all told. The remainder had gone to the rallying-points under the banners of Ismet, Irtik-Mergen, and other chiefs who had not yet given up their hopes of arresting the Russians in their progress, and of making them feel their strength, with the help of Allah, and thus extinguish for a long time to come all desire to invade their rich fields and pastures, heretofore considered beyond the reach of any enemy.

About fifteen carts, not yet hitched up, but ready for the road, were standing in several rows upon a small well-trampled space in front of a detached group of huts. The felt roofs had already been removed from some of the latter, and the bare concentric rafters resembled a huge bird-cage constructed of red poles. The women, in white turbans or with colored kerchiefs tied about their heads, were hard at work rolling the felt covering of the huts into cylindrical shape; others were collecting one by one the pegs and spikes and tying them into bundles, while others again were carrying to the carts large iron-bound chests, painted in bright colors, chiefly red and gold. All this was deposited there to be packed into the vehicles in a more systematic and orderly manner.

Domestic fowls—hens with their broods of chicks, tame pheasants, and guinea-hens—were noisily running about between the bundles and carts, getting under the feet of the bustling people. Emaciated greyhounds whined pitifully while looking at all this excitement. Half-naked children gathered in groups, gazing with wide-open, astonished eyes at what was going on before them, unable to understand the meaning of this strange, untimely move made by their fathers and mothers. Here and there, in the glaring sun, could be seen cradles for infants, and in these cradles were squirming and feeding dusky little bodies, with their small arms and legs entangled in wraps and rags. Several of them had succeeded in making their escape from their cradles, and, unnoticed by their toiling mothers, were groveling in the dust and digging into the piles of half-dried dung.

Another rider came up, the flanks of his horse white with foam, and shouting at the top of his voice, "Hurry, hurry! Aren't you ready yet?" He struck his horse with the whip and galloped on straight ahead, over bales and across ditches, not going out of his way to warn others. This cry caused everybody to work with redoubled haste and feverish activity. The loads on the carts rose higher and higher until they loomed up like small hills above the great wooden wheels. They began to lash them down with ropes. It was only necessary to drive up the horses and oxen to drag away all this property piled up for removal. Some of the carts had been provided with covers of cotton cloth, stretched over uprights; these vehicles were intended for the families—the wives and children; they were passenger-carts. A majority of the women, however, saddled horses for themselves and mounted them, sometimes two together, one in the saddle, the other on the horse's croup, holding onto the girdle of the woman in front.

More horsemen came galloping up. "What is the matter with you, you lazy cows? Are you coming soon? You must be off before the sun sets, and keep on all night so as to get well away!"

"Look out! They may catch you to-morrow morning; they are quite near. They have already captured the Budaï tribe; they cut them off from the road. Hurry, hurry!"

The oxen and horses were speedily driven up to the carts; clouds of dust arose over the settlement, stirred up by the feet of the animals. The confusion increased. The oxen were all small and low, but muscular and strong; each of them bore a saddle with a great wooden horn in front; on their necks were felt collars; the harness was of rope with wooden fastenings. The well-trained animals stood quietly among all this hubbub; the horses were snorting, stamping, and biting at each other whenever they came within reach; the oxen bellowed at times, and sniffed with their nostrils, cruelly torn by the iron rings or rough ropes fastened into them. For some of the vehicles there were not cattle enough.

"Well, those will have to be left." Another horseman came racing. "Not ready yet? Throw away everything!" But it was a pity to throw such things away. It seemed as if fate had willed it that the carts still left contained all that was most dear and precious to the owners — clothing and metallic utensils. Then was begun a hurried repacking. Bales were unlashed; cups and flasks and teakettles fell jingling and rattling to the ground; cloaks and shining silk trousers were ruthlessly trampled into the dust and dirt. The women were enraged over this waste, and reproachful and angry cries were heard.

One woman only in the whole community listened with calm apathy to all this uproar. She sat upon the ground like a statue; her hands were unconsciously stroking the hair of a child that was clinging to her.

"Why are you sitting there with idle hands?" an old Turkoman hag shouted into her ear. "Here, carry this!" throwing her a bag and hastening on farther herself, scolding, and threatening to beat somebody. The woman rose to her feet and seized the bag. It was too heavy; she could not lift it. She dragged it along — she did not know where. The child put up his little arms to help; he did not cry, but looked quite serious, as if he knew that this was no time for tears. The eyes of this boy did not resemble those of the other children — they were large and blue; and the hair on his head was fair, not black and closely cropped. His mother also had bright strands of hair hanging over her shoulders, entirely uncovered; but they concealed the rents in her garment, which was torn and worn and of indistinguishable hue.

"Bring it here, you Russian slut!" cried from the cart a stout, ruddy Turkoman woman with her arms set akimbo. Her turban had slipped to one side, and her braids, wound with beads, were fluttering in the wind; her face was covered with a paste of dust and perspiration.

"Not there! Here!" cried another, tall and well-shaped, rattling with bracelets and innumerable coins and trinkets sewed all over the bosom and border of her upper garment.

"Stand aside, or I run over you!" shouted a third,

laughing, and curveting upon a piebald stallion loaded from tail to ears with cloths and carpets.

" Where then? " muttered the poor woman.

" I'll show you! " some one snarled behind her, dealing her a heavy blow with the end of a rope.

" Do not bother with her," advised a very young girl, not yet fourteen, who was seated under the cover of one of the carts. "Leave her; she may stay here. The Russians will not hurt her; she is one of them. Leave her! "

"Yes—leave her—that would be well, indeed!" grumbled the old woman. " Ibrahim would probably ask me for her, and beat me on her account. Get up here on this cart, quick — take your brat —sit here!"

The sun was already very perceptibly declining toward the horizon, but the train was not yet under way. A few carts were strung out along the road, waiting for the others, when another cloud of dust arose in the distance. Horsemen came galloping by, repeating as they passed the old cry:

"Hurry! they are near now! Throw away all, and get on!"

It was already dark when the last cart filed into the road and hastened to catch up with the rear end of the train just disappearing over the nearest hill.

CHAPTER XLVI.

ENEMIES.

Sergeï Nikolaïvitch Rovitch had not known Golovin during his former sojourn in Central Asia. On the

present occasion he had easily guessed from the conversations in the officers' circles what were the feelings
of the lame Cossack for Natalia Martinovna, and that
knowledge was enough to arouse in Rovitch a strong
dislike of his rival. The dislike grew all the stronger
when he learned from the remarks and conversations
to which he so eagerly listened that Natalia, at least
partially, shared Golovin's feelings. The mere thought
of this goaded him to desperation. Thus far, however,
he had avoided all meetings with his rival — avoided
them very carefully, guarding against any accident
which might bring them together.

Sergeï Nikolaïevitch even held aloof from his old
Chiniaz acquaintances, and ever since the various expeditions formed a junction under the walls of Khiva,
when he had heard of their presence he had declined
all invitations to meet any of them or to enter into conversation about them.

Feeling instinctively how the part he had played
appeared in their eyes, and how these old friends of
Natalia Martinovna must look upon him, he brought
himself to hate and despise them with all the strength
of his evil mind. Even in the very midst of his ardent
dreams and silent vows of proposed self-humiliation, he
always cherished one idea which caused an ugly sneer
to wreathe his lips: "What a joke it will be if all
these friends and admirers, the lame Cossack included,
come out of this as losers; and what faces they will
make when I, Sergeï Nikolaïevitch Rovitch, shall own
their precious treasure, their 'holy angel'! I shall
probably not get out of this without a duel," he thought
at such times; and this after consideration threw some
ashes upon the flame of his desires.

The trifling character of Sergeï Nikolaïevitch displayed itself in all these musings. His superficial nature could not imagine or understand that if in one of his spells of self-accusation and humiliation he had openly revealed himself to this circle of Natalia Martinovna's friends, if he had confessed himself to be such as he saw himself in his remorseful, sleepless nights, he would probably have extinguished at once all jealousy in their hearts; and if they, on the other hand, should have observed a revival of Natalia's fondness for the father of her child, they would have been the first to extend to him a friendly, helping hand. But this natural, straightforward solution of the difficulty was not within the power of Sergeï Nikolaïevitch.

In the position assumed by the lame Cossack toward Rovitch there was nothing strained, nothing undecided. It had been clearly defined long since, before even Golovin laid eyes upon Sergeï Nikolaïevitch; but his feeling toward him grew in intensity the minute he was pointed out to him across a long table on the occasion of a breakfast at the general's headquarters.

"I do not want to be within a hundred paces of him," he had remarked to his neighbor, who had informed him of Rovitch's presence at the other end of the table. "My hand is itching to get hold of the beast!" And he had exchanged seats with another officer, so as to enable him to turn his back toward Rovitch and not look at that "beast."

After this breakfast, however, Golovin had never knowingly avoided any opportunity of meeting his enemy. On the contrary, he had sought him; and often, on perceiving Rovitch walking in the distance, he had gone out of his way and hastened his steps to come face to face with him, to look straight into his eyes (not impudently, however), thereby forcing the other to turn aside to avoid an unfriendly altercation.

The conflict, however, was sure to occur sooner or later — it seemed inevitable.

CHAPTER XLVII.

OVERTAKEN.

A LARGE detachment of cavalry, consisting of several "sotnias" of Cossacks, and extending over a distance of nearly two versts, was making its way through a part of the Yomud lands crossed and cut up everywhere by irrigating ditches. They did not know the road they were following; the whole region was new and strange to them — it was only just being explored, or, we might say, discovered. Some were moving ahead quite rapidly, others branched off to the right and left as if seeking for a better road, while others again halted at times as if in doubt, and then hurried on at increased speed when their doubts had been solved; hurrying as if it were of the utmost importance to make up for the time lost in their brief halt.

The detachment had guides, but these guides, whether intentionally or not, proved very poor leaders of a column; it would have been much better for the expedition if they had been without them. The guides only caused the loss of time by consultations, during which they made the most absurd and contradictory statements, though they were mostly natives belonging to the region through which the detachment was moving at this time.

This whole strong detachment, though moving rapidly enough to tire both horses and men, was evidently groping and feeling its way. This was no ordinary march from one well-known point to another, else there would have been no such frequent breaking into a trot, or even a gallop. Besides, the members of the expedition were acting in an unusual, independent manner which would not have been permitted on ordinary marches, when all proceed in a dreamy, half-dozing manner, moving in accordance with established rules and regulations, when the roads are all alike and the end in view always the same — to reach the camp selected for the night Here, on the contrary, all the horsemen were carefully and cautiously looking to either side, but chiefly ahead, as if searching for something along the wavy horizon, broken here and there by groups of trees and patches of brush ; their whole attention was fixed in that direction.

It was a pursuit, but a pursuit under very unfavorable circumstances, without any knowledge of the locality, of the roads, without proper guides, and beset with obstacles causing loss of time.

The pursued, on the other hand, were in a very different position. They knew the country well — they were settled there. They could move on without stopping for a certain well-known distance, and they could obstruct the road and make it impassable for the pursuer; but, for all that, the pursued were informed from time to time that the danger was approaching, and that their foes had already gained more than a day's march upon them — and a day's march means a great deal on such occasions.

But, in the words of one of the Turkoman Mullahs who subsequently described this flight, " Allah was

incensed against his true believers; he closed their eyes
and ears and enveloped their minds in fog. He sowed
among them confusion and fear, while he cleared the
eyes of the unbelieving enemy, gave them strength of
legs, speed, and power — and everything was lost by
the will of Allah, as an example to all, and to proclaim
his will in the future."   The will of Allah is certainly
enough to explain a total reversal of existing affairs by
means such as could not be available in the natural
course of events.

This was a force which had been detached from the
main body of the army that was marching for the purpose of punishing the unruly Turkomans.   The object
of the movement was to penetrate into the heart of
their pastoral and agricultural lands, to flank them
and surround them, cutting them off from farther
flight.

At the first glance this detachment appeared to have
but little in common with regular troops — there was
such a jumble of types and costumes; and the very
character of their movements reminded one of something Asiatic — half-savage.   The Cossacks went along
at a gallop, now going in single file, one after the other,
over narrow, barely perceptible paths, and then again
gathering in groups when those in advance halted to
look about or to remove some obstacle in the road.
Cannons would have been out of place in such a movement, and therefore none were to be seen.   In their
stead each company had a group of men carrying over
their shoulders, in place of their carbines, long poles
with round knobs at the end — this was the rocket
detachment, with their noisy and thereby effective
weapons, which are in reality as harmless as they are
expensive.

Here and there the colored guidons of the various "sotnias" and the personal flags of commanders fluttered in the breeze. Nearly every company was marching separately, exploring and selecting its own road. At a certain point a group of Orenburg Cossacks had assembled, in their loose gray homespun blouses and yellow leather trousers; they dismounted to remove with their hands a barricade constructed of broken carts and of trunks of trees felled across the road. In another place some Siberian Cossacks, in their ungainly shaggy caps with red cloth tops, were describing a long circuit in order to avoid a rice-patch which had been purposely flooded to convert it into an impassable swamp. There, again, some Caucasian Cossacks, in helmets, were jumping like goats across an irrigating ditch on their slender-legged mountain horses. Native mounted militiamen, in bright-colored cloaks and Turkoman caps and turbans, on untrained horses covered with cloths, were galloping to and fro, mingling with the Cossacks, shouting and talking in their own language, enlivening the scene and adding much to its wild, Asiatic character. One of the "sotnias" which had been detained for some time by an obstruction in the road, finally gave it up, turned aside, and, happening upon a practicable path, gave loose rein to their horses, to catch up, at a full gallop, with the others and to make up for loss of time. Dense clouds of dust were rising from under their horses' feet, hiding the company entirely from sight; only the soiled, torn square of the guidon could be seen fluttering above. A patch of liquid mire lay in their course, the horses sinking to their bellies, and all from head to foot being covered with mud. The tails and manes of the horses were clogged with it and the clothes of the riders bespattered, the men saving their guns and cartridges only by lifting them up. At last they reached solid ground again, and the burning sun immediately dried the mud, restoring the rider almost to his previous condition, until they should meet with another bath or submersion in dust or mud, the common incidents of a forced march in pursuit.

Energy must at last adjust itself to physical powers, and these powers were weakening. Both horses and riders began to feel the effect of overexertion. The horses' sunken sides were heaving; they were snorting and sniffing with their red, inflamed nostrils. They had been in motion for nearly ten hours — since daylight, and now it was nearly evening. They had covered a great distance, but how much there was still to be made was not known. Possibly a day, or two days, perhaps only an hour, might end the chase — not more. Who knew what lay there before them? It might be only just beyond that undulating line that they would see what they had been pursuing so long.

The shrill sound of a bugle came from the direction in which could be seen a large red flag with diagonal white stripes. It was an unwelcome, and even unexpected sound, though nearly every one had been unwillingly listening for it long ago. The signal was, " Halt! ' followed by, " Close up on the leading company! " It was necessary to rest, to breathe, or the horses might be permanently injured. The "closing-up" movement began; the companies in rear were gradually approaching those in advance. A few companies who had drawn ahead of the leading command turned back slowly and reluctantly, and a vast irregular bivouac was formed, as irregular and unconventional in all its arrangements as the march had been. Fires were lighted, from which rose huge columns of black smoke.

Tea was being made and meat roasted upon the coals. By good luck a few exhausted calves and sheep had been found on the road. The horses stood still in their places, hanging their heads from weariness—a few were rolling on the ground. In the dirty ditches the men bathed and washed, taking the same water for cooking and drinking. In places extemporized shelters and tents were even put up as a protection against the burning rays of the sun. Wherever there was a solitary tree or a clump of bushes giving shade, there crowds gathered; and noisy and animated conversation was carried on by the men—some grumbling and scolding, some happy and full of irrepressible and irresistible vigor.

It was not purposed to stop long; two hours at the most would give the hardy, strong horses of the steppe time to recuperate sufficiently to enable them to set out again upon another "heat" of the forced march.

An exchange of news and suppositions was going on on all sides. Everything was listened to eagerly, with feverish anxiety and impatience. The news was so abundant that one piece of it overtook another, the last exceeding all former in absurdity.

"Now we are close to them," explained one man with some heat; "that is plainly to be seen. But why, in the devil's name, are we stopping? We might just as well rest later on. Ah, it's too bad!"

"How do you know they are near? If you founder your horse, everything has to stop; that has happened before."

"If we had only gone on for half an hour, to those trees—see!—where the plantains are looming up."

"I am sorry Golovin is not with us," was the complaint in another group. "He is an expert in finding

18

out things ahead of the column. Do you believe me?
Once some one told him he thought the enemy was
only a little ahead. ' Be easy,' he said; 'in an hour
and three quarters we'll be up with them.' And, true
as fate, in just one hour and three quarters we had
them. We saw that with our own eyes. He is a knowing one! He follows them up, and catches them!"

" He has the devil's own scent. I know him — something like a hound. You remember when we went to
Ukhum, after the attack on Djusak?"

" Didn't he march with us? I thought I saw him —"

" No; he is laid up. He is very weak and poorly.
Ah, he was such a tough fellow once."

"Gentlemen, some Cossacks have found a fallen
horse from a cart. They were taking off its collar
when they found the neck still warm — it did not have
time to cool. It is evident they are near," said a Cossack as he was hurrying by.

"Well, now; do you see? I told you they were quite
near. Now it is clear!"

"Some of the advance have just come back. They
found hot cinders — the fire had been put out, but the
ashes did not have time to cool. They also found
a kettle, and brought it back with them."

" Now what are we dawdling here for? The colonel
ought to be told. Does he know it yet?"

" They have gone to report."

" See there! the Siberians are mounting. There goes
the bugle!"

" To horse! Blow, bugler; sound the advance!"

The latest news of the horse's neck still warm and
the glowing cinders somewhat shortened the time
intended for rest. The companies mounted again and
began to string out.

The country was still very much broken and difficult to travel over. Narrow paths meandered here and there, sometimes between walls of mud, and then again between deep ditches or through thickets of brush, and these paths seemed to cross each other and change direction every few steps, often apparently leading back to the rear. Such surprises were met with every few minutes. To the right and left, among fields planted with wheat and rice, there were traces of huts only just taken down. These round spots, well tramped down, with a pile of ashes in the center, were striking objects upon the surface of the landscape. They were carefully examined, in the hope of finding in them some indications.

And now they found fresh cart-tracks. The heavy wheels had been dragged through the yielding soil, leaving deep furrows. There they had crossed a ditch, and were stalled; they got out again with difficulty, as shown by the number of tracks of oxen and naked feet about the spot. Fowls began to start up from under the Cossacks' horses, but no attention was paid to them; that kind of booty was too insignificant when compared with what must be ahead. Now a cart comes in sight! The horses had been unharnessed and taken away, but the cart remained, with all its load, standing there alone in the road.

Men galloped up to it from all sides; they looked at it, felt it, smelled it. "What have you found?" "The devil knows what! I can never wash off the smell. There, boys; I see cattle grazing over there — they are driving them. Cut them off, quick!"

Far away, on one side of the road, there really could be seen some moving dots on the fields. Perhaps they were cattle, perhaps something else. The Cossacks asserted that they saw cows, and men driving them off somewhere.

"No, brother; you lie! Those are ours — some of the Orenburg fellows."

Again they came across a cart, and then another; then they saw three together, one of them lying on its side with a broken wheel — and there were the people!

Beside one of the carts there stood a large willow basket, and from it protruded two heads of young goats and one of a human being. The latter belonged to a boy not more than a year old. The black eyes looked full of apprehension at the strange men galloping around the carts — the little mouth half-open and the small hands clinging desperately to the rim of the basket, as if this diminutive son of the steppe were afraid that they would pull him out of his refuge.

Now they must be near if they were in such hurry as to forget their little ones. There were some huts not yet taken down; they had not time to take them away. One remained without its felt covering, the other had been stripped. The people were still rushing about, trying to take them down — too late! There, they were running.

Interpreters were now sent out to tell the people, "Whoever remains at home will be left undisturbed; only those are punished who run away or offer resistance!" But the flying crowd do not understand — perhaps they do not listen to these reassuring phrases. The women gathered in crowds, sat down and covered their faces. Some of the men threw themselves down, pretending to have been killed; one fired straight at a Cossack who was pursuing him, dropped him from his saddle, and spurred on his own faltering beast, trying to escape — vain attempt!

Shots were now heard farther ahead. " The rocket corps to the front!" Two wounded officers were being carried back. Some Caucasians were retreating before a stronger body of natives. " To the rescue, boys!"

There seemed to be much promiscuous fighting, but nothing definite could be made out for some time. Ahead of them, beyond those hills, was strung out an apparently endless chain of carts upon carts. Cattle and horses were being driven along, while mounted men circled about them, keeping up a desultory fire. A few rallied in groups, endeavoring to beat back the onslaught of the Cossacks; the others seemed to have but a single thought — to fly, to save themselves.

They were surrounded at last, and were being driven together. The road to the steppe — their only salvation — was cut off and closed to them. Flight was no longer possible.

Orders were issued at once, " For the least disorder the culprit will be shot like a dog. Women and children must not be touched with a finger."

" Gentlemen," said the commander of the expedition, somewhat excitedly, to his officers, "we must bring order into this chaos." And he passed on, followed by his staff, by his red and white standard, and by a motley crowd of native militiamen, staff-buglers, and others.

The sun was about to sink beyond the horizon in a crimson haze, and darkness was coming on. All tried to make use of the last rays of light to bring some system and order into this noisy turmoil. At night that would be impossible. The horses were unhitched from the carts and led aside. With the vehicles a compact square was formed, the unhappy inmates of which submitted to the will of Allah, but still carefully watched their property. The whole was surrounded by a chain of sentries, the Cossacks extending their bivouacs in a circle around the entire train.

The horses were not unsaddled all night; nobody slept; all were on the alert and ready for battle. For who knew but that fresh masses of the enemy might at any moment make their appearance from beyond those sand-hills in front, coming to the rescue of their wives, children, and property?

On the horizon, to the right and left, there blazed up suspicious-looking red reflections as if from conflagrations. Flames could be seen shooting up, and black clouds of smoke arose into the darkening sky. Was the steppe on fire? No; those were the fields and the ricks of the Turkomans, which they had ignited, in their blind fear and rage, destroying in a few hours the winter's store, upon which depended the lives of these now sorely punished nomads.

CHAPTER XLVIII.

FOUND.

SERGEÏ NIKOLAÏEVITCH ROVITCH was with this detachment. One may easily imagine the feverish condition in which he had passed this day. He was tortured by impatience and doubt. Would they catch up with them, or not? If they came up with them, would he find there what he was searching for, or not? Would he come upon some trace of Natalia Martinovna, or would he still be left in this unbearable state of uncertainty?

He was now galloping about the train looking into

the vehicles, listening, trying to question the prisoners, but all in vain. They would not answer — he could not get a word in reply to all his inquiries. How could they answer, these unfortunate women and children whom fear had robbed of their senses? The train was very large — several thousand carts; all the space in sight was filled with them. To count them and inspect them a whole day, at least, was needed, and here was the cursed night, with its darkness, precluding all possibility of farther research. There was nothing left but to submit to necessity and wait.

What a dreary wait! But if she was not here — if she was with some other train which succeeded in escaping — what then? This idea came into his head unbidden, and greatly increased Sergeï Nikolaïevitch's sufferings.

He was by no means the only one in a similar condition. All the officers of the commands hailing from Tashkent experienced almost the same feelings, though perhaps not in the same degree. The officers of the Caucasian expedition, who had never known Natalia Martinovna, but had heard of her, also were ready to take an active part in the search, but they went at it more calmly. In the heads of the former still another idea had taken root: " If she should be no longer among the living? " But this unwelcome thought was speedily put away by every one, without permitting a word or even a hint of it to escape through his lips. "That would be altogether unjust!" they considered. Unjust on whose part? Nobody cared to go into such details. It only seemed to every one that this affair could not, must not, end in so sad a manner.

The square of carts was surrounded by a chain of sentries, who were strictly forbidden to admit any one

to the interior, with the exception of officers. Sergeï
Nikolaïevitch was wandering about on foot, looking
into the nearest carts, at the dark figures sitting motionless in them and under them — he was waiting for
the dawn.

"If she were here," said some one not far from Rovitch, "she would have come out herself. She has not
weaned herself completely from the Russians — she
would not hide herself from us; she would have come
out long ago."

"But," replied another voice, "if she should be lying
ill and could not stir? No, brother; we shall have to
search."

Sergeï Nikolaïevitch looked around and observed two
other officers, who had evidently come for the same
purpose he had in mind. He felt an absurd, insane
jealousy of these two dark shadows; he would have
been willing to annihilate them that very moment. "I
alone," he thought, "have the right to seek her, to wait
for her. What did they come here for? By what
right?" He was fully convinced of the logic and just-
ness of his own ideas on this subject.

"It is a pity there is no lantern," came from some
other voice, evidently a soldier's. "Now would be the
time to look from cart to cart — we might ask permission!"

"Don't think of it. You would probably have a knife
thrust into you that would finish you. Those Turkoman women are tough ones!"

Two others walked up, stood for a few minutes, and
then walked on along the line of sentries. "They
also," groaned Rovitch, biting at the fingers of his
gloves in his rage.

"Tokhta!" (halt) cried the nearest sentry, bringing

his carbine to a "ready." Rovitch trembled, and stared into the darkness — he could see nothing.

"What did you say?" he asked the sentry.

"Some one came up toward the line from over there, but she went away again. I do not see her now."

"Where, where?"

"Who is commander of this detachment?" came in a feeble voice not far from Sergeï Nikolaïevitch. It was the voice of a woman. She spoke Russian. Several dark figures rushed out to meet her. Rovitch's head was turning around, sparks were whirling before his eyes, his legs trembled under him, and he fell to the ground unconscious.

The woman, with a child in her arms, was surrounded in a second. A dozen hands were extended; they seized her, these hands, and lifted her up, and with a shout of triumph and a hoarse "hurrah!" they carried her to the nearest bivouac.

"Some fire — light a fire! we must have some light!" was the cry all around. "Hurrah!" The shout was carried all over the camp in endless repetition; hundreds heard it and took it up without knowing what it all was about, but all came running to the place where the shout originated.

Natalia Martinovna laughed and wept, her tears being again followed by smiles. She talked much, and rapidly, and the others talked to her all at once. Nobody could hear, and nobody wanted to hear — all were foolishly merry and happy. If anybody had been asked the following morning how it happened, what was said or done, nobody would have been in a condition to give a correct and truthful answer to these questions.

Sergeï Nikolaïevitch, regaining consciousness, quickly sprang to his feet and hurried away in the direction from which the shouts of triumph were coming. The bright light of a camp-fire illuminated Natalia Martinovna's figure with an almost blinding glare. She was still in the old torn Turkoman garment, partly exposing her body; she was seated upon a carpet, holding a large cup of tea in her trembling hands. Little Petka was passing from arm to arm, his musical, silvery laughter ringing through the air. The officers were crowding around. Some Cossacks were busy putting up a fantastic tent of carpets, blankets, and horse-cloths — whatever came to their hands.

Sergeï Nikolaïevitch looked upon all this and stood apart. He felt that he could not join them. For such a step he lacked resolution.

CHAPTER XLIX.

A VERY DISAGREEABLE AND DIFFICULT SITUATION.

Yes; there certainly could not exist a more provoking situation than that in which Sergeï Nikolaïevitch found himself ever since that night when the first part of his hopes, his most ardent desires — the finding of Natalia — had been fulfilled. Now that she was found, there remained only the second part to be realized. How easy appeared this second part formerly, and how difficult, almost impossible, it seemed now!

To go to her, to confess his fault, and to pray for her forgiveness, and finally to receive it — Sergeï Nikolaïevitch never had a doubt on that point; then to propose to her, humbling himself by getting down upon his knees; to ask for her hand, and to receive it — of that there could also be no doubt; to gain possession of her as his wife, and to become the lawful father of his child; and at the end of all that —

This phrase "at the end of all that" was especially attractive to Rovitch. In spite of the serious disturbance of his moral nature, and of his real heartache, which had even affected his health, this "at the end of all that" suggested an idea so seductive, so pleasing, that it called an involuntary smile to his lips, and sometimes even an audible laugh, between his teeth — a laugh in which there was a note of mocking joy and of self-satisfaction. What a trick he would play *them*, and *him* especially. When *they* had been giving up hope and pining away, he simply came, took and carried away, perhaps telling them, to console them for their loss, "*Pardon, messieurs; que faire!* You see, if it had not been the wish of Natalia Martinovna herself, I might perhaps — but you see for yourselves, gentlemen, and therefore I trust that our friendly relations will not be interrupted; and if it should ever happen that fate brings you to St. Petersburg, I shall be only too happy — and my wife also — to entertain you." And much more of this character would Sergeï Nikolaïevitch have told *them;* only it was necessary in the first place that the thing should happen, but to bring it about was so simple a matter, it was only necessary to make a beginning.

The matter now stood like this: Natalia had already passed a whole night and a morning in the camp; after that she had, of course, accompanied the detachment on its next march, which occupied another day and night and half of the following day, or altogether

nearly three days. During this time not only all the
officers of the detachment, but also nearly all the common soldiers, had succeeded in talking *to* her, if not
with her — all whom she had previously known, and
even many who had not known her; while he, as if it
had been managed on purpose, had never yet succeeded
in saying half a word to her, much less in summoning
the necessary resolution to get near enough to her for
a serious conversation. What was still worse, he had
not even greeted her yet, and must therefore appear as
the only man who felt no interest in her and kept aloof.
He always felt like turning away whenever it appeared
to him as if she were looking in his direction. Did she
know, he wondered, that he, Sergeï Nikolaïevitch, was
here? Evidently she must know it. It was impossible
that she should not have been informed of his presence.
But there were those confounded fellows. *They* would
always hang about her like a constant guard of honor.
How could one talk with her under such unfavorable
conditions? It was out of the question to think of the
stupidity of a public declaration. There was certainly
much between them which could only be discussed face
to face. It was to be hoped that she would think of
that; that she would recognize the anomaly and incon-
venience of his position, and understand it and feel for
him. He understood how burdensome and annoying
must be to her these uninvited and undesired pages in
her train — pages with unshaven chins, in red leather
trousers and dirty shirts! Why would they not keep
away, these ill-conditioned idiots!

Thus pondered Sergeï Nikolaïevitch, and in his anger
smoked cigar after cigar, and viciously drove his spurs
into the sides of his horse, which certainly was innocent of any fault in the matter.

"Well, the devil is in it!   But there must be an end
to it.   I must come to a decision, and that at once!
What is the use of letting the matter drag along or of
beating about the bush?   I might, for instance, simply
tell them, " Excuse me, gentlemen; it is necessary that
we should talk without witnesses."   Then they would
go away.   I'll do it!"

But nevertheless the sun had now set three times,
and had risen as often, and still Sergeï Nikolaïevitch
had failed to act up to his resolve, or to summon at the
proper moment his courage and energy, which hitherto
had never failed him.

In the meantime Natalia Martinovna, surrounded by
her old and new friends, was traveling along with every
comfort which could be procured for her under the circumstances.   They selected for her use the best cart —
and there were many to choose from.   The cart was
lined with a thick layer of carpet, and they erected over
it a high shady cover.   The kind Cossacks even
greased the axles of her vehicle with Koordistan butter
in order that the squeak of the wheels might not annoy
the passengers.   Two strong Cossack horses were har-
nessed to the cart, enabling her to travel rapidly, without delaying the movement of a detachment in light
marching order.   Happy and contented, Natalia sat
there with her son, the constant object of the greatest
care, the most delicate attentions, such as one would
never expect to originate with the uncouth, dusty
figures that surrounded her vehicle.   The pock-marked,
homely "sotnik" Podprugin invented some way of
tying up the sides of her cart-cover by which, as he
expressed it, "the sun would not burn, while the wind
would be free — blowing through just a little, you

know!" The "esaul" Masloboinikof, who for himself
had never refused the slimy, disgusting water from the
desert-wells, designed for the "little mother" a sort of
filter, constructed from a large gourd, in which the
muddy water from the irrigating ditches was filtered
during the march, and by camping-time was clear and
pellucid enough for the most fastidious tea-drinker.
The bald sotnik Mashkin, Kuzma Fedossovitch, and the
junior ensign Kolobkof took a ride of about five versts
away from the road, at the risk of their lives—for at a
distance from the column the people were hostile—and
returned with some fresh apricots, almost ripe, and a
few bunches of grapes, entirely green and unfit for
use.

"You can't eat them that way," kindly explained
Mashkin, "but if you were to put them in your tea
instead of lemons—if you please, I will mash you some
in a cup."

Ensign Kolobkof brought from the same raid a whole
basket of roses, packing them very tightly, as they had
to get back the best they could, at full speed. Well,
the roses were "just a little" squeezed, and compressed
into an almost solid mass.

"Ah! I am so sorry they are crushed a little," he
complained; "they do not look right, somehow, but
their perfume is excellent—it seems better now than
when we gathered them."

"They smell terribly of tar," said Natalia, laughing
heartily.

"That is nothing—that is from the basket. Those
good-for-nothings! I told them to give me a clean
basket. Never mind; that will soon pass away—the
wind will freshen them. See, there are some buds—
please look at them. Now, if you would put them in

water, they would open over night; they would, by
God! "

Little Petka honored the cart with his presence only
to sleep with his mother; during the whole march he
passed from hand to hand, from one saddle to another.
He was in his glory when his little hands got hold of
the thick, clumsy reins, which he seized with a very
serious expression, not very far from reverence. At
times, however, the laughing, merry eyes of the boy
assumed a wistful, not at all childlike expression. He
would carefully examine the features of the Cossacks
around him, and then look down and think — the little
fellow was searching for some other face that was not
present; a face that had somehow survived in his
memory. When, however, at such times one of his
companions would get up some new game or call his
attention to something in view, the boy would brighten
up at once, laugh heartily, and, passing again from saddle
to saddle, would forget for a time his childish memories.

Natalia Martinovna, also, in the first moments after
her appearance in the Russian camp, had cast a searching, inquisitive glance around. The glance was understood, and they answered it, hiding from her as much
as possible the serious nature of Golovin's illness, and
telling her that he was with another expedition. In a
short time, however, she learned all that had happened;
that was easily done, as the Cossack officers proved
themselves very poor diplomats in such an emergency.
They also talked to her openly of Sergeï Nikolaïevitch,
with all the freedom from restraint that characterizes
the etiquette of the steppes. They did not know
whether this news would be welcome to her or not.
They even pointed him out to her, and Natalia had
several glimpses of the dejected figure of the once

dashing officer, who always kept himself at a very respectful distance.

In spite of the pleasant circumstances of her journey, Natalia Martinovna began to grow more and more thoughtful. She was troubled about something, and this mood of hers did not long remain unnoticed. The simple Cossacks seemed to understand what was disturbing her, but they knew of no way of helping her but to send ahead to the camp a native messenger with a letter for Golovin, of which the subjoined is an exact copy:

"OUR BELOVED CHUM: We found the lady, and we are bringing her. It is all right; she is well, and her son also, thanks be to God. That you are sick grieves her, and therefore, brother, if you are still breathing, and your strength has not left you altogether, try to pick up quickly. Get on your horse and come out to meet us. But if she should find you still in bed — what God may prevent! — it will grieve her more; she is now fretting, though we, all of us, are trying to divert her, and sometimes succeed in our attempts. That 'Petersky' (St. Petersburgian) is going along with us, and is never far off; he looks sideways at us. Natalia Martinovna has seen him; we pointed him out to her, but it was nothing! To judge from her expressions on that subject we may suppose that she would 'spit at him' if the black-leg were to say a word. Little Petka, thank God, is well, and he is asking for you. He is a boy of the best kind — he'll make a smart Cossack. We write this unknown to Natalia Martinovna; that is why she sends you no message. We inform you of this to ease your mind.

"SOTNIK IVAN PODPRUGIN.
"ESAUL PAVEL MASLOBOINIKOF."

The native who was intrusted with this missive carefully concealed it in his tobacco-pouch, which in turn he thrust into his bosom; then he mounted his horse and galloped ahead over the well-known road. He received ten kokans (one dollar) on his departure, and was promised another ten if he reached the Russian camp the same day. Twenty kokans was quite a respectable sum — enough to induce the native to push his tall racer and not to spare the whip.

"I must come to some decision!" thought Sergeï Nikolaïevitch, and at last he actually decided what to do. Just then a very favorable opportunity presented itself; the expedition halted for a rest. The locality was much obstructed and cut up with walls and ditches. It was impossible for the whole command to close up into a solid body, and the companies were scattered along the road at some distance from each other. Natalia Martinovna's cart had been drawn into a shady little garden a little removed from the road. While the Cossacks were attending to their horses or building fires and cooking, the officers, each with his company, were giving the necessary orders, and thus Natalia Martinovna was left alone with Petka. She had left the cart, where two Cossacks were busying themselves about something, and seated herself upon a piece of carpet, on the bank of a small pond, under the shade of a tree. Petka was still sitting in the cart, watching the Cossacks at their work. Sergeï Nikolaïevitch saw all this, and resolved to dally no longer. How could he postpone his attempt any longer when the next day, by noon, they would be at home and it would be too late? He was waiting there, and the devil only knew how they stood toward each other. Rovitch

rode along swiftly between the picket-ropes, jumped
across ditches, and coming up to the cart, alighted from
his horse, throwing the bridle to one of the Cossacks.
Petka looked at him doubtfully, opening wide his great
blue eyes. " Ah, this is excellent! " thought Sergeï Nikolaïevitch, and at once experienced an astonishing rush
of paternal love and kindness. " With the child, my
son, in my arms, I will go to her, and then —"

" Don't want to! " cried the boy, holding on convulsively to the carpet. " Don't want to! Mama ! "

" My darling ! my own child," cajoled Sergeï Nikolaïevitch, trying to kiss the struggling youngster, and to
hold his hands; but all at once there appeared before
him, as if sprung from the earth, the pock-marked face
of Podprugin, looking at him over a wall with a glance
such as people bestow upon unwelcome visitors. It
even seemed to Rovitch as if he smiled — yes; it was
an evil, diabolical smile, from ear to ear, with teeth
grinning and eyes glistening.

" D — n him! " muttered Sergeï Nikolaïevitch, almost
audibly.

" Why did you touch him ? " suddenly asked a familiar, musical voice behind him.

Rovitch's hands fell to his side. Petka toddled away
triumphantly and climbed upon Podprugin's shoulder.
Two officers came up (and where the deuce did they
come from ?), and two others dismounted from their
dust-covered horses and began to brush themselves.

" Look! what a carp I've pulled out of that pond,"
Masloboinikof shouted from somewhere. " Get ready
to fry it at once. Didn't I hook him nicely ? Eh, Vassutka, bring the lard, some salt, and a frying-pan —
quick! "

There was nothing to be done. Sergeï Nikolaïevitch

had failed again. At first he imagined that when Masloboinikof spoke of the carp he hinted at him.

"Natalia Martinovna," began Rovitch, "you will pardon me for not having thus far —"

"Never mind!" interrupted Natalia. "Tea will be ready immediately; we shall breakfast here. Will you join us?"

"Well, really—"

"Sit down! why don't you?" shouted Masloboinikof. "Never mind, Brother Vassutka; try to find another cup somewhere."

In a moment all was bustle. They dragged forth a large carpet and spread it out, and upon this they placed a horse-blanket for a table-cloth. Dishes were collected from all sorts of receptacles. Natalia Martinovna herself took an active part in the arrangements. It was positively impracticable to talk to her, and there remained to Sergeï Nikolaïevitch but two modes of procedure — either to withdraw quickly and unnoticed in this bustle, during which no attention was being paid to him, or to stay and take breakfast with the whole company, and during the general conversation to convey a hint to Natalia as to the necessity of a private audience. Very likely she could bring about such an interview much more skillfully than he could, and assist him in his efforts. Having considered the advantages of these propositions, Rovitch waited for the turmoil to subside to hear Natalia Martinovna's definite invitation, which, however, was not addressed to him, but to all present.

"Gentlemen, we ask a blessing!" she said, loudly and joyously, seating herself near the teapot, and around her crowded at once the others, forming a semicircle, the most distant point of which only was left for the hesitating Rovitch. He sat down, though he would have preferred a more graceful pose, as it happened that his feet were in a higher place than the other parts of his body. The carpet had been spread over some hummocks, and his tight trousers inconvenienced him considerably. At last he got himself into a better position, and cast upon the hostess of the improvised feast a look full of feeling and secret pleading, then sighed and lowered his eyes, playing absent-mindedly with the tassel of his sword-knot.

" Do you prefer head or tail? " asked Podprugin, who was carving the carp with his knife and counting the number of guests present. They were among themselves, but Sergeï Nikolaïevitch was a comparative stranger, a guest, and therefore the Cossack thought proper to ascertain his preference.

Sergeï Nikolaïevitch was somewhat startled; the prosaic question had recalled him from the realm of poetic meditation, but he managed to stutter, "Thank you; I have already breakfasted."

"When did you do it — on the road?" inquired the attentive Cossack. "I'm sure I did not see anything."

"What is the use of lying and standing upon ceremony? Eat, and may it do you good. Be pleased to take this," said Masloboinikof, holding out to him a piece of fish on the point of his Tartar knife. "Take it — it has roe in it."

Sergeï Nikolaïevitch was dumfounded at this breach of table etiquette, but he rallied, and took the fish in his hand, like all the others, but he forgot to take off his white gantlets, and when he noticed this mistake he found it difficult to repair it. There was no place to put down the piece of fish. On the carpet — that was full of dust, and there was even a fragment of dried dung clinging to it. On his knee—that was also inconvenient; and Natalia Martinovna was looking, and probably smiling — though Rovitch could not see it he felt it — and he was ready to fling away this miserable greasy piece of fried fish. He was already withdrawing his hand a little to do it unobserved, when the black bob-tailed dog Medvedka got him out of his difficulty. The dog had been sitting there for some time, looking at the appetizing morsel; now the opportunity came, and he made use of it. A general laugh ensued, the clear baby-voice of Petka ringing out above all others.

"Well, now you are without fish," one of the officers condoled with him, "and it is all given out. It was your own fault."

Sergeï Nikolaïevitch sprang to his feet. "Excuse me, gentlemen; I should be only too happy, but — but it is absolutely necessary that I should see the commander of the expedition immediately. There is so much work —"

"But your tea?" suggested Natalia.

"No; thank you. I have —" Rovitch once more essayed to convey to her in a glance all that he would have said in words, bowed gracefully, and stepped back, but came near falling over that cursed dog, which managed to get between his legs. At last he succeeded in getting safely out of the little garden, cursing almost audibly the various accidents which had thus far prevented him from carrying out his sacred, righteous intentions.

Suddenly another idea came into his head — why not write? It was true that in a letter he could not express all that he would have said to her face to face, but he could say much. It really seemed to be his only

outlet from a rather embarrassing position, but an outlet which must be used quickly, in view of their
approaching return to the permanent camp.

Through all that march, from the midday halt to the
night camp, Sergeï Nikolaïevitch was considering the
contents of this letter.   He finally came to a conclusion,
and the camp had scarcely been established when he
went to work at his task.   At first he wrote the whole
letter in French, but subsequently remembered that
Natalia was not very strong in that language and probably would not understand it at all.   It had to be translated into Russian, but the result was not satisfactory,
and he began anew.   How many sheets of paper were
spoiled by Sergeï Nikolaïevitch while concocting this
second letter!

"What is the matter with me?" he thought.   "How
easy it came to me formerly to write such letters, and
now — but wait!   Something has to be done.   I have
simply become stupid — I am a fool!"

What troubled him most was the question how to
address her; the remainder would come to him easily
enough, but these few words were difficult to frame —
they always appeared to him stilted and formal, not
feeling enough.

The entire night was consumed in his struggle with
this letter, but at last victory perched upon Rovitch's
banner — the letter was finished, sealed, and addressed.
His Cossack orderly was dispatched with the missive,
and nothing remained but to submit to fate and wait.

When the column started upon its march, Sergeï
Nikolaïevitch managed to watch his orderly from a dis-
tance as he delivered the letter to Natalia Martinovna.
He saw her take it and open it, looking around inquir-

ingly, and finally read it, blushing up to her ears, when her "body-guard" crowded around her.

What was that? Merciful God! she gave the letter into their hands; they read it aloud — that was clear! Now they were all getting down from their saddles to listen. They were laughing and she smiling. Ah! if that were the treatment he was to receive, they, and she also, should smart for it!'

Sergeï Nikolaïevitch held on to the pommel of his saddle with both hands, feeling as if he were losing consciousness and about to fall from his horse.

However, he held on.

CHAPTER L.

THE LETTER OF SERGEÏ NIKOLAÏEVITCH AND THE ANSWER TO IT.

"My Dearest Madam Natalia Martinovna."

This was the beginning of Rovitch's letter, a beginning which had caused him so much trouble, and which, in his opinion, formed the most difficult part of the whole composition.

"My treasure; my dear one, ever to be remembered; my own; my fondly loved one; my passionately beloved"— all these epithets flowed easily from the pen, as they came from the heart; but it would not do to embody all these terms of endearment in a fatal message upon which depended the future fate of the writer, his future life, as it appeared to Sergeï Nikolaïevitch. It was necessary to consider well, he thought; to weigh every word. It would be best to begin plainly, or even coldly, in order not to act too suddenly upon her kind, easily inflamed heart; to induce her, also, to take the letter seriously, to weigh every word, and to appraise at its true value every hint. It was necessary to write in such a way that when she should rest her hand with the letter in it upon her knee, lowering her glistening eyes and sinking into profound meditation, this letter would serve to guide her thoughts, and to assist her in giving answers to its questions and in overcoming any hesitation that might still incumber her mind, as well as in conquering the unfavorable promptings which would probably be conveyed to her from those fellows *who cat fried fish with their fingers* — those uncouth, ragged pages and knights. Later on, little by little, passion, possessing itself of the writer's whole being, would have to assert itself more and more clearly to act upon her heart after her head had been duly prepared by moderate and sensible phrases.

This was the plan, of campaign conceived by Sergeï Nikolaïevitch for his attack by letter; no wonder that he considered it so long. It was a cunningly conceived plan, before which even more experienced and worldly ladies would probably have succumbed — why not a simple-minded daughter of the steppe, who once had given him her trustful, unbounded love?

In conformance with this plan, the letter began with a formal address:

"My Dearest Madam Natalia Martinovna:

"Forgive me if I begin by recalling memories which may not be altogether agreeable to you, and perhaps even sorrowful. How can I help it? These memories must create in me a still greater anguish and sorrow — the anguish of the criminal in remembering his

crime. But if the criminal finds grim consolation in
confessing his fault, it must be surely permitted to one
to seek forgiveness before the face of an angel, to confess to you, and to disperse all the doubts and distrust
which I experience at the present moment.

"A few years ago we met, and you loved me. You
even preferred me to a man who subsequently died on
account of this preference. I also loved you, and was
consumed by a passion in the ardor of which I was
unable to weigh the possible consequences of the consummation of our love. I was still very young, and did
not know how to appreciate the sincere feelings of the
woman who evidently had been destined for me by
Providence.

" Under the influence of the maxims and requirements
of the circles to which I belong I was induced to sacrifice the consummation of my love. Circumstances
weighed upon me to such an extent that our marriage
became impossible, and I was forced to go away without taking leave of you in order to avoid, for my own
sake as well as for yours, the anguish of the parting
moments. I wrote you a letter which may have seemed
to you a little cold, but believe me when I say that the
words of that letter were far from giving expression to
the voice of my heart, or to what I felt in those minutes
full of anguish.

" It appeared as if all were over between us. A distance of several thousand versts separated us. There
was no prospect of our ever meeting again. Little by
little you could have forgotten me, loved another, and
even been happy; and I also, in my turn, hoped to
extinguish little by little the flame of my passion, the
fire which was consuming my heart, and perhaps to
meet a woman fit to eliminate your bright angelic

image from my soul. But things do not happen as we expect. Grim conscience troubled me; your image pursued me everywhere: in the glare and glitter of life in St. Petersburg, in the splendors of theaters and halls — in all the noisy recreations of the great world which surrounded me I could not forget you. I could not still the voice of my heart. I passed untouched by tens and hundreds of women — women before whom all fell down and worshiped, ready for any sacrifice. I could not even look upon them — you filled my whole soul; and I wandered in loneliness, with pain in my heart, full of cruel reproaches which gave me no rest for even a minute."

("If you must lie, do it well!" thought Sergeï Nikolaïevitch; but after he had written it he really did not think that he lied, but that all this was true, and must be true — only he had never thus far happened to notice his own sufferings. Now he saw them, and convinced himself of their existence.)

" At last my condition became unbearable. I dropped everything and resolved to visit once more this savage country, to search for you, to fall upon my knees and to regain my lost happiness. I have come.

" You may imagine the terrible shock I received when I heard of all that had befallen you. At first I felt as if I could not bear it — I was near self-destruction; but my strength of will saved me from that pitiable end, and I resolved to devote all that remained of my life to the search for you if you were alive, and to solitude within the walls of a monastery if you no longer existed in this world.

" Providence brought me here, and the same Providence preserved you. Let us not act contrary to its holy will, but let us calmly consider all the circum-

stances. I am guilty before you, and for that I have
suffered much. You will forgive me my guilt, because
there exists no crime that can not be forgiven, and
this crime has already been expiated by my sufferings.
You will find in me a faithful and devoted husband;
our child a father and a name. Oh, how I love that
boy! With what envy I look from afar upon those who
may caress him unrestrainedly, while I, his father, do
not dare even to approach him!

"We will, all three of us, be happy — I am fully convinced of that — and our life will be one endless,
merry, bright holiday.

"Upon your glance, in which I already read forgiveness — upon a single word from you now depends all
this happiness. Throw, then, that little glance; speak
that little word which must decide my fate.

"You are dearer to me than anything in this world.
You are necessary to me; and, on the other hand, I feel
that I may say that only I can make you perfectly
happy. My means are such that neither you nor our
boy will ever know want or privations. I will surround you with luxury and contentment, and will lead
you into the brilliant circle of my equals in society, in
which you will occupy the most honorable position.
Have compassion on me. Do not take from me that
one bright, sweet hope; do not deprive your son of his
father, but extend to me once more your honest, much-
prized hand.

"Every moment of waiting for your answer seems to
me an eternity — do not impose an additional burden
of pain upon one already well-nigh worn out. I shall
follow you at a distance, and I shall read my answer
upon your angel face before I hear it. Oh, God! how
passionately, how ardently I love you! I feel that my
heart may break — I feel it!

"I fondly kiss your feet, your hands, your garments, my cherished, only, worshiped Natalia Martinovna— my Natasha!"

The word Natasha was underlined twice, and near it there appeared a yellowish wrinkled blot. This was an actual, real tear of Sergeï Nikolaïevitch — nothing else — only it had not fallen quite accidentally; it had been carefully prepared by the writer and spread out a little with his finger. Here and there upon the sheet of letter-paper a few more similar blots could be seen — weighty arguments that were to strengthen the impression of the entire sincerity of all that had been written.

At the end of the letter came the unavoidable postscript, which read as follows:

"Please try to keep those who generally surround you at a distance, that I may talk with you face to face — it is necessary. You will agree with me that there are subjects of which we can not speak before witnesses."

The letter was not signed. "Why sign, when she knows very well where it comes from?" very justly considered Sergeï Nikolaïevitch.

On receiving this letter, Natalia Martinovna was at first somewhat disconcerted. She was turning the missive between her fingers, undecided whether to open it or not. She looked about her doubtingly, and finally asked, mechanically, "From whom?"

"From his honor Troop Commander Rovitch," reported the orderly. "His honor's orders concerning an answer were, that if it were given quickly I was to wait for it." The last clause the orderly added himself.

"Oh!" said Natalia, smiling, and began to break the seal, her fingers trembling slightly. "How long it is, and what small writing!"

"It would be interesting to read what he may have to say," said Podprugin, inquisitively, coming nearer. "Very interesting."

Natalia Martinovna did not seem to think this unceremonious curiosity at all strange; she even found it very natural.

"Let us go away," Masloboinikof whispered to his neighbor. "Why should we trouble her?" He nudged the other, who did the same to a third, and in a few seconds they all rose and prepared to walk away.

"Where are you going, gentlemen?" Natalia Martinovna asked, quite mechanically.

"We must make some arrangements about our commands and call the sergeants. We'll be back immediately."

"There seems to be some movement in the rearguard. Perhaps we are going to march."

Natalia Martinovna had in the meantime opened the letter and was reading it; the officers, in spite of their many reasons for going, were still waiting about. What happened next was seen by Sergeï Nikolaïevitch standing in the distance, and it caused him to break out in a paroxysm of rage.

"It is outrageous! To show it to all and to boast of it! To laugh at me!" He was repeating these phrases to himself almost throughout the day's march, riding at some distance from the column, and venting his anger upon his innocent horse. "Ah! they do not know me yet. I will show them!"

In the evening of that day, a few minutes after going into camp, he received his answer. It was brought by Masloboinikof.

"I was ordered to deliver this to you, Mr. Troop Commander," said the ensign, bending from his saddle to hand him the letter, and with a certain grace peculiar to the Cossacks he placed the fingers of his right hand against the visor of his cap. "You need not trouble yourself about an answer," he added, as he turned his horse.

"I thank you," replied Sergeï Nikolaïevitch, pressing his teeth together, while seizing the square-folded piece of paper which was not even sealed, and answered the other's salute by bringing his forefinger to his cap. After waiting until Masloboinikof had gone some distance he began to peruse the letter.

Natalia Martinovna's answer was written in pencil, in a large and not very regular hand, and was not altogether without errors in grammar.

"Dear Sir— Sergeï Nikolaïevitch:

"You remind me of the past, and ask me to pardon you for thus reminding me. I freely forgive you this indelicacy, but hope that you will not repeat it.

"I am not at all angry with you. I am even thankful to you for the lesson which taught me to esteem people at their true value. This has since been of the greatest service to me, and for this I am under some obligations to you. You write that in the ardor of your passion you did not duly consider consequences. I agree with you, and even go further. You are allowing yourself to be carried away again now by the 'ardor of your passion,' and it is my business to repair the mistake of your new fancy.

"I refuse all your requests. I am sure that later you will thank me for this refusal.

"The luxuries which you so kindly offer are unknown to me, and consequently they do not attract me; neither does your brilliant society, in which I would find myself an entire stranger."

When Natalia wrote this last line she smiled ironic-ally.

"Write to him, matushka, that you would like to spit on his society!" was the advice given by Podprugin, who had taken a violent dislike to Rovitch. "How is our society worse than his in St. Petersburg? The coxcombs and striped pheasants! Just write that you will spit on them, and then finish up!" Natalia Mar-tinovna did not take the advice of the enraged officer.

"Could I intrust my fate and that of my boy to a man who has once betrayed me?" she wrote. "And who can vouch for you that though you did not forget me you were not carried away by 'the ardor of your passion' for more than one woman? It is also very possible that I was not always constant, and may have been 'carried away' anew, or found a man who could make me forget my first mistake and love him suffi-ciently to finally eliminate your image, which, how-ever, has never troubled me very much.

"On the other hand, I am constantly pursued by another image — you know of whom I speak — and out of respect for this image I could never accept your propositions.

"As to a name for my son, you must know that he does not bear yours, and I would ask you not to trouble yourself about it. He will have his own name; not as brilliant, perhaps, but perfectly honorable and worthy of respect.

"Who has told you that Petka is your son? That he is mine — of that there can be no doubt, but that is all. I ask you to understand that in any sense you like.

"It only remains for me to hope that with this letter may end all correspondence between us, and I feel sure

that you will spare me in the future all further perse-
cution, by killing glances or sighs as well as by spoken
or written words."

Natalia Martinovna's letter was also unsigned, and
also accompanied by a postscript:

"I send you this letter unsealed. You observed yourself that the reading of yours was somewhat public.
This ought to convince you that I act openly and freely,
and am not at all inconvenienced by the presence of
my friends, whom you seem to dislike. Why I do not
understand, and do not care to know."

"That's it! The good-for-nothing! That is good for
him!" said the ensign, as he jumped into the saddle.

"Hurrah!" shouted Kolobkof and Masloboinikof.

"I am only sorry," complained Sotnik Mashkin,
"that I did not take a copy of the letter, as a
memento, especially the last lines. You may believe
me, Matushka, I would have sewed it up in a little-
bag and carried it under my shirt — upon my honor!"

"We are getting into Chandir!" a voice was heard to
say, in the advance.

On the horizon appeared rows of trees and scattered
half-destroyed dwellings — beyond them were columns
of smoke that rose from the bivouac-fires of the large
Russian camp.

A dense cloud of dust was now seen ahead, advancing rapidly to meet them. Through the dust the heads
of horses could be distinguished, shaking their manes;
arms and accouterments glistened, and the tunics of
officers shone white through the dust. Shouts of
"hurrah!" could be distinctly heard above the thunder-
ing tramp of the approaching horses.

"They are ours coming out to meet us — all the
officers!" shouted Masloboinikof.

"Look, look! There come some soldiers running — they are getting ahead of the mounted men!"

Natalia Martinovna, deeply moved, bent forward from under her cart-cover, and shading her eyes from the sun with one hand, she looked eagerly ahead. Her bosom was heaving violently and her eyes glistened. This woman, dressed in her ragged red Turkoman gown and a white kerchief around her head, felt that she, and she alone, was the object and cause of all this uproar, all this excitement. She could restrain her feelings no longer, but broke into tears, pressing her boy to her heart. But these were happy, joyous tears. Such tears do not sear the face or give it a sorrowful, suffering expression, but, on the contrary, they increase the effect of the happy smile as the slanting summer shower increases the brightness of the sun behind it.

"Ah, well! We'll see what he will have to say to-morrow when we fight!" muttered Sergeï Nikola-ïevitch between his teeth, glancing at Golovin, whom he had noticed at once at the head of the cavalcade coming to meet them.

The native messenger had reached the Russian camp at Chandir in safety, reporting directly to the general, and the news of the successful issue of the expedition rapidly spread through the camp. All were full of excitement, and everybody was moving about.

Pugovitzin was at the moment engaged in raking in the winnings of his one hundred and fourth cut — an unusual streak of luck for him; he had played his third jack and was preparing to put down the fourth, having before him quite a respectable little pile of crumpled, greenish paper money. "Easy, brother!" he exclaimed when Kustikof came flying into the tent, all out of

20

breath, nearly upset the table, and shouted, excitedly,
" Natalia Martinovna — here! "

" What! " cried the major, opening his eyes. The
other officers, forgetting to count up winnings or losses,
hurried away in various directions, stumbling over the
tent-ropes.

" They are bringing her! they are bringing her! "
cried the lieutenant. " A native has come. They are
bringing her; they are already near! "

Pugovitzin carefully examined Kustikof's face, and
saw that there must be some truth in the report. The
whole camp was already in an uproar. He could hear
excited phrases and the noise of horses being hurriedly
saddled. The major took off his cap — he had been
playing cards with his head covered — reverently made
the sign of the cross, and then shouted, " Arkhip, saddle up! " Without hurrying, he walked over to the
tent of his friend, the lame Cossack.

" They will surprise him! " he pondered, as. he went
on his way. " It will come to him with a shock, and
the doctor said only yesterday, ' May God prevent
any sudden emotion! ' How can we keep it from him?
It will shake him up — it would shake a well man —
that is as true as that twice two is four. I must go to
him at once. There, they are rushing in to him — the
fools! Gentlemen, gentlemen! carefully — not too suddenly! He must be prepared — listen! "

But nobody listened. Four men had already rushed
ahead of the corpulent major and stumbled into Golovin's tent before his very eyes. He could already hear
the excited exclamations of Kustikof, who had preceded
everybody.

" They are near, quite near! " he heard him saying.
" The native told us. They'll be here soon — to-day

perhaps.   Some have already seen dust rising.   It must
be they!"

When the major entered the tent it was already so
crowded that one could turn round only with the greatest
difficulty.   Golovin, with a bright hectic flush upon his
cheeks, was dressing hurriedly, drawing a pair of high
top-boots upon his feet, but rather unsuccessfully; his
feeble hands would not serve him, and trembled pitifully.   Great drops of perspiration stood upon the sick
man's forehead.   In sharp contrast with the hectic
cheeks was the deathly pallor of the remainder of his
face.   His eyes shone with a feverish luster.

"You are not strong, my poor fellow!   Hey! why
don't you help him to dress?" said Pugovitzin.   "You
are overdoing it, brother; you will hurt yourself.   Now,
what is all this talk about?   Why are you hurrying so?
They have found her, thanks be to God!   But be quiet!"

"I felt it in my heart!   I felt it in my heart!" muttered Golovin.   "My horse, for God's sake, my horse!
Saddle the bay — he can run better!"

"You are going yourself, are you?   What are you
thinking of?   Sit down and wait.   I declare — you burn
like fire!"

"Do you think I am dying?   I am well, don't you
see?   I can stand quite strongly on my legs.   I am perfectly well — look!"   And Golovin squeezed the major's
arm until he made him frown against his will.

"Ah!" grumbled the major, "why did they tell him?
They wanted to cheer him!   They have been stupid
asses.   Well, perhaps God will help you — I will not
keep you back.   Hold on, though; let me help you to
mount!   Hold the horse, Cossack!   Why did you not
bring mine, you devil's imps — quicker!"

"Here! the horse is ready, your honor," reported

Arkhip, pushing through the crowd and leading the major's charger by the bridle. "Here! will you please to seat yourself?"

"You must not run him, however," Pugovitzin warned Golovin. "You will meet them in good time." But the lame Cossack, who had just been staggering with weakness, seemed completely transformed when he found himself astride of a saddle. He sat his horse quite firmly, and soon let him break into a full run, taking the lead of the cavalcade crowding through the narrow avenues between the bivouacs.

In the ranks of the soldiers the news of Natalia Martinovna's rescue created no less excitement. The white blouses came running, without caps or hats, just as they were, and by cutting "across lots," climbing over fences, jumping across ditches, sometimes wading and sometimes on hands and knees, they were outrunning the mounted men.

"If the Turkomans were to fall upon us now when we are in such a mess!" said a discontented sentry to an orderly; not so much disgusted with the crowd as with the fact that his duties prevented him from being with it, and from taking part in the joyous meeting with the "little mother benefactress."

This was the crowd of mounted and foot men that was seen pushing forward to meet the Cossack detachment returning from its joyful march, or rather its successful reconnaissance.

CHAPTER LI.

THE DECISION OF NATALIA MARTINOVNA AND THE RESULTS OF ROVITCH'S CHALLENGE.

DURING the same evening an interesting scene was being enacted in Golovin's tent.

The lame Cossack, after withstanding a tremendous shock not at all commensurate with his strength, lay upon his bed weak, motionless, white as a sheet, with barely perceptible respiration. Anybody looking in upon him at that moment would have felt sure that he saw a corpse before him; but by looking more closely and attentively one could see that there was much life still left in those eyes that were so fondly gazing upon a woman seated close to his couch. These eyes alone spoke of the feelings that filled this sick man's soul to overflowing, and had reduced him to this sorry plight.

Golovin lay there silent, but how much he would have wished to say! But he said nothing, not only because his tongue was not strong enough to move in his fever-dried, inflamed mouth, but because of another man sitting at the foot of the bed, in a white blouse, under which a yellow silk shirt could be seen, and a doctor's epaulets upon his broad but somewhat rounded shoulders.

This man had been repeating a single sentence nearly a hundred times. He repeated it every time that he noticed an inclination on the part of his patient to use his tongue.

" Do not dare to speak! " commanded the doctor. " If you only open your mouth to talk some foolishness

I shall send Natalia Martinovna away at once, and will
not permit her to visit you again without my written
permission! Do you understand?"

But at this moment the hand of Natalia Martinovna
gently covered the mouth of the sick man, who made
use of the opportunity to kiss the slender emaciated
fingers.

Upon a camp-stool in the center of the hut sat
Pugovitzin, also repeating over and over a single
reassuring phrase.

"Ah, never mind! He will be quite a man yet. You
will see whether we do not put him on his legs within
a month! Remember my word — as true as that twice
two is four!"

Kustikof was also in the tent, and had so cunningly managed to seat himself that he could easily
seize Natalia Martinovna's unoccupied hand, which she
did not withdraw, being convinced that he was fully
aware to whom that hand belonged.

Podprugin and Masloboinikof, passing by, looked in
to ascertain how matters were progressing in the tent,
which was easy enough to do as all the walls but one
had been hoisted up to procure ventilation.

At the entrance of the tent stood Major Birnaps, who
had tried so hard to have his battalion ordered to join
the expedition. The good-hearted but self-satisfied
"Estlander" stood with his legs apart and his hands in
his pockets, and was blowing great white clouds of
smoke from his long pipe, which he had just filled with
his special brand of plug. His broad, red face, framed
in stiff yellow side-whiskers, was completely hidden
behind this curtain of tobacco-smoke.

Natalia Martinovna had already exchanged her Turkoman costume for her own gray dress, with black apron

and white cape of muslin. Her clothes had been preserved by Golovin after her flight, and had ever since
that time lain in his trunks, jealously guarded as sacred
relics.

"Now listen!" said Natalia Martinovna to the sick
man, laying her hand upon his cold though perspiring
brow. "I shall cure you, together with the doctor. He
will cure your body and I will cure the soul. I want to
cure you, and I shall do it. I am very selfish, you know,
and I shall cure you for my own sake only. Nobody
but you, my dear, shall be my husband. Now you
know it, and you must make an effort to get better."

"Oh, never mind! He will be a good man yet.
You'll see how we will get him upon his legs in a month.
I shall be acting as father—what a wedding we shall
have!"

"And I will be best man!" chimed in Kustikof.
"May I be best man, Natalia Martinovna? You could
not select anybody but me. Yes, will you have me?"

"And how I shall drink at that wedding!" exclaimed
Major Birnaps, through the cloud of tobacco-smoke.
"How I shall drink!"

"That will help us more than any drugs," said the
doctor; "if this great power can not accomplish his
cure, what could our medicine-chest do? I shall bring
you a little powder, all the same, and some drops, and
all this will be taken in strictest conformance with
instructions as pasted upon the bottle."

"Am I alive?" whispered the patient almost inaudibly.

"'Sh!" Natalia Martinovna once more closed his
mouth. "Not a word!"

"Silence, or I shall immediately send away all, without exception!"

"You owe the doctor just as unquestioning obedience

as you do the general — the relations between doctors and patients may be compared —"

"Have you not finished your pipe?" Natalia Martinovna interrupted Birnap's tedious philosophizing. "The whole tent is full of smoke!"

"I have finished and am now placing it in my pocket," prosed the major, slowly packing up his smoking-apparatus.

"Here is a letter for your honor," said a soldier, coming to "attention" in front of the tent and extending with one hand a sealed envelope.

"From whom is this?" asked Pugovitzin, seizing the letter.

"From his honor Mr. Troop Commander Rovitch."

"For Golovin!" muttered the major, frowning. "Well, excuse me, brother; I will open it for you and read it. Oho!"

The patient was "not up to letters" at this moment wherever they came from, and he paid no attention whatever to this little occurrence.

As Pugovitzin read, an expression of anger came over his face. He handed Rovitch's letter to Birnaps, who also read it, and exclaiming, "Coxcomb, beast!" he passed it on to Kustikof, who again read it, passing it in silence into the doctor's hands. In this way the contents of the missive became known to all but the one to whom it was addressed. Natalia Martinovna also became very much interested in it when she saw the angry expression of those who read it. She held out her hand for it. "What is it? Give it to me!"

"This does not concern you at all, matushka," said Pugovitzin, and unceremoniously walked out of the tent, seizing the paper, which was then in the doctor's hand.

The letter was very brief — only a few straggling lines written in a nervous, uncertain hand:

"DEAR SIR: All explanations are unnecessary. You must feel convinced that the business between us can only be settled by a duel; therefore, if you are not a coward, I shall await you to-morrow at daylight, behind the grove of Chandir, two versts from the camp.

"I have no seconds — you may bring your own, as many as you like; it is all the same to me.

"ROVITCH."

Half an hour later, after consultation with several officers called together for the purpose, an answer was composed, copied, and dispatched to its destination. This answer, not less brief than Rovitch's letter, was as follows:

"You, my dear sir, must be either a fool or an impudent clown. In the first case God will forgive your stupidity, but in the second case you deserve to be soundly thrashed, and in order to avoid this we advise you to immediately leave the expedition and to return to wherever you came from.

"(Signed)   By general request,

"PUGOVITZIN."

" I ought to go and shoot them all like dogs! " angrily exclaimed Sergeï Nikolaïevitch, after reading the answer to his challenge; but then he began to reconsider. He was thinking and considering for a long time, nearly all night, and by morning he had arrived at the following conclusions: To embroil himself with them was impracticable for many reasons. In these wild places, with manners and morals of savages, bereft of all civilized influences, one might deteriorate or be seriously injured in health. It would really be better to go while still in good health and unaffected in any way by life among savages. And, strange coincidence, he had no sooner made up his mind to this when he experienced a radical change in his own feelings. The flame of his great passion for Natalia Martinovna suddenly began to flicker, and subsided with astonishing rapidity. And thus he made up his mind. That scandalous, libelous letter, Pugovitzin's answer, was immediately burned in the blaze of a match, and Rovitch's faithful orderly received orders to pack his master's trunks.

All that still remained to be done was to send in his request for a furlough, to receive it, and to depart. While attending to these details he received another letter from the same persons, in which he was assured that the whole affair would be kept secret, and that he would not be compromised if he behaved himself in the future and gave no further provocation. This second letter was very consoling and quieting to Sergeï Nikolaïevitch's soul; he even came to the conclusion that though these knights of the steppe were a little savage, they were also good fellows, and did not bite promiscuously like enraged dogs.

Sergeï Nikolaïevitch's request for a furlough was not refused.

CHAPTER LII.

EPILOGUE.

THE old gunner's house at Chiniaz was waking up.

For a long time — ever since the death of the gunner, Martin Fedorovitch Chishikof, and the subsequent taking off of his scolding helpmeet, the shutters which protected the numerous windows of the little house had been closed, as well as the doors, over the locks of which great seals of red wax, suspended by strings, had been placed by the authorities, to await the appearance of heirs.

The interior of the little house was dark and damp. Slender threads of sunlight sometimes passed through the cracks of the shutters, gliding over the walls hung thickly with cobwebs, over the angular protuberances of furniture softened in outline by thick layers of dust. How much time had passed away since a single foot had entered here — or since a single hand armed with a brush had carefully dusted and rubbed this furniture! All was covered up — hidden, forgotten. The place had been left a playground for mice and rats, and a workshop for the spiders, who had filled all corners with the product of their diminutive looms, and taken possession of the whole room. From the stove to the cupboard, from the cupboard to the little hanging lamp, from there to the neck of a bottle that had been forgotten on the window-sill, from there again to the corner their fine frail nets were suspended.

And now, all at once, there came a revolution.

The doors had been unsealed and stood wide open;

the fresh air was penetrating into the long-neglected dwelling, passing through it at will, stirring up the rags and remnants that had outlived the past. The furniture was carried into the yard and carefully overhauled. Two women with petticoats triced up to their belts were throwing water over the floors, wading about with cloths and buckets; the walls were being plastered anew until they shone in snowy whiteness. The alarmed mice looked askance upon all this turmoil from a crack in the floor. The poor things probably wondered what all this chaos was about — these uncalled-for, untimely reforms; how much better it was when they had their own way, in the good old times! And the spiders? They had long since been made to submit to fate, and were swept away and carried off with the other litter into the yard, where the chickens had made short work of most of them. A few that escaped made their way laboriously over the grass-grown yard to some outhouses, where they set up their shop and continued to labor, complacently saying to each other, " The world is large, and there is room for all! "

But those who were effecting this complete upheaval and attending to the resurrection of the little home — the two women and a soldier, who were subsequently reinforced by two Cossacks from Golovin's sotnia — they did not care what became of the mice and the surviving spiders. They had only one object, one thought.

" Lively there, children; lively! The master will be here in two days from Tashkent. Let everything be ready!" And they did hurry and strive to prepare, freshen up, and cleanse the house in time for the arrival of its owners from Tashkent. They had come to Tashkent from Kazalinsk, and had reached Kazalinsk, coming from the banks of the Amu, on the steamer

Perovsk, by way of the Aral Sea. These owners were Golovin and his wife, Natalia Martinovna, with her son Petka.

The united efforts of an able physician and a loving woman had conquered the lame Cossack's malady — a disease which had been caused chiefly by moral and mental anguish and excitement. Quiet and loving attention aided in restoring the patient's lost strength; his pale cheeks resumed their bright, healthy color, and he was soon upon the high road to perfect recovery.

The happy, but, under the circumstances, necessarily quiet and modest wedding of Golovin and Natalia took place in the camp. The lame Cossack's term of active service was approaching its end, and for many reasons he thought it better to remain there, in Central Asia, where fate had given him happiness, than to return to his own home, at Yaïk, where he had no ties. As their place of residence they had selected Chiniaz, on the Syr Daria. This was the cause of the bustle of cleansing and restoration of order in the long-forgotten house of the old gunner.

A year or two ago, during my last journey in Central Asia, I visited Chiniaz, and there met the happy couple. The old gunner's house was altered almost beyond recognition; the change was as great as if a feeble old man had by some secret charm been transformed into a blooming youth of fifteen.

A dense screen of green climbing vines covered the outer walls of the little house, and between the emerald foliage sparkled and glistened bright windows with clean white curtains. The picket-fence shone in bright colors; over the sand of the cleanly swept yard prome-

naded the hens, escorted by their conceited rooster-
husband; horses snorted and neighed in the shady
stable lately filled by their master who was a great
lover of those animals. · Some one stepped out upon
the porch to greet me — my host himself. Stately,
ruddy with health, contented, and happy — who would
have recognized in this brawny fellow the sick man
dying of supposed, though never really existing, consumption? "Only that leg of mine still gives me
trouble," he says; " I can not walk even slowly without
limping. Well, that is nothing — I am not an infantryman."

Natalia Martinovna, having abandoned at last her
half-mourning, half-monastic costume of a Sister of
Mercy, was still more improved in looks.

It only remains for us to wish all three of them in the
future such contentment and happiness as they enjoy
at present, and which — to draw a moral — they have
fully deserved.

Very recently I happened to come in contact with
still another hero of my tale; during the present winter
in St. Petersburg.

I happened to turn into Borelli's for supper. At one
of the tables, still covered with the remnants of a luxurious preliminary course, sat several officers — if their
lounging attitude may be designated as sitting. They
were awaiting the supper they had ordered, and passing
the time in badinage not altogether devoid of " res-
taurant " witticisms.

"Yes, gentlemen," one of the officers continued a
story he was relating; "yes, that was an exalted, ardent
love, entirely disinterested and self-sacrificing."

"You should have brought her here, Sergeï!" interrupted another, straightening out his lanky figure.

"Well, I found she was foolish. She was bound to the steppe and could not think of going anywhere else. What could I have done here with this 'Gretchen'?"

"All right!" shouted a third listener. "Gentlemen, make room! Here comes our lobster — a monster, a colossus! Make room!"

"And then," continued the officer telling the story, "my Don Juanic adventures in Central Asia came to a close with a very singular experience, which might have resulted very disagreeably to me. They were six men — I was alone. I conceded them the right of the first fire. I waited. Six pistol-barrels were aimed at me. I must frankly acknowledge that I do not consider myself a coward, but to see six such black little openings gaping before you is, to say the least, disagreeable. I looked at my watch. The first report came — the ball almost grazed my temple; the second, also the third, missed — I did not even hear the bullets; the fourth struck the sand and covered me with dust; the fifth went somewhere over my head; the sixth shattered my revolver.

"'Gentlemen,' I said, 'fate has saved you!' and displayed to them my disabled weapon. 'Let us hope that all misunderstandings between us are at an end!' They shouted 'hurrah!' threw themselves upon me, lifted me upon their hands and prepared to toss me up in triumph — a foolish custom they have. Then they went to drinking like swine; but I came back to St. Petersburg — I was tired of savage life!"

"Are you not lying, Sergeï?" curiously interrupted some skeptic. Sergeï Nikolaïevitch only shrugged his shoulders contemptuously.

The Tartar waiter, in swallow-tail coat and white necktie, brought a tray with some covered dishes — and the gentlemen began to satisfy their fastidious stomachs.

THE END.